LOYALTY LEGENDS

...living a life of abundance through the anointing!

TOBE MOMAH

WESTBOW
P R E S S®
A DIVISION OF THOMAS NELSON
& ZONDERVAN

WestBow Press books may be ordered through booksellers or by contacting:

WestBow Press
A Division of Thomas Nelson & Zondervan
1663 Liberty Drive
Bloomington, IN 47403
www.westbowpress.com
1 (866) 928-1240

ISBN: 978-1-5127-6856-5 (sc)

Print information available on the last page.

WestBow Press rev. date: 2/23/2016

CONTENTS

PART IV
TYPES OF LOYALTY

PART V
TRAITS OF THE LOYAL

PART VI
TEMPTATIONS OF THE (SUPPOSEDLY) LOYAL

PART VII
TRIUMPH OF THE LOYAL

PART VIII
TOOLS FOR LOYALTY

PART IX
CONCLUSION

DEDICATION

This book is dedicated to my father, General. Dr. Sam Momah. An epitome of humility, service and the quintessential mark of loyalty I grew up watching him serve the "least of these" without a wimp and graciously stretching himself over and over again to help the poor, the orphans and the widows.

Today, he is a testimony of God's greatness on the earth. He has maintained fidelity to his marital partner, having been married to my mother for up-wards of Forty eight years, and led our home with excellence and an excruciating work ethic.

He paid his younger brother's school fees through post-graduate school, protected his sisters' without eroding their spouses chivalry, reached the epoch of a military career by attaining the two-star General status, led the Nigerian Federal Ministry of Science and Technology for five years without blemish and carved a niche for himself as an entrepreneur after thirty five years of meritorious service to the Nigerian army.

His loyalty to the Nation, Nigeria, is unwavering. As a fall out of the Nigerian civil war that took place between 1967 and 1970, he was demoted in rank and ended up serving men that were, prior to the war, his juniors. He, however, never balked or betrayed his Nation, Nigeria, but serves with distinction till date.

FOREWORD

I have followed the weekly internet postings of Dr. Tobe for a long time and admire the passion and doggedness with which he pursues the exposition of biblical truths. For a season, he wrote consistently every week particularly on Prayer and Deliverance. When he, a budding legend, approached me to write this foreword to this book, I knew I had a tough work on my hand because it must be as good as the content of his book in your hand.

When *legendry* and *loyalty* come together we see excellent or brilliant loyalty at work. Loyalty exists when there is commitment, perfect allegiance and dedication to one another.

The Bible contains great stories of legendry loyalty. For example in 2Samuel 1: 26, we read part of the lamentation of David when his friends Jonathan, son of Saul died in battle.

> *"I am distressed for you my brother Jonathan; you have been pleasant to me, your love to me was wonderful, surpassing the love of a woman."*

A bible character called Ruth made Naomi popular. Her story is that of loyalty per excellence. Now read her pledge of loyalty to the mother- in- law:

> *"Entreat me not to leave you or to turn back from following after you; for wherever you go, I will go, and wherever you lodge, I will lodge; your people shall be my people, and your God my God. Where you die I will die, and there would I be buried. The Lord do so to me, and more also, if anything but death separate you and me". (Ruth 1: 16-17)."*

Loyalty is beautiful to behold, pleasant and enjoyable to receive. It is honorable and commendable that any Christian who is mature should possess and display genuine loyalty. The world is empty and lonely without loyalty. It takes loyalty to serve God well, loyalty to be a good friend, loyalty to belong to a winning team, loyalty to demonstrate faithfulness and commitment. It takes loyalty to be faithful to your spouse in marriage and to your friends in life. We need it to belong to a local Church for a long time, to serve anyone or organization, and even your country and to produce remarkable results in life.

Martin Luther once wrote:

> *"Where the battle rages, there the loyalty of the soldier is proved".*

Colin Powell wrote, *"Success is the result of perfection, hard work, learning from failure, loyalty, and persistence.*

Zig Zigler once wrote:

> *"The foundation stones for a balanced success are honesty, character, integrity, faith, love and loyalty."*

Great men arrived faster at the rare heights they climbed to with the help of the ladder of loyalty of true friends and supporters. We all need it as part of our character and as a gift from all. To be trusted, loved and cherished, we all owe it to each other not just for a short period of time, but for life. Dr. Tobe's book will guide you as you navigate your way to becoming a world class legend of loyalty.

Apostle Mossy Madugba
Port-Harcourt, Nigeria
November 2016

ACKNOWLEDGEMENTS

God inspired this book. He gave the words and allowed me to put them in print. It, however, would not have been possible without some other invaluable assets along the journey who saw value in it and spurred me on.

More than anyone else, my wife of thirteen years, Rita Uchenna Momah, provided a setting that encouraged and sharpened me to write. She persisted and prodded me to continue, even when contending obligations nearly "froze" book-writing out of my busy schedule.

My church, the Assembly West Monroe, Louisiana, and my pastor, Shane Warren, inspired me to keep writing with their heartfelt worship, exceptional warmth and care, and the trail blazing word. These enabling surroundings helped the dream of this book become a reality.

My parents General (Dr.) and Mrs. Momah continue to inspire me with their unconditional love and steadfast loyalty to family. They have supported my outlandish projects again and again and can be relied upon for untiring camaraderie whenever I need it. My brothers and sisters - Amaka, Ada, Emeka and Nkem - were all instrumental to this book's completion. I cannot over-emphasize the importance of theirs' and their families' help.

Finally, I want to thank supporters of my ministry-Faith and Power ministries—for their ardent support and steadfast loyalty. They spurred the publishing of this book with their fervent enthusiasm and spirit when I shared portions of it at our monthly Holy Ghost Night meetings or in correspondence. May what you have made happen in my life be multiplied many times in yours, in Jesus' name. Amen.

INTRODUCTION

Growing up in the home of a military general, I was surrounded by commands not suggestions, orders not opinions and mandates not maybes. In the military the adage is "*Obey before complain,*" and I soon found that out that any attempts at subverting the authority of *Generalissimo* Dad would not be tolerated.

It was, therefore, shocking when I received Jesus as Lord and Savior in January 1989, to see the Church debate their *Generalissimo's* demands and question His commands. As Dr. Jesse Duplantis once said, "*When there is hesitation in the pulpit, there will be confusion in the pew.*" It is the loyal Church that births legends, not the dilly-dallying or double-minded church.

In the summer of 2015, God started to instruct me from Deuteronomy 15:12-17 about the value of loyalty to the Christian experience. It wasn't sugar-coated, ear-tingling stuff but hard-hitting truths with bitter repercussions when left unattended.

He showed me that loyalty has become a rarity in the world. For example, the average American changes profession – not jobs - six to seven times in a working lifetime. Seventy per cent of married individuals change marital partners at least once in the course of a lifetime and, even in the church, two-third of first-time-church-attendees in one church are members of another church. The average church member stays in one congregation for about three years while the average American pastor continues in a congregation for less than six years.

There is a rapid erosion of loyalty as a valued virtue in society today. Commitments are rarely kept, fidelity to agreements are few and far between and more and more youth want freedom but without faithfulness. In the words of Apostle Paul, people today are "*...trucebreakers, traitors,* *heady, high minded, lovers of pleasures more than lovers of God"* (2 Timothy 3:3-4).

The price for a legendary-Christian-life is loyalty! In this book the Bible's prescription for a life of loyalty in secular and spiritual circles are elucidated. This book is a word from heaven to change, challenge, and characterize the last day church as a loyalty legend for God. Happy reading.

*Your Loyalty to Him
determines His lethality
to your enemies!*

PART I

YOUR CAUSE, YOUR CROSS, AND YOUR CALL!

- ٠ THE CAUSE
- ٠ THE CROSS
- ٠ THE CALL

*A life without a
cause is a curse!*

CHAPTER ONE

THE CAUSE

"...To this end was I born, and for this cause came I into the world, that I should bear witness unto the truth..." (John 18:37).

Everyone has a cause for which they were born. Jesus, while answering Pilate's question on His identity as the Son of God said, *"Thou sayest that I am a king. To this end was I born, and for this cause came I into the world,..."* (John 18:37).

Jeremiah the prophet testified about his cause in life having been established even before his birth. He said the word of the Lord came unto him saying, *"Before I formed thee in the belly I knew thee; and before thou camest forth out of the womb I sanctified thee, and I ordained thee a prophet unto the nations"* (Jeremiah 1:5).

Paul the apostle, was established as a preacher to the nations in his mother's womb. He said, in Galatians 1:15-16, *"...when it pleased God, who separated me from my mother's womb, and called me by his grace, to reveal his Son in me, that I might preach him among the heathen..."* he went forth into ministry.

Your cause is the reason you are alive, and it is what you live for! It is, in one word, your destiny; and until you discover and do it, life is mundane, mediocre, and muddled.

CREATE A VACUUM NOT A VACANCY!

As believers, we are enjoined to live a life that leaves vacuums not vacancies on our absence! We are not supposed to be easily replaceable in absentia, but rather be a void that is hard to fill.

Believers are not called to fit the mold but to break the mold! *Status-quo* Christians who don't challenge standards or shift expectations cannot be God's standard bearers. Isaiah 10:18 says, they "*...shall consume the glory of his forest, and of his fruitful field, both soul and body: and they shall be as when a standard bearer fainteth.*"

Those who set standards and elevate expectations herald glory and bring about new heights of excellence. When Peter was captured by Herod and about to be killed, the Bible says "*...Herod the king stretched forth his hands to vex certain of the church. And he killed James the brother of John with the sword*" (Acts 12:1-2).

Our lives are not ordinary but extraordinary! We are not just a *certain of the church,* but a critical part of God's end-time heavenly army! God, in Isaiah 41:15, calls the church "*...a new sharp threshing instrument having teeth* (that) *shall thresh the mountains, and beat them small....*"

ACCURACY OF ASSIGNMENT!

One of the greatest deterrents to a life of loyalty is ignorance of the assignment given. As a wise man once said, "*If you don't know where you are going, you will get there every time.*" Many believers live their lives as a gamble when God invites them to a guaranteed life of distinction if they will follow His path.

The prophet Isaiah cried out, in Isaiah 40:6, "*...What shall I cry? All flesh is grass, and all the goodliness thereof is as the flower of the field.*" He was not given to preaching a generic gospel to all comers, but he wanted the word of the Lord that was distinct and accurate.

As a result, God's word came to Isaiah. He said, "*The grass withereth, the flower fadeth: but the word of our God shall stand for ever. O Zion, that bringest good tidings, get thee up into the high mountain; O Jerusalem, that bringest good tidings, lift up thy voice with strength; lift it up, be not afraid; say unto the cities of Judah, Behold your God*" (Isaiah 40:8-9).

There is a God-given route to accomplishing a believer's cause on the earth. **Until believers' locate their destination, they can't download their divine allocation.** Isaiah 62:2-3 says, "*...thou shalt be called by a new* *name, which the mouth of the LORD shall name. Thou shalt also be a crown of glory in the hand of the LORD, and a royal diadem in the hand of thy God."*

Accuracy is, however, integral to the assignment. Apostle Paul, for example, said "*...I was not disobedient unto the heavenly vision*" (Acts 26:19). God had shown him to go "*...to the Gentiles...to open their eyes and to turn them from darkness to light, and from the power of Satan unto God...*" (Acts 26:18).

As a result of his obedience, Paul wrote more than two-thirds of the New Testament and heralded an awakening of the Gentile church that continues by the spirit of God unabated today. If he had done anything else, no matter how well-intentioned, he would have failed because it was not his cause in life!

WHAT IS IN A NAME?

My grandfather was impoverished, even by his own primordial standards, after a sudden change in job circumstances in the 1940s'. His brother, on the other hand, was a wealthy produce seller and in order to avoid public knowledge of any acquaintance with my paternal grandfather, he once contemplated changing his and his family's surname.

Eventually, thanks to the industry of my grandmother, my grandfather was able to rediscover his niche and provide for his family as a teacher and bible lay reader. His children, including my father, have gone on to attain enviable heights in society that have made them the envy of other families.

My grandfather's brother, who wanted to change his name because of the appalling poverty in the home of his brother at their outset in life now has a family that wants to associate with the success story that has emanated from my grandfather's family.

From that experience, my father – General Sam Momah - learned the beauty of loyalty. It showed him that even when family is fickle, God is always true. As the current patriarch of the family, he reaches out, with altruistic intentions to serve, to all members of the Momah family no matter their social or material cadre.

Acquaintance without allegiance is aggravation!

CHAPTER TWO

THE CROSS

"Whosoever will come after me, let him deny himself, and take up his cross, and follow me. For whosoever will save his life shall lose it; but whosoever shall lose his life for my sake and the gospel's, the same shall save it" (Mark 8:34-35).

Loyalty costs everything! It cost Jesus his life on the cross of Calvary, and it will cost believers' everything to follow Jesus in this life. The Christian life, according to Mark 8:34-35, must involve carrying the cross no matter the cost if it is to succeed.

Loyalty has rewards, but it also has responsibilities. In fact, according to Mark 8:37, if it does not cost everything it may not be the cause to which God has called! The cause of Christ is not cheap to obtain, even though it is free.

The cross represents sacrifice. It represents a life lived in accordance to God's will regardless of the cost. Daniel, for example, had the spirit of excellence but it took sacrifice to attain it.

In Daniel 1:8, the Bible says *"But Daniel purposed in his heart that he would not defile himself with the portion of the king's meat, nor with the wine which he drank: therefore he requested of the prince of the eunuchs that he might not defile himself."*

Even though almost everyone else was eating the meat that was offered to idols from the king's table, Daniel knew he couldn't do the same because he had a call to accomplish. He forfeited the king's banquet and instead opted for *"...pulse to eat, and water to drink"* (Daniel 1:12).

As a result of this sacrifice testifying of his loyalty to God, Daniel developed wisdom and understanding that was ten times better than that of "...*all the magicians and astrologers...in all* (the King of Babylon's) *realm"* (Daniel 1:20).

Human loyalty produces divine liberality. In Matthew 13:44, Jesus said, *"Again the kingdom of heaven is like unto **treasure** hid in a field; the which when a man hath found, he hideth, and for joy thereof goeth and selleth all that he hath, and buyeth that field."*

Loyalty is the reason there is liberality; therefore, anytime believers' display obedience there will always be overflow! Those who sell all they have, in loyalty and love for the Master receive life's hidden treasures that otherwise would have remained unexplored and non exploited.

REJECTION IS NOT DENIAL!

Barnabas was rejected as the twelfth apostle in Acts 1:26. He was, however, a loyalist notwithstanding the position occupied and he went on to become a legend in his own right. He headlined Paul's ministry that reached the whole of Asia in two years (Acts 19:10), was a significant giver to the cause of Christ (Acts 4:36-37) and as an accomplished orator (Acts 14:12) was widely known as the son of consolation (Acts 4:35).

Barnabas never saw his rejection as a denial but an opportunity for other duties in the ministry, and went on to have a far reaching ministry outside the stratosphere of the other twelve apostles. The man or woman who believes there is nothing else to live for, because he or she has been rejected, does not know God yet.

God says, *"the vessel...made of clay (that) was marred in the hand of the potter (will) He make again (into) another vessel, as seemed good to the potter to make it"* (Jeremiah 18:4). God is the potter and we are the clay. No matter how deformed or malformed a believer gets, God is committed to correcting and restoring us back to good function!

Barnabas may not have become the twelfth apostle, but he reached more people and affected more lives as a loyal "side-kick" of Paul's than some apostles did in their lifetime. He was, like Jesus, *"...a rejected corner stone who became the head of the corner..."* (see Acts 4:11; Luke 20:17 and Psalm 118:22).

It is not over because the world rejected you. It is only over because God says so and wants something better for you. In Ezekiel 21:27, God says *"I will overturn, overturn, overturn, it and it shall be no more, until he come whose right it is and I will give it him."*

PAUL: LOYALIST, LEGEND AND LEGACY

The apostle Paul said in 2 Corinthians 6:10, *"As sorrowful, yet always rejoicing; as poor, yet making many rich; as having nothing, and yet possessing all things."* He added, in 2 Corinthians 11:24, *"Of the Jews five times received I forty stripes save one. Thrice was I beaten with rods, once was I stoned, thrice I suffered shipwreck, a night and a day I have been in the deep."*

As a result of his fortitude, however, Paul went on to become the apostle to the Gentiles from his generation. He confronted adversaries, fought evil beasts (1 Corinthians 15:32) and *"in weariness, painfulness, watchings often, hunger, thirst, fastings, cold and nakedness"* (2 Corinthians 11:27) persisted to arrive at his place of destiny.

The cross of ministry cost Paul everything; but because he persisted, he gained his destiny! He suffered mind-boggling physical and psychological assault but at the end of his journey, he could say *"I have fought a good fight, I have finished my course, I have kept the faith: and henceforth there is laid up for me a crown of righteousness..."* (2 Timothy 4:7-8).

Paul stayed tenacious till the end! He refused to throw in the towel, notwithstanding the odds and as a result, he made a legendry mark on ministry that still reverberates today in the Pauline gospels. He is an example of a man who *"...endured unto the end* (and as a result) *the same shall be saved"* (Matthew 24:13).

MY DAD AND GENERAL AJAYI

My father, as a Major in the Nigerian Army, was the procurement officer for the military barracks cantonment in Yaba, Lagos, Nigeria. In the course of his duties, he was summoned to the office of his immediate superior - Colonel Ajayi - and tongue lashed for something that was not his fault.

Before telling his own side of the story, however, Col. Ajayi slapped him and dismissed him from the office with a summary wave of the hand.

In his physically assaulted and emotionally crestfallen state, my father returned to his office but did not tell anyone about the incident.

Fourteen years later, in 1989, the tables had turned. My father, now Col. Sam Momah, was brigade commander of the 42nd Engineering Brigade in Ibadan, Nigeria. When he heard of the death of his erstwhile boss, retired General Ajayi from a protracted illness, he took a cow as a gift to the family and personally attended the funeral in Ijebu-Ode, Ogun State Nigeria as a mark of respect to his late superior officer.

About thirty years later my Dad broached the topic again. He had remained tight-lipped about it to everyone (including my Mother) but while writing his biography, aptly titled *a General and a gentleman*, he relived the incident to my humble self with nostalgia instead of negativism.

He considered the marks on his face, from his superior's slap, as evidence of loyalty, life sacrifice, and desire for longevity in the Nigerian Army. He went on to serve the Nigerian army for thirty five years and rose to the epoch of his career as Adjutant-General of the Army and Federal Minister of Science and Technology.

In further discussion, he postulated that many marriages, jobs, and careers that were salvageable were shipwrecked because the parties involved bailed at the slightest provocation. He attributed his legendary fame in Nigeria today to his unalloyed loyalty to his respective bosses and the nation, notwithstanding their intermittent aggravation.

Talk is cheap, charm
will fade but loyalty will
reap eternal rewards

CHAPTER THREE

THE CALL

"Moreover whom he did predestinate, them he also called: and whom he called, them he also justified: and whom he justified, them he also glorified" (Romans 8:30).

Everyone has been called by God to live for a cause, but not everyone has obeyed that call! Jesus said, in Matthew 22:14, *"For many are called, but few are chosen."*

God calls everyone to a life of glory (Romans 8:30), but not all attain that glory because they have not heeded that call on their lives. If they take heed and obey, they will be glorified but if they ignore the call to pursue alternative interests, they miss their destiny.

Paul said in Philippians 3:14, *"I press toward the mark for the prize of the high calling of God in Christ Jesus."* There is a high mark of the call of God on every individual's life. It behooves all who want to achieve God's will of glory for their lives, therefore, to take heed to it.

CYRUS: CREATED FOR CHANGE!

God called Cyrus before he was born to change the future and the fortune of the coming generations of Israelites. God said, in Isaiah 44:28, *"That saith of Cyrus, he is my shepherd, and shall perform all my pleasure even saying to Jerusalem thou shalt be built; and to the temple, thy foundation shall be laid."*

This prophecy by Isaiah spoke of Cyrus's emergence more than a hundred and fifty years before Cyprus's birth, while the Jews were in captivity to the Babylonians, reputed at the time as the strongest nation on the earth.

Eventually, according to Ezra 5:13-14, "*in the first year of Cyrus the king of Babylon a decree was sent out saying build this house of God and the vessels also of gold and silver of the house of God, which Nebuchadnezzar took out of the temple that was in Jerusalem, and brought them into the temple of Babylon, those did Cyrus the king take out of the temple of Babylon, and they were delivered unto one, whose name was Sheshbazzar...*"

Cyrus's destiny of glory was tied to the rebuilding of the temple in Jerusalem. He achieved it by pursuing that objective till it was accomplished. It was an against-the-tide and across-the-grain decision that several of his associates resisted (see Ezra 4:5), but Cyrus's steadfastness left him a legend in his time.

King Cyrus's proclamation in Ezra 6:3 and 2 Chronicles 36:22-23 set the stage for the return of Israel to their homeland. Even though Cyrus had opportunities to disregard his divine call to free the Jews and rebuild Jerusalem he didn't take any of them. Rather he set out a decree for the house of God in Israel to be built and the treasures stolen to be repatriated (see Ezra 5:13-14).

What it took for King Cyrus to obey God and restore Israel to Jerusalem was a call that bore a cross for its cause in which Cyrus wholeheartedly believed. Too many believers quit on the edge of their call's manifestation, and as a result they forfeit their (promised) legendary status.

THE JOSHUA GENERATION!

After the death of Joshua, the Bible says "*...Israel served the LORD all the days of Joshua, and all the days of the elders that over lived Joshua, and which had known all the works of the LORD, that he had done for Israel*" (Joshua 24:31).

Joshua had become an *alterego* of sorts to Israel. Without him, or the elders who had lived before, during, and after his life Israel would have been doomed to destruction.

The secret of Joshua's success was his unalloyed loyalty to God. He preceded a generation of fellow archloyalists, who outlived him, by following God fully. NUMBERS 32:11-12 SAYS, "SURELY, *None of the men that came up out of Egypt, from twenty years old and upward, shall see the land…SAVE CALEB..AND Joshua the son of Nun: for they have wholly followed the LORD."*

These *under-twenty starlets* followed Joshua back into the promised land, conquered territory, overthrew kings, and left an enduring legacy in Israel because they made a commitment to serve God and Him alone. He was fiercely loyal, famously saying in Joshua 24:15, "*….as for me and my house, we will serve the LORD."*

Joshua was also fiercely loyal to his mentor and master Moses. He once told him, in response to Eldad and Medad's prophesying in the camp, "*…My lord Moses, forbid them*" (Numbers 11:28) to which Moses replied "*Enviest thou for my sake? Would God that all the LORD's people were prophets, and that the LORD would put his spirit upon them*" (Numbers 11:29).

A generation that protects the dignity and reputation of their masters, rather than discard them in the dust heaps of history when they are gone will leave a posterity for future generations to follow! Joshua finished strong because he stayed loyal to his call.

THE BLOOD SPEAKS!

On my way back from a church's small groups meeting, I meditated on the word God had given me that morning. He had told me in my secret place, "I will cover you," Now as twilight approached, I wondered from what God intended to cover me.

As a house officer at the Nigerian Army Reference hospital Yaba (NARHY) Lagos Nigeria, I was staying at a nearby guesthouse since my quarters were not yet ready. I drove up to the guesthouse in ebullient spirits, but pitch darkness met me, as had become customary in Lagos.

I honked at the gate, but there was no response. I disembarked and attempted to open the gate myself, but it was firmly locked. I called out to the guards all to no avail. So I walked into the reception of the guesthouse aghast at the state of disregard incoming guests were made to suffer.

On entry, I saw seven of the guesthouse employees prostrate on the floor and three men wielding fierce looking pistols over them. They immediately pushed me to the ground and asked me to throw my car keys over to them.

I did as commanded. Soon I felt the cold nozzle of a gun at my temple as one of the men asked me to give them every valuable I had.

I emptied my wallet, gave them my gold rimmed glasses, wristwatch, and all the money I had on my person. Meanwhile, they were frisking me for my car keys having forgotten I had given it to them earlier. After thirty minutes of frantic searching, they left our guesthouse in another commandeered car.

Immediately they left, I found the keys to my car on the floor, and with my dazed eyes clearly now adjusted to the dark, I understood what God meant by "I will cover you." The car they commandeered and used as their getaway car was later found, abandoned and beat-up, in a neighboring west African country.

God had covered my car keys with Jesus Christ's blood, and through its saving power, delivered me from untoward men who wanted to destroy my destiny. I soon moved out of the hotel and into an apartment in the hospital. I shall never forget that day when God covered and saved me by the power of the blood of Jesus.

PART II

LOCATION, LOVE, AND LOYALTY

- Loyalty vis-à-vis Liberality
- Loyalty vis-à-vis Location
- Loyalty vis-à-vis Love
- Loyalty vis-à-vis Legends

*Are the things you live for
worth Christ's dying for?*

CHAPTER FOUR

LOYALTY VIS-À-VIS LIBERALITY

*"And if thy brother, an Hebrew man, or an Hebrew woman, be sold unto thee, and serve thee six years; then in the seventh year thou shalt let him go free from thee. And when thou sendest him out free from thee, thou shalt not let him go away empty. Thou shalt furnish him **liberally** out of thy flock..." (Deuteronomy 15:12-14).*

The servant who had served his master meritoriously, in Deuteronomy 15:12-18, was considered *"...worth a double hired servant to* (the master for)*... (dutifully) serving* (him) *six years,"* As a redeemed servant, he walked out of his master's house free and liberally lavished upon for according to God's law, the master must give liberally to an outgoing redeemed servant to such an extent that their value in life doubles.

Like that servant, the church has been redeemed from the abyss of sin by the blood of Jesus Christ (1 Peter 1:18; Galatians 3:13). Through redemption, believers have been elevated to a higher form of life than that which a natural man can ever understand. Titus 2:14 says, Jesus Christ *"...gave himself for us, that he might redeem us from all iniquity, and purify unto himself a peculiar people, zealous of good works."*

Loyalty, however, imparts to the believer an even higher level of spiritual armamentarium than just an owner's liberality. **Loyalty makes a believer a blessing, while liberality blesses the believer** (emphasis added). Loyalty turns one, who once was a servant, into an heir while the liberality of an owner keeps a hired servant hired but at twice the income.

Loyalty is what changes the equation! Until the servant in Deuteronomy 15:12-17 decided to *"...take an aul, and thrust it through his ear unto the door, and...be thy servant for ever"*, all he had access to was the master's liberality. He understood there was more and decided he wanted everything in the house, and not just the hand-outs. He was more interested in being in his master's presence, than just the presents his master brings.

LACK OF LOYALTY: THE BANE OF A GENERATION

According to Barna 2012 research, about one third of young adults between 18 and 29 years of age are unaffiliated with a religious association (compared to 12% in 1979) and about 43% of these group drop out of church attendance by the age of adulthood1. This totals eight million 20-something year olds who give up on church. These ones are otherwise called NONES meaning no religious affiliation1.

The growth in the number of religiously unaffiliated Americans – sometimes called the rise of the NONES – is largely driven by generational replacement and the gradual supplanting of older generations by newer ones2. A third of adults under 30 have no religious affiliation (32%), compared with just one-in-ten who are 65 and older (9%). This connotes that young adults today are much more likely to be spiritually unaffiliated than previous generations were at a similar stage in their lives.

This demographics show a startling deterioration in commitment among the millennial generation. The average member of the millennial generation will change professions, not just jobs, six to seven times in a lifetime and will have twice to thrice as high a risk of divorce compared to earlier generations. Statistics show crude divorce rates rose from 2.2 in 1960 to 5.3 in 1981 - a 141 percent increase – and peaked at 22.6 divorces per 1,000 marriages in 1980[3].

There is a generation that wants benefits without commitment. Apostle Paul speaks about them in 2 Timothy 3:1-5, describing them as *"...lovers of their own selves, covetous, boasters, proud, blasphemers, disobedient to parents, unthankful, unholy, without natural affection, trucebreakers, false accusers, incontinent, fierce, despisers of those that are good, traitors, heady, high minded, lovers of pleasures more than lovers of God; having a form of godliness, but denying the power thereof.…"*

The lack of loyalty, it seems, is the bane of this generation. So many want the liberality of God, but they fail to give Him their unalloyed loyalty. Such ones will always be under servitude and never in command structure positions. In Matthew 24:45-47, Jesus said, *"Who then is a faithful and wise servant whom his lord hath made ruler over his household, to give them meat in due season? Blessed is that servant, whom his lord when he cometh shall find so doing."*

LARGER THAN LIBERALITY!

The redeemed servant was *"…worth a double hired servant…"* (Deuteronomy 15:18), due to the liberality of his master. There is a dimension that is larger than double that is hardly gleaned by believers, however, because of lack of loyalty.

Moses prayed for the Israelites saying, *"The LORD God of your fathers make you a thousand times so many more as ye are, and bless you, as he hath promised you"* (Deuteronomy 1:11). Apostle Paul wrote in Ephesians 3:20, *"Now unto him that is able to do exceeding abundantly above all that we ask or think, according to the power that worketh in us."*

God wants to do more than the eye can see or the mind can conjecture, but the church will never get there if they only depend on liberal hand-outs' from benevolent masters. 1 Corinthians 2:9 says, *"Eye hath not seen, nor ear heard, neither have entered into the heart of man, the things which God hath prepared for them that love him. But God hath revealed them unto us by his Spirit.…"*

It is when God sees true loyalty that He unravels these supernatural mysteries to His church for *"…we have received, not the spirit of the world, but the spirit which is of God; that we might know the things that are freely given to us of God"* (1 Corinthians 2:12).

A loyal church receives secrets from the master that a servant is not privy to. Jesus, speaking in John 15:14-15, said *"Ye are my friends, if ye do whatsoever I command you. Henceforth I call you not servants; for the servant knoweth not what his lord doeth: but I have called you friends; for all things that I have heard of my Father I have made known unto you."*

The loyal church is not an-attention-seeking church, but all-for-God centered church that seeks to obey Him in all things. As the church pursues this goal in a single-eyed manner, Jesus says, *"…(you) should go and bring forth fruit, and that (your) fruit should remain: that whatsoever ye shall ask of the Father in my name, he may give it you"* (John 15:16).

EXPANDING THE KINGDOM

Critics in London, United Kingdom (UK) vilified and slandered Pastor Matthew Ashimolowo, the Senior Pastor of Kingsway International Christian Center (KICC) London, when the charity commission slammed sanctions on him personally and on the church for breaching Charity Laws in the UK.

His opponents told anyone who cared to listen that it was over for Pastor Matthew. His church finances were impounded, and the government took over his land for the 2012 London Olympics. Between 2004 and 2012, KICC shuttled in and out of a 1,000 seat auditorium, called Land of Wonders, in Walthamstow England utilizing six services to provide a home for its burgeoning congregation.

Pastor Matthew, however, never stopped dreaming. He expanded the number of churches under the KICC banner to over one hundred and made inroads into foreign countries like Ghana, South Africa, Namibia and Nigeria. He purchased a satellite station and became the first church-based-television-network satellite broadcaster in Europe. At the same time, he also began work on a state of the art University in his home town in Nigeria.

As his enemies angled for the kill, Pastor Matthew made an offer in 2012 for a 24 acre property in Essex, United Kingdom. The property, valued at over 50 million pounds was sold freehold for 5 million pounds to the church and since then a seven thousand seat auditorium, alongside adjoining facilities for offices and Bible school, have been erected.

Pastor Matthew, who was an outcast following the London Development Authority forfeiture of his land and the charity commission's indictment, has now become the cynosure of all eyes in London. He was recently awarded an award as the most influential Black Briton in 2014 and has, even amidst his travails, metamorphosed into an-impossible-to-ignore equation in London's socio-political life.

1. Kosmin, Barry A. and Ariela Keysar, with Ryan Cragun and Juhem Navarro-Rivera. 2009. "American Nones: The Profile of the No Religion Population, A Report Based on the American Religious Identification Survey 2008." Trinity College.

*It is not proximity or place
of birth that matters but
persuasion in His promises!*

CHAPTER FIVE

LOYALTY VIS-À-VIS LOCATION

"...And it shall be, if he say unto thee, I will not go away from thee because he loveth thee and thine house, because he is well with thee; then thou shalt take an aul, and thrust it through his ear unto the door, and he shall be thy servant for ever" (Deuteronomy 15:16).

As described in the previous chapter, the avowed servant who had an opportunity to leave and start his own life as a result of his master's liberality (see Deuteronomy 15:12-14), chose instead to stay with his master. Then, rather than accept his commitment to their location as a loyalty indicator, the servant allowed the master *"...take an aul, and thrust it through his ear unto the door, and* (so) *shall...*(he) *be* (his) *servant for ever"* (Deuteronomy 15:17).

Too many believers view church membership or social acquaintance as a true test of loyalty, unaware that location does not mean loyalty. Location may play a crucial part in proving loyalty, but it cannot be the sole yardstick by which loyalty is determined.

Jesus was careful to emphasize that being near Him did not make one a Christian. He said, in Luke 13:26-27, that on judgement day several who are unable to gain entry to heaven shall *"...begin to say, We have eaten and drunk in thy presence, and thou hast taught in our streets. But he shall say, I tell you, I know you not whence ye are; depart from me, all ye workers of iniquity."*

It is not where one is but to whom one belongs that matters in the Kingdom of God! True servant hood requires a commitment that is beyond fraternal or familiar. It is one that is faithful or loyal that becomes the carrier of His blessings. Proverbs 28:20 says "a *faithful man shall abound with blessings: but he that maketh haste to be rich shall not be innocent.*"

JESUS: FORSAKEN BUT NOT FORGOTTEN!

In Mark 15:34, "*Jesus cried with a loud voice saying, 'Eloi, Eloi, lama sabachthani?' which is, being interpreted, 'My God, my God, why hast thou forsaken me?*'" This cry from the Son of God to His Father was His defining moment. This one hue and cry was the true test of loyalty that defied all conundrums, including our sin condition.

Jesus had said, in John 8:29, "*...He that sent me is with me: the Father hath not left me alone; for I do always those things that please him.*" The cross was necessary, but it cost God the Father his location beside His son on the cross of Calvary.

God is "*...of purer eyes than to behold evil, and canst not look on iniquity...*" (Habakkuk 1:13) not withstanding upon whom sin was found. Jesus took the sins of the whole world upon himself, so that he became "*... sin for us, who knew no sin; that we might be made the righteousness of God in him*" (2 Corinthians 5:21).

In that momentary substitution, God forsook Jesus! He changed location, but He did not change loyalty for after three days He raised Jesus from the dead to sit at the right hand of God His father. In Matthew 22:44, the Bible says "*The LORD said unto my Lord* (Jesus Christ), *sit thou on my right hand, till I make thine enemies thy footstool.*"

God the Father's loyalty to His son was tested and found unassailable. In His Son's darkest moments, when the Father forsook the Son as a result of sin, God sent the "*...Spirit...that raised up Jesus from the dead...*" (Romans 8:11).

Loyalty is found in spiritual communion, not physical contact. Loyalty is not proven by how close someone is physically but by what spirit knits those hearts to one another. Apostle Paul said, "*...though I be absent in the flesh, yet am I with you in the spirit, joying and beholding your order, and the stedfastness of your faith in Christ*" (Colossians 2:5).

ICHABOD THROUGH CONSEQUENTIAL INCORRIGIBILITY

The world wants to equate things or experiences to physical presence, but God is bigger than any experience, emotion or any extraordinary act. In Jeremiah 23:23-24, God questioned the Israelites asking *"am I a God at hand, saith the* LORD, *and not a God afar off? Can any hide himself in secret places that I shall not see him? saith the* LORD. *Do not I fill heaven and earth? saith the* LORD.*"*

God is more interested in the church's spiritual allegiance to Him than in a mere physical sobriquet that is akin to acquaintance. This error of form and familiarity over faithfulness cost Israel the glory of God, and birthed *Ichabod* meaning inglorious or where there is no glory.

In 1 Samuel 4:6-7, the Philistines reacted to the arrival of the Ark of the Covenant in the camp of Israel with fear. It says, *"...when the Philistines heard the noise of the shout, they said, What meaneth the noise of this great shout in the camp of the Hebrews? And they understood that the ark of the* LORD *was come into the camp. And the Philistines were afraid, for they said, God is come into the camp...."*

Unbeknown to the Philistines, God had long departed from the vicinity of the Ark of the Covenant because of the sins of Eli's sons, Hophni and Phinehas. In 1 Samuel 2:29, God told Eli, *"Wherefore kick ye at my sacrifice and at mine offering, which I have commanded in my habitation; and honourest thy sons above me, to make yourselves fat with the chiefest of all the offerings of Israel my people?"*

Eli's sons, through their consequential incorrigibility, turned the Ark of the Covenant from an asset into an object of apathy. Though it evoked fear in Israel's enemies, it was bereft of power as a result of their sin. 1 Samuel 4:10-11 says, *"...the Philistines fought, and Israel was smitten, and they fled every man into his tent: and there was a very great slaughter; for there fell of Israel thirty thousand footmen. And the ark of God was taken...."*

Ichabod means the glory has departed. Israel's glory was gone, and so was *Jehovah Sabaoth*, their Lord of Hosts and Man of war. They lost, in spite of the Ark, not because of it. The presence of the Ark is not tantamount to God's presence, especially when there is no loyalty among His surrounding armies.

As the wise man said in Proverbs 5:14, *"I was almost in all evil in the midst of the congregation and assembly."* The building does not make the body of Christ, but the body of Christ – if loyal – can make the building a habitation for His presence.

MY DAD'S DISLOYAL ORDERLY

In 1994, My father, General Sam Momah, had an enviable job as the Adjutant General of the 200,000 plus Nigerian army. As one of the country's top generals, he had several aides attached to him; but none was closer to him than his orderly. Being from the same tribe and with similar ethnic affiliations as my father, many saw this orderly as destined for a meteoric rise in the army but it was not to be.

Every morning, the orderly picked my dad's work tools and ensured they were safe as those work materials contained several files bordering on national security. He came early to work, left late and, with little in salaries and allowances, served dutifully or so we thought.

Unceremoniously and out of the blues, my father eavesdropped on this orderly as he dipped his hands into his briefcase. He was pilfering various sums of money from his wallet without permission, and immediately my Dad reported him to the authorities who jailed him for theft and summarily dismissed from the Nigerian army.

He was the closest person in terms of physical contact to my Dad, among his soldiers, but the farthest from his heart. Other military stewards, from other tribes and cultures than my Dad's, were fiercely loyal and as a result, thirty five years later, they are still in his employ.

"*He is no fool who gives up what he cannot keep, to gain that which he cannot lose*"

- Jim Elliot (1927 – 1956)

CHAPTER SIX

LOYALTY VIS-À-VIS LOVE

*"And it shall be, if he say unto thee, I will not go away from thee; because he **loveth** (emphasis added) thee and thine house, because he is well with thee"* (Deuteronomy 15:16).

The proof of love is loyalty to a person, the state, or a cause. Jesus said in John 14:21, *"He that hath my commandments, and keepeth them, he it is that loveth me: and he that loveth me shall be loved of my Father, and I will love him, and will manifest myself to him."*

The avowed servant, in Deuteronomy 15:12-16, who had wowed his superiors with six years of stellar service decided to remain in the master's house as a servant forever because, according to the above verse, *"…he loveth thee and thine house, because he is well with thee."*

The word used in the above scripture in the original Hebrew for Love means *affection* and for well it means *cheer*. **The servant was connected at the heart with the master, not just at the pocket book.** This servant went on to prove his love for his master by allowing his ear to be pierced indicating *"…he shall be thy servant for ever"* (Deuteronomy 15:17).

This servant epitomized commitment and dedication. To him it was not a materialistic and crass relationship about what he could obtain from his master. It was about upholding ideals that stirred his heart to serve in the first place!

MORE THAN DOUBLE

The Hebrew servant in Deuteronomy 15:16 was worthy of double honor. He had served meritoriously and according to scripture "...*the laborer is worthy of his reward*" (1 Timothy 5:18). This servant, however, wanted more! Instead of inheriting possessions, he opted for the master's presence; and instead of commodities he chose communion. As a result, he became an heir with the master of all his possessions.

Jesus said, in John 8:35, "...*the servant abideth not in the house for ever: but the Son abideth ever.*" The servant made a commitment to serve the master for ever, and by that act of loyalty inherited more than double! The reason many so-claimed lovers do not inherit more is lack of loyalty. They talk the talk but fail to walk the walk as their talk is cheap and their charm fading. **Loyalty stays for the journey and not just for the ride.**

Jesus so loved that he gave His life for humanity (John 3:16). What one gives is proof of love which in turn is proof of loyalty. The love that is loyal is not mere words, or what one says, but action. In 2 Corinthians 5:14-16, the apostle Paul describes this love saying, "...*the love of Christ constraineth us; because we thus judge, that if one died for all, then were all dead: And that he died for all, that they which live should not henceforth live unto themselves, but unto him which died for them, and rose again.*"

THE GREATEST LOVE

The Bible identifies the greatest love. It is not gifts, - not even the gift of the gab, but giving one's life for a neighbor. In John 15:13, Jesus said, "*Greater love hath no man than this, that a man lay down his life for his friends.*"

The true test of love is sacrifice, not showmanship. The greatest love is demonstrated not remonstrated over. In 1 John 3:16,18 Elder John says, "*hereby perceive we the love of God, because he laid down his life for us... we ought to lay down our lives for the brethren...(so) let us not love in word, neither in tongue; but in deed and in truth.*"

The Prophet Balaam, for example, spoke long about his credentials and commitment to God but was short in loyalty. He was told by God, in Numbers 22:12, "*thou shalt not go with them; thou shalt not curse the people: for they are blessed.*" Yet he "...*rose up in the morning, and saddled his ass, and went with the princes of Moab. And God's anger was kindled because he went...*" (Numbers 22:21-22).

The outcome of Balaam's disobedience was destruction. In 1 Peter 2:15-16, the Bible says, they *"...have forsaken the right way, and are gone astray, following the way of Balaam the son of Bosor, who loved the wages of unrighteousness but was rebuked for his iniquity: the dumb ass speaking with man's voice forbad the madness of the prophet."*

Many believers claim they love God, but they actually love men's praise and adulation more. What one loves more will determine where one ends in life. You can end up, like Balaam, on the ash heaps of history (Revelation 2:14) or love in deed and shine like the Sun as stated in Judges 5:31.

THE CHURCH IN SWEDEN

The largest church in the world in 1943 was the *Filadelphia* Church in Stockholm, Sweden. It was a pilgrim's delight, as many people from all over the world – including kings and queens of different countries - came to seek the Lord at its altar.

The spread of the gospel from Sweden was, however, abruptly cut off by Nazi Germany and their feudalistic leader Adolf Hitler. The people of Sweden sought God and in prayer vowed to serve God if He delivered them from the hands of Hitler.

Unfortunately Hitler triumphed, and Sweden was overrun by Nazi Germany. The Christians in Sweden were shocked and stunned into silence. At the end of the war, a spirit of apathy and coldness took residence in Sweden.

A nation that once was the quintessential evidence of Christianity lost her passion for God in a season of despondency and disappointment. She has since become pluralistic, embraced a post-Christian worldview and has 80% of its population as single parents and only 3-5% as regular church attendees.

The reason for their loss of relevance was the dearth of God's love in the hearts of the people. They were disappointed in their loss of territory to Nazi Germany, and as a result were offended. Their offence depleted their spiritual arsenal and capitulated the move of the Holy Spirit in that country until date.

Never in the Field of Conflict has so much been Owed by So Many to So Few!

CHAPTER SEVEN

LOYALTY VIS-À-VIS LEGENDS

"Of Zebulun, such as went forth to battle, expert in war, with all instruments of war, fifty thousand, which could keep rank: they were not of double heart" (1 Chronicles 12:33).

The word *loyalty* is defined by the Free dictionary as *a feeling or attitude of devoted attachment and affection*. In the original Hebrew, loyalty or allegiance (as used in 1 Chronicles 12:33) is interpreted as obstinate, and undivided attention.

The legend, on the other hand, is an individual account of awe-inspiring acts and breadth taking deeds. The word *legend* as used in the Bible in 1 Chronicles 12:33, means someone who is *"...expert in war..."* or in God's chosen sphere for their lives.

God has earmarked His church to live legendary lives! In Isaiah 26:18, the prophet Isaiah complained to God that *"...we have as it were brought forth wind; we have not wrought any deliverance in the earth; neither have the inhabitants of the world fallen."* He expected the evidence of his ministry to be worldwide deliverance and was aghast it was limited to just a few in Israel.

In Genesis 22:17-18, God gave Abraham a prophecy about the coming generations of loyalty legends. He said, *"...in blessing I will bless thee, and in multiplying I will multiply thy seed as the stars of the heaven, and as the sand which is upon the sea shore;* ***and thy seed shall possess the gate of his enemies; And in thy seed shall all the nations of the earth be blessed"*** (emphasis added).

The Believer's calling is to bless the nations of the earth, and not just local areas of operation! That is the reason *"Christ...redeemed us from the curse of the law, being made a curse for us: for it is written, Cursed is every one that hangeth on a tree: That **the blessing of Abraham** might come on the Gentiles through Jesus Christ: that we might receive the promise of the Spirit through faith."* (Galatians 3:13-14).

There is no more excuse for insignificant living! Jesus broke the limitations of life and equipped the church with the power of the Holy Spirit (Galatians 3:14b) to take territories and conquer countries. The Church was not designed by God to just warm pews and watch the five-fold-ministries ministers engage in the battles for life and destiny. Rather, He said *"...Occupy till I come"* (Luke 19:13). The word *occupy* is the Greek word *pragmateúomai* which means pragmatic trading or being busy with business transactions that bear much fruit.

SHOWERS OF BLESSINGS

Loyal believers live a legendary life because God helps them. 2 Chronicles 20:20 says, *"The eyes of the Lord run to and fro the earth to sho himself strong on the behalf of those whose hearts are loyal towards Him"* (NKJV).

Such believers evoke terror in their opposition and triumph among the godly because they live to *"...satiate the weary soul, and...replenish every sorrowful soul"* (Jeremiah 31:25).

Loyalty legends are they who believe and, *"...as the scripture hath said, out of (their) belly shall flow rivers of living water"* (John 7:38). They are a showers of blessing, for according to Ezekiel 36:26, God *"...will make them (Israel) and the places round about my hill a blessing; and...cause the shower to come down in his season (so that) there shall be showers of blessing."*

God has given the church triumphant procession, no matter the opposition involved. In 2 Corinthians 2:14-15, He says *"...thanks be unto God, which always causeth us to triumph in Christ, and maketh manifest the savor of his knowledge by us in every place. For we are unto God a sweet savor of Christ, in them that are saved, and in them that perish."*

As Israel came out of Egypt, the surrounding nations were silent and still as a stone; Exodus 15:16 says, *"Fear and dread shall fall upon them; by the greatness of thine arm they shall be as still as a stone; till thy people pass over, O Lord, till the people pass over, which thou hast purchased."*

CITY SHAKERS AREN'T CONVENIENCE SEEKERS

No person shakes a city or changes a generation without strong loyalty. Apostle Paul, a man ascertained by the people of Thessalonica in Acts 17:6, as "*...these that have turned the world upside down...*" said in Galatians 2:20 "*I am crucified with Christ: nevertheless I live; yet not I, but Christ liveth in me: and the life which I now live in the flesh I live by the faith of the Son of God....*"

It cost Paul everything to serve Christ. He recalled his past achievements and merits in Philippians 3:4-6, and surmised it all in Philippians 3:8 by saying "*I count all things but loss for the excellency of the knowledge of Christ Jesus my Lord: for whom I have suffered the loss of all things, and do count them but dung, that I may win Christ.*"

The whining and weak-willed believers cannot shake a city or change a generation because they seek convenience, not commitment. They abhor sacrifice, but esteem sumptuousness unaware that every legendary figure in history paid a price to attain that achievement. The price is called loyalty.

King David, for example, ended his eulogy of God's benevolence to his heritage, by asking "*...what one nation in the earth is like thy people, even like Israel, whom God went to redeem for a people to himself, and to make him a name, and to do for you great things...*" (2 Samuel 7:23).

Israel's legendary acclaim in their new found land was however, at a cost. In 2 Samuel 7:24, David said "*For thou hast confirmed to thyself thy people Israel to be a people unto thee for ever: and thou, Lord, art become their God.*"

There is a city-shaking and generation-changing anointing on every believer, but it takes loyalty to release her. The last days are the church's programmed time to shine (Isaiah 60:1-6; Micah 4:1-3 and Zechariah 1:17), and she must not let comfort stand in her way.

Jesus Christ said, in John 12:24-26, "*...Except a corn of wheat fall into the ground and die, it abideth alone: but if it die, it bringeth forth much fruit. He that loveth his life shall lose it; and he that hateth his life in this* *world shall keep it unto life eternal. If any man serve me, let him follow me; and where I am, there shall also my servant be: if any man serve me, him will my Father honor."*

JIM ELLIOT: MARTYR TO THE AUCAN INDIANS

Jim Elliot (1927 – 1956) was born to the family of a Plymouth Brethren evangelist and his wife, who was a chiropractor in Portland, Oregon. He gave his life to Jesus Christ as a young boy, and told a friend of his father, who enquired if he would be a preacher, "I don't know, but I would like to tell someone about Jesus, that never heard of Him before!"

He enrolled in Wheaton college in 1945 and graduated with a degree in Greek in 1949. During his student days, Jim and his room mate David Howard, were members of the campus organization Student Foreign Missions Fellowship where Elliot spoke concertedly to the student InterVarsity Christian Fellowship on the role of the Holy Spirit in missions. He spent many vacations on foreign mission fields and attended the International Student Missionary Convention, where he met a missionary to Brazil that further convinced about the tribal work in South America.

He met his room-mates sister, Elizabeth Howard, at Wheaton and intimated her on his plans to preach the gospel as a missionary in South America, believing the American church was already "well-fed." She shared his passions, and even though he departed for Ecuador in February 1952, they continued correspondence. In October 1953, they got married in the jungles of Ecuador and in May 1955 they had their only child - Valerie Elliot.

Working with four other missionaries and their families, including Ed McCully, Roger Youderian, Pete Fleming, and their pilot Nate Saint, Jim and Elizabeth Elliot toiled in the jungles of the Quechua Indians. Their work was fruitful as several Quechua Indians became Christians. Among the converts was a young girl from the Auca Indians called Dayuma, who lived among the Quechua Indians. She told them about the heinous conditions the Aucan Indians lived in and the desperate need they had for Christ.

The Aucan Indians were a savage tribe who did not tolerate interlopers.

They had forcibly removed an oil drilling company from their grounds, by spearing several of their workers to death and were considered totally unreachable as a result. On January 8th, 1956, after three years of courting the Aucan Indians with gifts and voicing their messages of love from the airplane, they (Jim Elliot and his four male colleagues), were killed and left for dead by the spears of thirty Aucan warriors who violated their camp territory. Even though they had guns, they refused to use them against the natives' spears in order not to thwart the mission of winning the Aucan Indians for Christ.

Elizabeth Elliot was devastated and returned to the United States with her daughter. In October 1958, however, she and Rachel Saint (a sister to one of the Martyrs who died with Jim Elliot) returned and continued the work their husband and brother, respectively, commenced with the Aucan Indians. She worked with them until 1963, when she and Valerie returned to the US, and by the time of her departure they had seen several of the local natives saved.

One of the men who killed Jim Elliot and his colleagues later testified saying, "I have killed twelve people with my spear! But I did that when my heart was black. Now Jesus' blood has washed my heart clean, so I don't live like that anymore."

PART III

TRUE LOYALTY

Loyalty is not skin-deep or soul-steeped but spiritual indeed!

CHAPTER EIGTH

URIAH – THE STUFF OF LEGENDS

*"And this is the number of the mighty men whom David had; Jashobeam, an Hachmonite, the chief of the captains:... Ira the Ithrite, Gareb the Ithrite, **Uriah the Hittite**,..."* (1 Chronicles 11:11,41).

Uriah lived an exemplary life. He was one of David's mighty men (1 Chronicles 11:41), and he fought David's enemies to a standstill. He took cities (2 Samuel 11:17), conquered kingdoms (2 Samuel 12:29) but never made personal comfort his priority (2 Samuel 11:11).

He was opportune to have a privileged background as a Hittite. According to historians, the Hittites were a wealthy aristocratic nation who imported horses from Egypt (1 Kings 10:29), and from whom Abraham bought the cave of Machpelah (Genesis 23:3-20) for his wife's burial. In spite of these antecedents of wealth and power, Uriah was a down-to-earth man who wanted no more than to serve his country, king and immediate superiors.

Uriah was loyal to a fault. He refused to take advantage of David's suggestion to go home and sleep with his wife (2 Samuel 11:8), and highlights a life steeped in loyalty that made him a mighty man of war.

He chose to fulfill his duty, instead of being intimate with his wife, saying on one occasion *"...The ark, and Israel, and Judah, abide in tents; and my lord Joab, and the servants of my lord, are encamped in the open fields;*

shall I then go into mine house, to eat and to drink, and to lie with my wife? as thou livest, and as thy soul liveth, I will not do this thing" (2 Samuel 11:11).

Today, he is celebrated as a man of principle and passion who left a legacy of loyalty as one of David's mighty men. His loyalty was unequivocal and his legendary status so unassailable that Ahitophel, his wife's grandfather according to 2 Samuel 23:34, stirred up Absalom to topple David as the King of Israel (2 Samuel 17:1-3) in revenge.

BETWEEN DEATH AND LIFE

Uriah was not just any officer. He was a leading officer in David's army and as one of the leaders of the army, was not supposed to be placed at the forefront of a battle. In 2 Samuel 18:3, the people of Israel told King David *"...Thou shalt not go forth: for if we flee away, they will not care for us; neither if half of us die, will they care for us: but now thou art worth ten thousand of us: therefore now it is better that thou succour us out of the city."*

Uriah was, however, unilaterally positioned there by King David to kill him! In 2 Samuel 11:15, King David wrote to his army chief, saying *"...Set ye Uriah in the forefront of the hottest battle, and retire ye from him, that he may be smitten, and die."*

He was sacrificed to enemy fire because David wanted to cover up his affair with Uriah's wife who was now pregnant by him. Having refused the comfort and convenience of a palace invitation to sleep with his wife, and so appear to be the father of David's illegitimate-child-to-be (2 Samuel 11:5-19), Uriah had to be eliminated.

Uriah paid the ultimate price for loyalty to country, king and commander. In 2 Samuel 11:16-17, the Bible says *"...when Joab observed the city, that he assigned Uriah unto a place where he knew that valiant men were. And the men of the city went out, and fought with Joab: and there fell some of the people of the servants of David; and Uriah the Hittite died also."*

In death, however, Uriah still triumphed. He epitomized loyalty to the crown and fidelity to a kingdom that was not even his own. He died a legend, having been listed as one of David's mighty men in 1 Chronicles 11:41 and as one who left eternal repercussions to King David's lineage.

The Bible says in 2 Samuel 12:9-10 that God, through the prophet Nathan, told David *"...thou hast killed Uriah the Hittite with the sword,* *and hast taken his wife to be thy wife, and hast slain him with the sword of the children of Ammon. **Now therefore the sword shall never depart from thine house;** because thou hast despised me, and hast taken the wife of Uriah the Hittite to be thy wife"* (emphasis added).

Heaven has no unnoticed legends! If a person lives a life of loyalty, his or her death will not be silent or unrewarded. Uriah's legendary status lives on today in the Middle East crises that has bedeviled the house of David since the days of its founder's affair with Bathsheba, Uriah's wife.

In death or in life, loyalists become legends! Revelation 12:11 says, "… *they* (the saints) *overcame him* (the accuser of the brethren) *by the blood of the Lamb, and by the word of their testimony; and they loved not their lives unto the death."* What is worth dying for always outlives the life that died for it.

BREAKING BARRIERS

Uriah was a Hittite. They were descendants of Heth, the son of Canaan and the great grandson of Noah according to Genesis 10:15. They inhabited areas of modern day Syria, Turkey and Asia minor and battled for part of the promised land with Egypt, Babylon and Israel (Exodus 23:28). In Ezra 9:1, they were still considered a distinct nation.

In spite of the cultural, racial and spiritual barriers imposed on Uriah by his pedigree and history as a Hittite, he went on to become a foremost legend in the army of Israel. Spiritually, he had to overcome the curse Noah placed on Canaan, the father of Heth (who founded the Hittite tribe), in Genesis 9:25, and culturally he had to overcome the monolithic Jewish society that considered Hittites as outcasts.

Notwithstanding these monumental odds, Uriah proved his mettle to his new nation and family. Eliam, the son of Ahitophel, was the father of Bathsheba (2 Samuel 11:3) and also a mighty man of David alongside Uriah the Hittite (2 Samuel 23:34). He observed Uriah at close quarters, as both were in the mighty men of David's camp, and approved of his relationship with his daughter, Bethsheba, by giving him her hand in marriage.

The notion of loyalty being based on color, cast or culture is an abrogation of Bible truth. True loyalty is spiritual, not skin deep! Uriah came into Israel as a foreigner but rose to the highest echelons of that day's society as one of David's mighty men (2 Samuel 23:29). This was because he had spiritual, not skin-deep or soul steeped, allegiance to the God of Israel.

OVERSEAS' OVERCOMERS!

Forty per cent of Fortune 500 companies, according to the partnership for a New American economy, are immigrant start-ups. These include iconic brands like Google (Russia), Yahoo (Taiwan), Goldman Sachs (Germany), Home Depot (Russia), Kraft Foods (Germany/Canada), Well Care (Zambia), Du Pont (France), Honeywell (Switzerland), Capitol One Bank (England), Big Lots (Russia), Procter and Gamble (England/Ireland), Colgate (England), Comcast (Germany), Ebay (France), General Electric (England), AT and T (Scotland), Nordstrom (Sweden), Kohl's (Poland), Pfizer (German), and Intel (Hungary).

In addition, Mike Bloomberg of the partnership for a new American economy says "the top ten brands in the world currently are products of immigrants or of their children's ingenuity." This is not because local Americans lack instruction or innovation, but due to their foreign born counterparts' quest for the "American dream."

Many foreigners are shacked, disenfranchised and incessantly challenged in their native countries. When they come to the land of the free and the home of the brave called America, they begin to entertain dreams they otherwise would not have dared in their home countries due to political and economic instability. This is illustrated by the fact that foreigners make up 10% of the US population but acquire greater than 40% of all post-graduate degrees.

They are twice as likely as native-born Americans to be entrepreneurs, according to the Kauffman Foundation's Kauffman Index of Entrepreneurial activity3, with a business formation rate of 0.62 per cent compared to 0.28 per cent for native Americans. Many attribute this to the higher risk taking strategies of immigrants who have less to lose and everything to gain by developing start-up companies.

One of the root causes
of Disloyalty is
Discontentment!

CHAPTER NINE

RECHABITES – RESOLUTE AND REWARDED

"But they said, We will drink no wine: for Jonadab the son of Rechab our father commanded us, saying, Ye shall drink no wine, neither ye, nor your sons for ever" (Jeremiah 35:6).

The Rechabites were descendants of the Kenites who accompanied Israel into the promised land and were in-laws to Moses (Judges 1:16). They were a nomadic tribe who had made a covenant with God through their father Jonadab for the promotion of the laws of God.

Jonadab's instructions that had become binding on generations of Rechabites thereafter said, not to *"…drink wine,…build house, nor sow seed, nor plant vineyard, nor have any: but all your days ye shall dwell in tents; that ye may live many days in the land where ye be strangers"* (Jeremiah 35:6-7).

Their loyalty to the covenant turned them into legends, spiritually, and physically! As a reward for their obedience and fidelity, which contrasted with Israel's repugnance and rebellion, God made a vow to the Rechabites that conferred legendary status on them for life.

He said, through Jeremiah the prophet, *"…Because ye have obeyed the commandment of Jonadab your father, and kept all his precepts, and done according unto all that he hath commanded you:…Jonadab the son of Rechab shall not want a man to stand before me for ever"* (Jeremiah 35:18-19).

The Rechabites were a loyal and God-fearing group who, no matter how much intimidation and impoverishment they faced, kept to the dictates of their father's covenant with God. They followed the instruction of their father Jonadab, to such an extent, that God made them an example to Israel in the days of Prophet Jeremiah.

God told the prophet, in Jeremiah 35:16-17, "*Because the sons of Jonadab the son of Rechab have performed the commandment of their father, which he commanded them; but this people hath not hearkened unto me: Therefore thus saith the LORD God of hosts, the God of Israel; Behold, I will bring upon Judah and upon all the inhabitants of Jerusalem all the evil that I have pronounced against them:….*"

RIDICULOUS BUT REWARDED!

God rewarded the Rechabites for their loyalty to God's word. After several years of disregard and dishonor as a result of their vagrant living that left them with no fixed assets in the community, God recognized them. 2 Chronicles 16:9 says, "*…the eyes of the LORD run to and fro throughout the whole earth, to shew himself strong in the behalf of them whose heart is perfect toward him.*"

Loyalty may look ridiculous to some, but in God's end of the equation, there will always be rewards for the ridiculously loyal. The apostle Paul said, "*Let the elders that rule well be counted worthy of double honor, especially they who labor in the word and doctrine*" (1 Timothy 5:17).

A Christian's greatest rewards may follow their toughest ridicule in life, if they continue to trust and obey God every step of the way. Hebrews 6:10 says, "*…God is not unrighteous to forget your work and labor of love, which ye have shewed toward his name, in that ye have ministered to the saints, and do minister.*"

Obedience may not be convenient at the time, but it will be worth it if you hold onto your confidence in God. Those who labored in love, in Hebrews 6:10, were adjured to "*…be not slothful, but followers of them who through faith and patience inherit the promises*" (Hebrews 6:12).

In the eyes of some persnickety observers, these ones were laboring without rewards in ridiculous circumstances. The difference, however, was loyalty. Hebrews 6:11 says, "*…we desire that every one of you do shew the same diligence to the full assurance of hope unto the end:*"

Loyalty is laboring in love with a hope that lasts till the end of time. It has no expiration date and does not resign, renege or rebel in the army of the Lord. It is not a convenience-seeking attraction, but a city-shaking-and-taking anointing that does not stop hoping until it sees God's promises manifest.

THE NEXT GENERATION

In Romans 14:7-8, apostle Paul writes, "*...none of us liveth to himself, and no man dieth to himself. For whether we live, we live unto the Lord; and whether we die, we die unto the Lord: whether we live therefore, or die, we are the Lord's*".

Whether in death or life humanity is speaking for or against the gospel, and by their actions, they shape future generations. Loyalty is not just about you and your rewards, but the rewards that cascade through your unalloyed loyalty to redundant generations yet unborn.

God told the Israelites in Jerusalem and the surrounding towns of Judah, "*Because...*(the Rechabites) *have obeyed the commandment of Jonadab your father, and kept all his precepts, and done according unto all that he hath commanded you: Therefore thus saith the LORD of hosts, the God of Israel; Jonadab the son of Rechab shall not want a man to stand before me for ever*" (Jeremiah 35:18-19).

The future is guaranteed for a people with exemplary loyalty. Those who, in spite of all odds, stand on God's word without shifting the ancient landmarks save not only themselves but also rein in future generations to stay on the path of righteousness and holiness. The Rechabites instituted a never-ceasing legacy of living in God's presence for their next generations through their unalloyed loyalty to the words of their father.

The price a generation pays in loyalty to the Lord is repaid multiplied times by their next generation's longevity in God's presence. Psalm 112:1-2 says, "*Blessed is the man that feareth the LORD, that delighteth greatly in his commandments. His seed shall be mighty upon earth: the generation of the upright shall be blessed.*"

WILLIAM WILBERFORCE: A LIFE LIVED FOR ONE CAUSE

William Wilberforce (1759-1833) was born into an aristocratic family in England. After attending Eton High School and Oxford University, his eyes were clearly set on becoming the United Kingdom's youngest prime minister. He was schooled in the high-wire politics of the British parliament, as a Member of Parliament for Yorkshire, Kingston upon Hull, and Bramber between 1780 and 1825.

In 1787, however, the thrust of his public service was revolutionized by a conversation he had with a former slave. After hearing about the sordid living conditions the slaves were forced to undertake enroute the slave plantations in the Caribbean and the hedonistic life the slave owners subjected them to both in Europe and the Americas, William Wilberforce made it his life mission to abrogate slavery.

He said in 1787, "God Almighty has set before me two great objectives; the suppression of the slave trade and the reformation of manners (moral values)." Despite coming against the might and money of the merchants operating the trans-Atlantic slave trade, William Wilberforce persisted.

After 46 years of presenting twenty different bills which were defeated in parliament, he succeeded in 1833. The Bill, called the "Bill for the Abolition of Slavery", was approved by the Government on 26th July 1833, and passed by the House of Lords on 29th August 1833. It instituted abolishment of slavery in most of the British Empire starting August 1834.

By this time, however, William Wilberforce had died on 29th July 1833. He suffered from chronic Ulcerative Colitis, and with his last breadth was able to see the actualization of his life purpose – emancipation of all British owned slaves. He was buried in Westminster Chapel and, as described in his epitaph, came to be known as William the Emancipator for his role in the fall of the trans-Atlantic slave trade.

A career is what you are paid for but a calling is what you are made for!

CHAPTER TEN

ELIEZER – THE GAME CHANGER!

"And the servant put his hand under the thigh of Abraham his master, and sware to him concerning that matter" (Genesis 24:9).

The servant to Abraham, Eliezer, epitomizes loyalty to the highest ideals. He served Abraham as a servant after his parents were captured in the invasion of Damascus (Genesis 14:15), and rose to become the chief servant when Abraham was about one hundred and forty years old.

He served Abraham for at least fifty-five years. Mention is made of him in Genesis 15:2-3, as having been born in Abraham's house. It says, *"...Abram said, LORD God, what wilt thou give me, seeing I go childless and the steward of my house is this Eliezer of Damascus? And Abram said, Behold, to me thou hast given no seed: and, lo, one born in my house is mine heir."*

Eliezer was not a man of flimsy, whimsical and lackluster loyalty but one of deep devotion who served his master from the cradle to the grave. He was not a man of pretence, but a man of persistence. Rather than be flippant with his employers, he was faithful to the end.

When Abraham needed someone to entrust the task of finding a wife for Isaac, his son of promise, he chose Eliezer. He told him during their conversation, *"...if the woman will not be willing to follow thee, then thou shalt be clear from this my oath: only bring not my son thither again. And the servant put his hand under the thigh of Abraham his master, and sware to him concerning that matter"* (Genesis 24:8-9).

Abraham entrusted the future of his progeny to the capable hands of Eliezer because he had unalloyed loyalty! His word was his bond, and like the individual abiding in God's presence, Eliezer was one "...*that sweareth to his own hurt, and changeth not*" (Psalm 15:4). He was a loyal servant, and eventually grew to become a legend in the Abrahamic dispensation!

THE RULER OVER ALL!

Eliezer began as the son of refugees in Abraham's household (Genesis 15:3). His parents, according to Bible history, were probably captured or voluntarily submitted themselves to Abraham, when he invaded Damascus to rescue his nephew Lot in Genesis 14:15.

In a space of around ten years, thereafter, Abraham had handed over the possession of his house and all that he had to Eliezer. He said, in Genesis 15:2-3, "...*the steward of my house is this Eliezer of Damascus?... and...one born in my house is mine heir*."

The words steward and heir, used to describe Eliezer are interpreted in the original Hebrew as possessor and someone given prescriptive authority. Eliezer went from an alien to the *bona fide* authority in Abraham's house hold because of his uncommon loyalty.

In Genesis 24:2, Eliezer is described as Abraham's "...*eldest servant,... that **ruled over all that he had**"* (emphasis added). Eliezer did not "...*despise the day of small things...*" (Zechariah 4:10), but was faithful in the little and so became ruler over much (Luke 16:10).

Legends are not an overnight success, but through diligence and loyalty, they become pursuers and peruses of God's will for their lives. Eliezer had paid his dues in Abraham's household and, notwithstanding whether he got the inheritance or not, he maintained strict fidelity that rewarded him as the executor of Abraham's estates.

In Genesis 24:10, the Bible says that "...*all the goods of his master were in his hand....*" Eliezer was tried, tested and true and became great in Abraham's household because he chose to make Abraham great (Genesis 24:34-35). He was one of those "...*who keep(s) the fig tree...(by)...waiting on their master (and so are) honored*" (Proverbs 27:18).

LOYALTY, NOT LEVELS!

Eliezer was a man dedicated to the cause for which Abraham lived, notwithstanding the cost to him in terms of hierarchy or level attained. He believed in the perpetuation of the nation through Abraham's seed that would bless the nations of the earth and was willing to play second fiddle to see Abraham's vision accomplished.

In spite of being Isaac's superior in age and organizational hierarchy, and the purported original heir to Abraham's inheritance in Genesis 15:3, Eliezer understood loyalty enough to call Isaac "*...my master...*" in Genesis 24:65. He went further and reported his mission of seeking a wife back to Isaac (Genesis 24:66), even though he had originally been sent by Abraham. This submission signaled his support for Isaac and his desire to make his master's vision a reality.

He did not betray his loyalty to Abraham's cause because of a change in command structure but maintained faith and fidelity throughout his life. **Eliezer understood that true loyalty was self-effacing and not selfish.** He served gladly in any position he was given and eventually rose to become a true legend in Abraham's household.

His legacy was not in the possessions he had or in the positions he occupied. It was in the prosperity his service enabled the vision of Abraham to bequeath to future generations. Eliezer was never his own man, but in being who God called him to be, he became God's man!

In Galatians 3:13-14 the Bible says, *"Christ hath redeemed us from the curse of the law, being made a curse for us: for it is written, Cursed is every one that hangeth on a tree: That the blessing of Abraham might come on the Gentiles through Jesus Christ; that we might receive the promise of the Spirit through faith."*

If Eliezer had dropped the baton, when sent to find Isaac's wife, multiple generations of blessings would be non-existent today! Alas, the Abrahamic blessing on the church through Christ by faith would have had to be obtained through another man. But Abraham held to his loyalty and remained God's agent of blessing to countless generations following.

I WILL BE NUMBER TWO, IN GOD'S AGENDA!

Several individuals began ministry with Billy Graham in the mid

1940's. They included Charles Templeton, Cliff Barrows and George Beverley Shea. While Charles Templeton jettisoned the ministry after undergoing a personal-faith-in-God crises at the Princeton Seminary, Cliff Barrows stuck with Billy Graham and has remained a staunch associate and loyal ally till date.

Cliff Barrow's responsibility as music and program director in the Billy Graham Evangelistic Association (BGEA) involved leading the choir and public in praise and worship during Billy Graham's nearly five thousand crusades worldwide. He also served to introduce Billy Graham, George Beverly Shea and other guest ministers just before they ministered.

As his visibility at BGEA organized crusades grew, so did Cliff Barrow's worldwide fame and loyalty to BGEA. He was asked on several occasions, by numerous individuals, when he would start his own ministry since he was, like Billy Graham, a licensed Southern Baptist minister. He always replied, *"I would rather be number two in God's plan than be number one in my own plans."*

Today, Cliff Barrows is in his mid-Nineties and still very active with BGEA. His loyalty has never wavered, and his commitment to souls is still non-ebbing. His legacy lives on in the work BGEA has done in the last 60 years that saw more than two hundred fifty million people in over a hundred countries reached face-to-face with the preaching of the gospel. Even though he stayed in the background while Billy Graham was in the spotlight, Cliff Barrows's loyalty to the cause God called him to – serving Billy Graham to win souls – has made him a legend in his time.

True faith is not borne out of logic but loyalty!

CHAPTER ELEVEN

BARAK: THE SHOELESS GENERAL!

*"And what shall I more say? for the time would fail me to tell of Gedeon, and of **Barak**, and of Samson, and of Jephthae; of David also, and Samuel, and of the prophets: Who through faith subdued kingdoms..."* (Hebrews 11:32-33).

In the days of Barak, it was not the norm for a man to stand behind a woman as his leader. But Barak did! He told Deborah, *"If thou wilt go with me, then I will go: but if thou wilt not go with me, then I will not go"* (Judges 4:8). He was willing to risk everything on Deborah the prophetess's instruction.

In spite of the grave odds his ragtag army of 10,000 men faced against a Canaanite army that consisted of *"...nine hundred chariots of iron..."* (Judges 4:13) and perhaps millions of soldiers, Barak staked his and his soldiers' lives on whatever Deborah the prophetess said.

Barak re-defined loyalty in that age. At the mention of Deborah's assent in Judges 4:14, he (Barak) moved his army into battle. In Judges 4:14, prophet Deborah said, *"up; for this is the day in which the LORD hath delivered Sisera into thine hand: is not the LORD gone out before thee? So Barak went down from mount Tabor, and ten thousand men after him."*

The result was an unprecedented victory over the better equipped and much-fancied Canaanite army led by Sisera (see Judges 4:15). Barak was loyal to the letter of Deborah's instruction, and in the process, he became a legend whose deeds are recorded in the annals of history.

In Psalm 83:9-11, for example, God instructed Israel "*...do unto them* (her enemies) *as unto the Midianites; as to **Sisera**, as to Jabin, at the brook of Kison....*" The victory roadmap initiated by Barak is still applicable for today's end time battles. If this roadmap is followed, like Barak, the church can "*subdue kingdoms..., wax valiant in fight, (and) turn to flight the armies of the aliens*" (Hebrews 11:33-34).

LEAVING A LEGACY

Because of his loyalty to Deborah and God, Barak became God's benchmark of how enemies are destroyed, He reaped the rewards of victory by leaving a forty-year legacy of peace in Israel. In Judges 5:31, the singers proclaimed after Barak had routed the army of Sisera, "*So let all thine enemies perish, O LORD: but let them that love him be as the sun when he goeth forth in his might. And the land had rest forty years.*"

Barak went out, not for self-acclaim, but to win a war that would lead to a land he could bequeath to the next generation. It did not matter who received the acclaim as long as God's objectives were achieved.

Even though Deborah had instructed him that he would not get the honor for the death of Sisera (Judges 4:9), Barak persisted and prevailed thereunto. He marched forward, albeit with a disunited army according to Judges 5:14-17, and prevailed.

Even though he did not have the tribes of Reuben, Dan, Gilead or Asher with him, he had God on his side and won. Judges 4:10, 20-21 says, "*...Barak called Zebulun and Naphtali to Kedesh; and he went up with ten thousand men at his feet: and Deborah went up with him.... They fought from heaven; the stars in their courses fought against Sisera. The river of Kishon swept them away, that ancient river, the river Kishon....*"

When men fail you, God raises up supernatural agents from unfamiliar territory to help you! Barak is celebrated today as one of the great heroes of faith because of his legendary loyalty to the Lord. While Barak is celebrated in Hebrews 11:32, Meroz is cursed in Judges 5:23 for desisting from the same battle. It says, "*Curse ye Meroz, said the angel of the LORD, curse ye bitterly the inhabitants thereof; because they came not to the help of the LORD, to the help of the LORD against the mighty.*"

Those who refuse to fight God's battles, at His behest, lose their life prominence and power. Meroz is never mentioned in history after this incident! **Loyalty births legends but disloyalty gives rise to derelicts and devestation.**

RESULTS WITHOUT RESOURCES

Barak fought the armies of Sisera bereft of resources such as shoes and spears. In Judges 5:8, the Bible says "*...then was war in the gates; was there a shield or spear seen among forty thousand in Israel?*" In Judges 5:15, the Bible adds that, "*...Barak...was sent on foot into the valley....*"

While his enemies had iron chariots numbering nine hundred (Judges 4:13), amongst other exquisite armory, Barak refused to go by what he saw but based his convictions on the word of God.

He made a decision to"*...walk by faith, not by sight...*" (2 Corinthians 5:7). He believed the prophetess Deborah, and in accordance with 2 Chronicles 20:20, he prospered. Even though Barak's army of shoeless and spear less men were materially deficient, they were the mightier army because of faith.

In 2 Chronicles 20:20, the Bible says "*...Believe in the LORD your God, so shall ye be established; believe his prophets, so shall ye prosper.*" Barak won the battle of the mind and so won the battle of means. He conquered through sheer mettle and so overcame the metal of his enemies!

In Judges 5:21, Barak exclaimed, "*O my soul, thou hast trodden down strength.*" He triumphed in his soul – that is the mind, will and emotions - and as a result won against the strength of Sisera. The soul that believes God's report will fight a better equipped army, amidst a dearth of physical resources, and still come out triumphant.

REAPING A MULTIGENERATIONAL REWARD!

Barak changed a generation, but Deborah shaped multiple generations with her legacy of service (see Judges 4:3-4). Many "Deborah's" of our time abound. Three who left multi-generational deposits to upcoming generations, as did Deborah, are listed below.

Fannie Crosby (1820-1908), for example, composed over 9,000 songs in her lifetime. Acknowledged as one of the greatest song writers of all time, Fannie Crosby composed such legendary songs as *Blessed Assurance,*

Rescue the *Perishing* and *O Pass Me Not O Gentle Savior*. Her song sheets have been reproduced over a hundred million times, and even in death, she still affects millions of lives today with her songs.

Nancy Alcorn started *Mercy Ministries Multiplied* in West Monroe, Louisiana in 1983. She set out to change the care of juvenile, abused, and distressed girls between the ages of sixteen and twenty-five years of age after witnessing the beleaguered state of juvenile care at the Tennessee correctional Department where she worked. With no government support, and no family to call her own, Nancy Alcorn has taken in thousands of young girls suffering from low self-esteem, anorexia, bulimia, depression, child abuse, domestic violence and other mental health conditions from across three continents, free of charge. She gives them a six month mind renewal with the sword of God's Spirit (the word of God) and afterwards releases them back to the local church and society.

Lastly, a woman called Grandma Bauszuss gave a prophetic word about Reinhard Bonnke when he was eleven years of age. According to *Living a life of Fire, – an autobiography of Reinhard Bonnke*," she stood at the end of a mid-week prayer meeting and told the congregation about a vision she had just had. In the vision she saw a very large crowd of black people surrounding Reinhard Bonnke. He was giving them bread from a loaf that never seemed to be exhausted1. This vision sparked faith and belief in Reinhard Bonnke's heart to establish Christ For All Nations (CFAN) in 1963, an organization that has seen over seventy-four million souls saved and has heralded the greatest evangelistic campaign in the modern era.

You cannot be a good servant of Christ and a poor servant of man!

CHAPTER TWELVE

ONESIMUS – THE CHAMPION SLAVE

"With Onesimus, a faithful and beloved brother, who is one of you. They shall make known unto you all things which are done here" (Colossians 4:9).

Onesimus was a slave who became a Christian after being ministered to by Apostle Paul during one of his numerous travels. Hitherto meeting Paul, however, he had run away from his master Philemon. According to Philemon 1:18, he was indebted in cash or kind to him.

Onesimus was free in Christ, but he chose to return to his master as a slave in order to demonstrate his loyalty first to God, and then to his master Philemon. As someone Paul called, *"...profitable to thee and to me. Whom I would have retained with me, that in thy stead he might have ministered unto me in the bonds of the gospel"* (Philemon 1:11,13), Onesimus was an asset to both the kingdom of God and man.

The name *Onesimus*, in the original Greek, means to get the advantage, derive joy from or be profitable to someone. Onesimus was a champion slave who was profitable to whomsoever he joined. He evoked joy in his audience and caused increase wherever he went. The secret to the fortune and faith Onesimus exhibited was his loyalty to his master.

In Luke 16:10-12, Jesus told his disciples, *"He that is faithful in that which is least is faithful also in much: and he that is unjust in the least is unjust also in much. If therefore ye have not been faithful in the unrighteous mammon, who will commit to your trust the true riches? And if ye have not been faithful in that which is another man's, who shall give you that which is your own?"*

Even though a runaway slave, Onesimus returned to his master at great personal risk. According to Old testament tenets, *"thou shalt not deliver unto his master the servant which is escaped from his master unto thee: He shall dwell with thee, even among you…"* (Deuteronomy 23:15-16) because of the attendant physical and emotional maligning a returning runaway slave would be subject to.

In spite of this, Onesimus returned to Philemon and served him meritoriously. Paul wrote, in Philemon 1:15-16, to Philemon and said, *"…perhaps he (Onesimus)…departed for a season, that thou shouldest receive him for ever; Not now as a servant, but above a servant, a brother beloved, specially to me, but how much more unto thee, both in the flesh, and in the Lord?"*

SEDUCTION, NOT SEDITION!

It is believers' attitude toward leadership that determines their altitude in influencing their leaders. Those who become legends at their places of worship or work first became loyalists of their superiors. **They "seduce" them by their loyalty instead of causing sedition by disloyalty!**

Apostle Paul wrote, in 1Timothy 6:1-2, *"Let as many servants as are under the yoke count their own masters worthy of all honor, that the name of God and his doctrine be not blasphemed. And they that have believing masters, let them not despise them, because they are brethren; but rather do them service, because they are faithful and beloved, partakers of the benefit…."*

There is great reward in right service, but it takes loyalty and not just laboring to receive it. Colossians 3:22-24 says, *"Servants, obey in all things your masters according to the flesh; not with eyeservice, as menpleasers; but in singleness of heart, fearing God; And whatsoever ye do, do it heartily, as to the Lord, and not unto men; Knowing that of the Lord ye shall receive the reward of the inheritance: for ye serve the Lord Christ."*

Many believers do their work, with eye service or deceitfulness. As a result they lose their reward. In Jeremiah 48:10, Jeremiah says, *"Cursed be they that doeth the work of the LORD deceitfully…"* and in Ephesians 6:5-8, Paul adjures *"Servants, be obedient to them that are your masters according to the flesh, with fear and trembling, in singleness of your heart, as unto*

Christ; Not with eyeservice, as menpleasers; but as the servants of Christ, doing the will of God from the heart; With good will doing service, as to the Lord, and not to men."

In Titus 2:9, servants are adjured *"to be obedient unto their own masters, and to please them well in all things; not answering again; Not purloining, but shewing all good fidelity; that they may adorn the doctrine of God our Savior in all things."* The gospel that is lived and seen in all things a believer does is a gospel lived in loyalty to superiors, no matter their motives or manners. I Peter 2:17-18 says, *"Honor all men. Love the brotherhood. Fear God. Honor the king (and) servants, be subject to your masters with all fear; not only to the good and gentle, but also to the froward."*

If the service rendered is to the Lord, and not to man, it will generate rewards, but if it is unto man it brings a curse instead. A life of loyalty is a life of commitment towards God and man. As Matthew Henry said in his commentary, *"Christianity does not do away our duties to men, but directs to the right doing of them."* Eventually, Onesimus became the bishop of Ephesus (according to Church history), and was allowed by Philemon to flourish as a minister of the gospel who was highly respected by the local churches (see Colossians 4:9).

THE GREATEST GENERATION IS A GRATEFUL GENERATION!

What several historians call the Greatest Generation lived between 1920 and 1956. They are acknowledged as those men and women who having lived through the Great Depression and the Second World War went on to rebuild America not for their own personal fame or fortune but because it was the right thing to do1.

Today's generation of millennials, on the other hand, have been labeled the Entitlement Generation. In the eyes of modern society, they expect everything to be handed down to them with as little effort as possible on their part. They frown at apprenticeship and expect mastery without the pains of tutelage.

Unfortunately, this has produced half-baked entrepreneurs with bankrupted businesses midway through their lives. This spirit of entitlement is described by Apostle Paul as one of the signs of the last days.

He said, "...*men shall be lovers of their own selves, covetous, boasters, proud, blasphemers, disobedient to parents, unthankful, unholy, without natural affection, **trucebreakers*** (emphasis added), *false accusers, incontinent, fierce, despisers of those that are good, traitors, heady, highminded, lovers of pleasures more than lovers of God*" (2 Timothy 3:2-4).

A generation, however, that does not burn its bridges or despise those who lifted them up in the first place will be akin to the greatest generation. Jesus said, in the parable of the talents, "...*thou good servant: because thou hast been faithful in a very little, have thou authority over ten cities*" (Luke 19:17).

Nabal labeled David as one of "...many *servants...that break away... from his master...whom I know not whence they be*" (1 Samuel 25:10-11) to David's chagrin. In our generation, to the contrary, this statement from Nabal would be considered a compliment. This generation celebrates those who are "self-made" even if these so-called success stories have no obvious apprenticeship or loyalty trail to their name.

The Bible honors those who serve; it says, "*Whoso keepeth the fig tree shall eat the fruit thereof: so he that waiteth on his master shall be honored*" (Proverbs 27:18). It goes on to add that "...*he that is greatest among you shall be your servant*" (Matthew 23:11).

The life of loyalty is a life of fidelity that proclaims the gospel of legends to a world that abhors such sacrificial service. Onesimus became a general of the faith, in spite of his checkered background, because he waited on instead of wasting his master and was grateful not greedy concerning his position in the ministry.

THE WESTMINISTER "WANT-A-WAY"

One of such legends who served their generation was Dr. David Livingstone (1813-1873). A St-Andrews-trained-medical doctor, he lived and breathed missions. After medical school, he set out for Africa at a time when all that was known about it was that it was unknown. Africa in the early nineteenth century had not been explored. Apart from a few ships that had berthed at coastal towns in South Africa, no one had gone into the interior.

David Livingstone initiated inland missions on continental Africa by collaborating with the United Kingdom Geographical Society. While they wanted exploration for strictly geographical reasons, David Livingstone wanted to do it in order to discover souls for whom Jesus Christ died.

On his graduation, while every other medical doctor in his class was listing lucrative job offers that had been tabled before them, David shocked them all by saying he wanted to be a missionary to Africa. They mocked and derided him as flippant and foolish, but David Livingstone was firm in his convictions.

His brother, Charles Livingstone, as a physician in the then newly discovered land of America, asked David to join him and take advantage of the opportunities America had to offer. In his reply, David Livingstone said *"I will go anywhere, provided it be forward! The end of the geographical exploration is the beginning of the missionary enterprise. I shall open up a path to the interior or perish! Death alone will put a stop to my efforts because I am a missionary, heart and soul. God had an only son and he was a missionary and physician. I am a poor imitation of him or wish to be. In this service I hope to live; in it I wish to die."*

Throughout his lifetime, he labored under arduous circumstances. His left arm was paralyzed after his being attacked by lions. His boats were broken at sea leaving him abandoned and countless times he suffered hunger, pain, and loneliness. In spite of the travails he faced, David said *"if we wait till we run no risk, the gospel will never reach the interior."* In 1871, Stanley the explorer asked him to return to Europe but he said to Stanley's dismay, *"I am immortal till my work is accomplished and though I see few results, future missionaries will see conversions after every sermon."*

He died in May 1873 and his body was carried across the terrains of South Africa to the coastal city, Bagamoyo, by his African servants. He was interred at Westminster Abbey, the citadel of Kings and Archbishops, in recognition of his numerous accomplishments in opening Africa to the gospel and the outside world. In retrospect, his classmates who chastised him for pursuing a missionary calling to the detriment of his medical career lined the streets of London to accord him a martyr's burial in honor of a "Westminster want-a-way" who ended up in Westminster!

Those who address their mountains will be dressed by their decision, but those who ignore their mountains will be destroyed by them!

CHAPTER THIRTEEN

JONATHAN: DAVID'S ALTEREGO

*"So Jonathan made a covenant with the house of David, saying,
Let the LORD even require it at the hand of David's enemies. And
Jonathan caused David to swear again, because he loved him: for
he loved him as he loved his own soul"* (1 Samuel 20:16-17).

Jonathan, prince of Israel and the heir to the throne of King Saul of Israel
never constituted any obstacle to David attaining his father's throne. In
fact, he told David *"…thou shalt be king over Israel, and I shall be next unto
thee;…"* (1 Samuel 23:17).

At the cost of his relationship with his father, Jonathan supported
David's meteoric rise from shepherd to statesman. He told David, *"Go in
peace, forasmuch as we have sworn both of us in the name of the LORD, saying,
The LORD be between me and thee, and between my seed and thy seed for ever"*
(1 Samuel 20:42).

While his father, King Saul, wanted David dead, Jonathan *"…went to
David into the wood, and strengthened his hand in God* (saying) *fear not for
the hand of Saul my father shall not find thee"* (1 Samuel 21:16-17).

In true loyalty, Jonathan was willing to suffer retribution and disgrace
for the sake of his relationship with David. After his father called him the
"…son of the perverse rebellious woman…" (1 Samuel 20:30), he *"arose from
the table in fierce anger, and did eat no meat…for he was grieved for David,
because his father had done him* (David) *shame"* (1 Samuel 20:34).

True loyalty seeks to absolve a compatriot from shame, even at

65

personal expense. It loves uncompromisingly and suffers inconsiderably in true loyalty fashion. Jesus, *"...a friend that sticketh closer than a brother"* (Proverbs 18:24), *"...laid down his life for us and* (so) *we ought to lay down our lives for the brethren"* (1 John 3:16).

SWIFTER THAN EAGLES, STRONGER THAN LIONS!

Jonathan and David had a covenant relationship just like the church has with Jesus Christ. Hebrews 12:24 says the church reaches unto, *"... Jesus the mediator of the new covenant, and to the blood of sprinkling, that speaketh better things than that of Abel."*

Jonathan was so loyal to David he covenanted to protect him (and *vice versa*) to everlasting generations. In 1 Samuel 20:16, *"Jonathan made a covenant with the house of David"* that stipulated Jonathan *"...shall not cut off...kindness from (David's) house for ever"* (1 Samuel 20:15).

Jonathan jettisoned his opportunity to the throne because of his loyalty to David, and prayed that David's enemies treat him as well as he would (see 1 Samuel 20:16). At Jonathan's death, David said *"I am distressed for thee, my brother Jonathan: very pleasant hast thou been unto me: thy love to me was wonderful, passing the love of women. How are the mighty fallen, and the weapons of war perished!"* (2 Samuel 1:26-27).

The result of such uncommon loyalty between friends was that, at Jonathan's death, David described him as *"...lovely and pleasant in life, and...swifter than eagles,...(and)... stronger than lions..."* (2 Samuel 1:23). Those attributes are not those of a wayfaring jobber, but those of a man with commitment, faith and loyalty.

Any person who in life was stronger than a lion or swifter than an eagle is a legend. Jonathan was one of such; he and his armor bearer single-handedly attacked a garrison of Philistine troops that eventually sparked an Israeli victory in 1 Samuel 14:1-15, 46.

In the aftermath of that victory, the Israeli soldiers responded to King's Saul murderous intent of killing Jonathan for tasting honey, by saying, *"Shall Jonathan die, who hath wrought this great salvation in Israel? God forbid: as the LORD liveth, there shall not one hair of his head fall to the ground; for he hath wrought with God this day..."* (1 Samuel 14:45).

Jonathan commanded unusual loyalty from Saul's soldiers because he was a man of unequivocal loyalty. He kept his promises, and in the process, God gave him a legendary status in Israel that outlived him. At his death, David asked *"Is there yet any that is left of the house of Saul, that I may shew him kindness for Jonathan's sake?"* (2 Samuel 9:1).

After getting an answer in the affirmative, David sought out and restored Mephiboshet, Jonathan's son, to the palace giving him everything his father and grand father owned (see 2 Samuel 9:6). The name *Mephibosheth* means shame destroyer and is akin to what happens to the seed to those who remain loyal to their covenant.

THE POWER OF COVENANT

God is a God of covenant. He said, in Hebrews 8:8-10, *"....I will make a new covenant with the house of Israel and with the house of Judah: Not according to the covenant that I made with their fathers in the day when I took them by the hand to lead them out of the land of Egypt;...For this is the covenant that I will make with the house of Israel after those days, saith the Lord; I will put my laws into their mind, and write them in their hearts: and I will be to them a God, and they shall be to me a people:"*

This covenant is irrevocable and binding eternally on both sides, just like the covenant made in God's presence between Jonathan and David in 1 Samuel 20:12-17 was binding on both of them. A covenant is not just legally binding on both parties involved, but also on their children forever. God said, in Psalm 89:34, *"My covenant will I not break, nor alter the thing that is gone out of my lips."*

The Gibeonites, for example, during the reign of Joshua entered into covenant by subtlety with Israel forever. They beguiled the advancing armies of Israel into making a peace pact with them and as a result *"...the children of Israel smote them not, because the princes of the congregation had sworn unto them by the LORD God of Israel"* (see Joshua 9:15-18).

Four hundred years later, in flagrant violation of this covenant, King Saul killed multitudes of the Gibeonites. In 2 Samuel 21:2, the Bible says *"... Saul sought to slay them in his zeal to the children of Israel and Judah."* As a result a famine arose in Israel because of *"...Saul, and...his bloody house, because he slew the Gibeonites"* (2 Samuel 21:1).

The curse causeless does not come (Proverbs 26:2). Several times the cause of the curse was breaking of covenants or disloyalty to long-held vows and promises. Until David sacrificed seven sons of King Saul to the Gibeonites, the famine ravaged the land of Israel (see 2 Samuel 21:14).

God, as a God of covenant, expects His church to abide by covenant. He expects exemplary loyalty, commitment, and faithfulness to that agreement or covenant from His Church. **The mark of a true legend is loyalty.**

David and Jonathan were accorded the status of legends in their time because they abode by the terms of their covenant. King Saul, on the other hand, dilly dallied between banning mediums and using them (1 Samuel 28:9) and taking the land of the Gibeonites or slaying them (2 Samuel 21:1-9) and as a result ended up derided, even in death (1 Samuel 31:9 and 2 Samuel 1:21). **A life of loyal decisions makes for a legendary destiny!**

THE TRAP OF THE TRICKSTER

Col. Sam Momah had just received the phone call he had been dreading. His wife, Christy Momah had just called to inform him about the latest list of military governors, and she was not a "happy camper."

His name was once again not on the list. She reminded him of the litany of recommendations she had made for him to follow in order to get on the list, but which he had failed to adhere to.

Because another wave of political appointments by the military administration had come and gone, she reeled off countless opportunities that had gone begging because he would not cozy up to the powers-that-be.

When she suggested they go to see a "prayer man," Col Momah reticently agreed hoping to create some space to maneuver out of the tight spot he was in. Unfortunately, he was about to get into the trickster's trap albeit surreptitiously.

They saw the "prayer man" and he prayed for them. Within a few years, Col. (now General) Momah, was appointed as Federal Minister of Science and Technology. As was to be expected, my family were elated.

Unbeknown to us, however, the "prayer man" was also aware of the appointment and expected my Dad (General Momah) to allocate a huge portion of the ministry's budget to him.

When my father refused, he resorted to blackmail and deadly espionage to make my father divert state resources to him. Consequently, my father had him apprehended by the police. On his arrest, he confessed to being a con artist who used blackmail to rough-shod prominent society bigwigs to forfeit their wealth and property.

My parents earned an invaluable lesson from their experience. They saw that some wolves come clothed in sheep's clothing and that true promotion comes only from God. My Dad, now General Momah, then went on to have a successful tenure as the longest serving Federal Minister of Science and Technology till date.

What you compromise to keep, you will ultimately lose!

CHAPTER FOURTEEN

ELIAKIM – THE LIFE OF GLORY!

"And I will fasten him (Eliakim) *as a nail in a sure place; and he shall be for a glorious throne to his father's house. And they shall hang upon him all the glory of his father's house,"* (Isaiah 22:23).

God took a Levite, Eliakim the son of Hilkiah, and elevated him to glory. In Isaiah 22:20-22, God said *"…I will call my servant Eliakim the son of Hilkiah and I will clothe him with thy robe, and strengthen him with thy girdle, and I will commit thy government into his hand: and he shall be a father to the inhabitants of Jerusalem, and to the house of Judah. And the key of the house of David will I lay upon his shoulder; so he shall open, and none shall shut; and he shall shut, and none shall open."*

He gave unprecedented authority and power to Eliakim, so such so that *"they shall hang upon him all the glory of his father's house, the offspring and the issue, all vessels of small quantity, from the vessels of cups, even to all the vessels of flagons"* (Isaiah 22:24). When a man becomes the cynosure of all eyes and the accumulation of the family blessings, he has truly become a legend of his times.

Eliakim followed Shebna as treasurer or overseer of the king's household (an office comparable to today's chief of staff). Unlike Shebna, however, who was deposed by God for pride and security in vanity (see Isaiah 22:15-19), Eliakim served with no axe to grind. Since his allegiance to the throne was never in question, King Hezekiah entrusted him with major matters of state, including war negotiations with the Assyrians (Isaiah 36:3-22) and prayer requests to the prophet Isaiah (Isaiah 37:1-6).

As a result of his unalloyed loyalty, Eliakim became a landmark and a yardstick by which to measure glory and power in Israel. In Isaiah 22:22, God says Eliakim "*...shall open, and none shall shut; and he shall shut, and none shall open*" because he had allowed God to "*...fasten him as a nail in a sure place*" (Isaiah 22:23). He wasn't wavering in opinion or insubordinate to authority, but stayed in his place and reaped a life of unprecedented glory.

THE REIGN OF GLORY

Before Eliakim could live a life of glory, however, God had to "*...clothe him with thy robe, and strengthen with thy girdle...*" (Isaiah 22:21). This robe, according to Ephesians 6:14 and Isaiah 61:10, is the believer's robe of righteousness, and the girdle is the truth of God's word (Ephesians 6:14). Without these two qualities, legendary loyalty is impossible.

Eliakim was, first and foremost, righteous before he became regaled in glory! There can be no true glory without grace, and there is no legitimate honor without holiness. In a world that celebrates counterfeit Christianity, nothing has shorn the church more from being legends with true glory than divided loyalties towards the word of God. **Sin is the ultimate glory stopper!**

Until believers put the word of truth in their hearts and wear the robe of righteousness through the atoning work of Christ on the cross (2 Corinthians 5:21) in their daily lives, they will forfeit the apportioned life that God has called them to which is full of His glory.

Truth is the believer's master key to freedom from shame and oblivion. Jesus told a group of believers in John 8:31-32, "*...If ye continue in my word, then are ye my disciples indeed and ye shall know the truth, and the truth shall make you free.*" Truth shows a believer what, who and where to live. **Until he or she believes and lives the truth, he or she will always believe and live a lie!**

TOTAL LOYALTY IS IMPOSSIBLE
WITHOUT TRUE LOVE!

No man or woman can walk in great glory without love and loyalty. Not just blind loyalty, but a loyalty that is birthed first and foremost in love. In 1 Peter 5:1-4, the apostle Peter warns elders to "*feed the flock of God which is among you, taking the oversight thereof, not by constraint, but willingly; not for filthy lucre, but of a ready mind; Neither as being lords over God's heritage, but being examples to the flock…and when the chief Shepherd shall appear, ye shall receive a crown of glory that fadeth not away.*"

Love is the undergirding reason for a life of loyalty – not lordship. Eliakim was one who would be "*…a father to the inhabitants of Jerusalem, and to the house of Judah.*" As a result, God said "*…the key of the house of David will I lay upon his shoulder; so he shall open, and none shall shut; and he shall shut, and none shall open*" (Isaiah 22:21-22).

Unlike Shebna, who was more preoccupied with protecting himself in a sepulcher (see Isaiah 22:16), Eliakim was a father to all in Israel and committed to protecting and praying for their peace. In Isaiah 36:11, he told Rabshakeh, the emissary of the King of Assyria, to couch his words of propaganda and aggravation toward the listening Jews but Rabshakeh stood and "*…cried with a loud voice in the Jews' language, and said Hear ye the words of the great king, the king of Assyria*" (Isaiah 36:13).

Rather than respond in like manner, Eliakim (and his ancillary staff) "*…held their peace, and answered him not a word for the king's commandment was, saying, Answer him not*" (Isaiah 36:21). Those who become loyalty legends in life treasure peace and walk in love no matter how provocative their enemies are toward them. In Psalm 37:8-11, the Psalmist adjures believers to "*Cease from anger, and forsake wrath: fret not thyself in any wise to do evil. For evildoers shall be cut off: but those that wait upon the LORD, they shall inherit the earth. (And)…the meek shall inherit the earth; and shall delight themselves in the abundance of peace.*"

Faith works by love (Galatians 5:6), and without faith it is impossible to please God (Hebrews 11:6) or see the miraculous (Mark 11:23-24). **Love is the turn-around that changes lords to legends!** As a tribute to the kind of love Eliakim possessed, Shebna (his predecessor in the office of chief of staff) remained one of his aides during King Hezekiah's reign (see Isaiah

36:3). Eliakim was not vindictive or punitive towards his predecessors, including Shebna, but chose to build on their legacy instead. **Tomorrow's legends are today's lovers!**

FROM SHAME TO FAME

As one of the top students in my home economics high school class, I was expected to coast smoothly to an excellent grade. I was, however, a poor student in the practical aspect which involved sewing clothes together from the scratch. I wanted to prove to all and sundry that I could do more than an average grade, and so even though I could not thread a needle properly, and had little hope of sewing a pajamas all by myself, I submitted a perfectly sewn multicolored pajamas in pursuit of my home economics assignment.

The work was, however, too good to be done by a student and my teacher new it! I had purchased multicolored material and given it to a nearby tailor to finish in his embroidery and sewing institute. He had used a sewing machine on the job I gave him, a fact easily noticed by my home economics teacher. As a result of this fraudulent activity, I was given me a zero score in home economics practical. Due to this unexpected but deserved action, I was faced with possible failure and repetition of the class unless I scored above ninety five per cent in the theoretical paper.

My home economics teacher publicly shamed me, and told me that I would most likely repeat the year. I was, however, determined not to fail. I studied for the theoretical paper diligently and achieved a perfect score of one hundred per cent that pleasantly amazed my home economics teacher and fellow students. My home economics teacher said afterwards to her colleagues, *"I have never seen a student who failed my practical aspect with a zero score still pass the final course."* I was a first in her book and became famous among my classmates as a result. My shame became fame, my disgrace became His grace and those who despised me began to delight in me!

PART IV

TYPES OF LOYALTY

- , LOYALTY TO THE COUNTRY
- , LOYALTY TO THE CHILDREN
- , LOYALTY TO THE CARRIER
- , LOYALTY TO THE CAUSE
- , LOYALTY TO THE CITIZENS
- , LOYALTY TO THE CHRIST
- , LOYALTY TO THE CHURCH
- , LOYALTY TO THEIR CHOICES

Loyalty is not antiquated
but archetypal of
every Christian!

CHAPTER FIFTEEN

LOYALTY TO THE COUNTRY

"Let every soul be subject unto the higher powers. For there is no power but of God: the powers that be are ordained of God. Whosoever therefore resisteth the power, resisteth the ordinance of God: and they that resist shall receive to themselves damnation" (Romans 13:1-2).

When a man or woman is loyal to their country, they are obedient to the laws of the land and not disobedient. Paul, writing to Titus, said, *"Put them* (the church) *in mind to be subject to principalities and powers, to obey magistrates..."* (Titus 3:1).

The Bible describes a ruler as the *"...minister of God to thee for good... he beareth not the sword in vain: for he is the minister of God, a revenger to execute wrath upon him that doeth evil"* (Romans 13:4).

Loyalty to the country is a commandment that must be obeyed. In Romans 13:2, Apostle Paul says that those who fight the authorities fight God unwittingly. He says, *"Whosoever therefore resisteth the power, resisteth the ordinance of God: and they that resist shall receive to themselves damnation."*

Loyalty to the country is not an opinion, therefore, but an ordination from heaven for our welfare. That is the reason Paul adjured *"...first of all, supplications, prayers, intercessions, and giving of thanks, be made for all men; For kings, and for all that are in authority; that we may lead a quiet and peaceable life in all godliness and honesty"* (1 Timothy 2:1-2).

PATRIOTS DO NOT PRACTICE PERFIDY!

Loyalty to one's country is called patriotism. Patriotism is defined as love for or devotion to one's country. Patriotism is, however, contingent on the nation or country's loyalty to God. In Psalm 33:12, the Psalmist exclaims, *"Blessed is the nation whose God is the LORD; and the people whom he hath chosen for his own inheritance."* If a nation turns her back to God, however, God will curse instead of bless her!

Perfidy, on the other hand, is defined as a deliberate breach of faith or trust. It is a violation of loyalty and is demonstrated by acts of treachery. Patriots fear the Lord and so honor authority, but those who practice perfidy forsake God's word and live by human impulses and vagaries.

The prophet Jeremiah, writing to the exiles in Babylon, adjured them to obey God's instructions and *"...seek the peace of the city whither I have caused you to be carried away captives, and pray unto the LORD for it: for in the peace thereof shall ye have peace"* (Jeremiah 29:7).

Mordecai, for example, chose to pray for the Kingdom of King Ahasuerus instead of assault it with rebellion and resistance (see Esther 4:16). In spite of the fact that King Ahasuerus had signed an edict exterminating all Jews from the land (Esther 3:12-14), prayer remained Esther and Mordecai's choice weapon.

In deference to God, Mordecai refused to bow to Haman (Esther 3:3-5). He was loyal to his adopted country, as proven by his exposure of the plot to assassinate the king in Esther 2:21-23, but refused to abdicate his loyalty to God because of Haman (Esther 3:2).

A believer's loyalty is first to God, before a country or an individual. David, for example, covenanted to sacrifice seven descendants of King Saul to offset the famine in Israel, but yet *"...spared Mephibosheth, the son of Jonathan the son of Saul, because of the LORD's oath that was between them, between David and Jonathan the son of Saul"* (2 Samuel 21:7).

All other loyalties must be in tandem with allegiance to God for it to be obeyed. That is the reason Daniel defied King Darius's commandment not to pray to anyone but the king in Daniel 6:10, and the three Hebrew boys – Shadrach, Meshach, and Abednego – refused to bow to the golden idol erected by King Nebuchadnezzar (Daniel 3:16).

SUPPORT, NOT SUPPLANT!

God advocates that the Church make "...*supplications, prayers, intercessions, and giving of thanks,...for all men; For kings, and for all that are in authority...for this is good and acceptable in the sight of God our Savior*" (1 Timothy 2:1-3).

Our responsibility is to plead, not pillory, our leaders! The quicker the church prays, the quicker God turns the nation and its leaders toward Him. Paul said, in 1 Timothy 2:2, that those who pray for their leaders "...*lead a quiet and peaceable life in all godliness and honesty.*"

To live in peace, believers must pray for their leaders, not curse or complain over them. They should not sponsor sedition or encourage trauma, turmoil and tirades that are designed to push the government out of office.

Absalom, for example, usurped his father's authority in a "palace putsch" but ended his life tragically. At his death, a Cushite messenger sent to relay the tidings of the war to King David, told him, "*The enemies of my lord the king, and all that rise against thee to do thee hurt, be as that young man is*" (2 Samuel 18:32).

Absalom did not desire peace in the nation, and so lost any semblance of peace in his life. The Psalmist said, "*Pray for the peace of Jerusalem: they shall prosper that love thee. Peace be within thy walls, and prosperity within thy palaces*" (Psalm 122:6-7).

When you desire peace in the nation, it will promote you; but if you are only interested in the balkanization of a nation and the dismemberment of its citizenry, your destiny will be pulverized.

FLIGHT #93

On September 11th 2001, forty passengers and crew boarded United flight #93 en route to San Francisco. They embarked on the journey from Newark airport, New Jersey as passengers but ended their journey in Somerset county, Pennsylvania as patriots. They entered as laymen and lay women but died minutes later as legends.

These forty, without any weapons of their own, stopped four brazen terrorists from crashing flight #93 into the White House or Capitol Building in Washington DC. These four men named Ahmed Alnami,

Jarrah Ziad, Ahmed Alhaznawi and Alghamdi Saeed had seized the cockpit of the plane thirty minutes after takeoff and redirected the plane toward Washington, D.C.

These forty passengers learned similar developments had earlier that morning resulted in the destruction of the Twin Towers and the Pentagon Building. They were determined to stop the terrorists' repeating their script with Flight #93. They stormed the cockpit, which the terrorists commandeered, disarmed them, and forced an emergency crash landing of the plane in Somerset county, Pennsylvania.

Though more than three thousand people lost their lives at ground zero and other terror stricken sites, even more would have died but for the heroic intervention of these forty passengers. They made the supreme sacrifice for their nation, and today are considered legends because of their unalloyed loyalty to God, their nation and their fellow humans.

Mentorship Is Makeover Without The Mistakes!

CHAPTER SIXTEEN

LOYALTY TO THE CHILDREN

"Lo, children are an heritage of the LORD: and the fruit of the womb is his reward. As arrows are in the hand of a mighty man; so are children of the youth. Happy is the man that hath his quiver full of them: they shall not be ashamed, but they shall speak with the enemies in the gate" (Psalm 127:3-5).

America is currently at a crossroads in respect to teenage delinquency. With the highest teenage pregnancy rate in the western world (34 pregnancies per 1000 teenage girls)[1], a substance abuse rate of 40% among its teenage population[2] and more teenagers raised in single parent homes than at any other time in its history[3], American youth are stymied in a myriad of poverty, violence, and drugs.

This grim future is believed by some public commentators to be the result of a loss of loyalty by parents to the next generation. The terms "sperm-donor", "baby-daddy," and "deadbeat pop" represent aphorisms that reflect this dearth of parents, especially fathers, in our modern society[4].

The Psalmist described children under the tutelage of their parents as *"...arrows in the hands of a mighty man..."* (Psalm 127:4). Without parental guidance, however, these arrows become blunt and are directed amiss. The responsibility of parents to their children is to be spent for them, and not to spend from them.

In 2 Corinthians 12:14-15, Apostle Paul understanding these dynamics, challenged the church in Corinth saying *"...I will not be burdensome to you for I seek not yours but you. For the children ought not to lay up for the parents, but the parents for the children. And I will very gladly spend and be spent for you…."*

Too many homes are rudderless and aimless because selfish parents spend their patrimony on themselves, rather than to spend it on their children. Paul called true fathers in the faith those willing to serve without being served, and those who give without being given anything in return. It is these individuals who leave indelible footprints and become legends of their time.

THE FAILURE-PROOF HOME

The Psalmist describes a failure-proof home in Psalm 128:1-4. He says, *"Blessed is every one that feareth the LORD; that walketh in his ways. For thou shalt eat the labor of thine hands: happy shalt thou be, and it shall be well with thee. Thy wife shall be as a fruitful vine by the sides of thine house: thy children like olive plants round about thy table. Behold, that thus shall the man be blessed that feareth the LORD."*

There must, however, be a man who fears the Lord for the rest of their family to be blessed (see Psalm 128:4). God gives individuals to change families, and He gives families to change the church and the nation. The panacea for the world of corruption are God-fearing individuals who lead their families to church and by so doing change the world.

The spate of divorce, domestic violence, child abuse, teenage pregnancy, and youth incarceration is a result of the broken-family system in America today. In the last fifty years, the rate of single parent families has increased from less than twenty percent in 1935 to above fifty percent in 2015. As a result, the rate of child abuse and domestic violence cases has escalated tenfold[6].

Never in the history of the world have children been more unsafe! In 2014, 366 teenage girls were abducted from their classrooms by the *Al-Queda* sect called *Boko-Haram* in Chibok, Nigeria, and married to several terrorists. In 2012, at an elementary school in Sandy Hook, Connecticut, USA, twenty-seven children were killed by a deranged youth adding to worsening violence-to-children statistics.

The reason for this non-scripted behavior is the infiltration of the family unit with strange spirits. In Psalm 144:11-12, the Psalmist prayed

"…deliver me from the hand of strange children, whose mouth speaketh vanity, and their right hand is a right hand of falsehood: That our sons may be as plants grown up in their youth; that our daughters may be as corner stones, polished after the similitude of a palace."

The dearth of the parental figure in the home has led to a loss of defense for many children. **The failure-proof family thrives on parental loyalty to their children.** These parents defend, direct, and demonstrate a lifestyle of faith that their children emulate. Psalm 112:1-3 says, *"Blessed is the man that feareth the LORD, that delighteth greatly in his commandments. His seed shall be mighty upon earth: the generation of the upright shall be blessed. Wealth and riches shall be in his house: and his righteousness endureth for ever."*

JOCHEBED: THE LOYALTY OF A MOTHER!

Moses, the deliverer of the nation of Israel, was born to Jochebed, a woman of the tribe of Levi (Numbers 26:59). Even though the Bible is silent on the role Amram, her husband, played in safeguarding little Moses from the evil draconian decree of Pharaoh to kill all Israeli male infants, it gives prominence to the cost Jochebed paid to nurture Moses.

Exodus 2:2-3 says, *"…when she saw him that he was a goodly child, she hid him three months. And when she could not longer hide him, she took for him an ark of bulrushes, and daubed it with slime and with pitch, and put the child therein; and she laid it in the flags by the river's brink."*

Her child was designated for death on delivery, but she defied Pharoah's orders by having the baby, hiding him for three months and then putting him in the bulrushes of the river and eventually nursing him till he was weaned (Exodus 2:3-9). She risked her life, defied the law and spent Moses formative years framing his mind-set with the word of God.

In Hebrews 11:23, she is listed as one of the heroes of faith. It says, *"By faith Moses, when he was born, was hid three months of his parents, because they saw he was a proper child; and they were not afraid of the king's commandment."*

Without the loyalty of Jochebed, Moses - the man who became a prince of Egypt and eventually led Israel out of Egypt -, may never have become *"… mighty in words and in deeds"* (Acts 7:22). She gave up all she had to give him the opportunity to change his generation. Only such loyalty can produce such legendary faith as demonstrated for following generations by Moses (Hebrews 11:27-29).

LEESVILLE TEST

While working at the Louisiana State Penitentiary, Angola, Louisiana, as a family physician, I met an inmate at the gate of the hospital treatment center. He was serving a life sentence and worked as a cleaner in the clinic. While waiting for transportation to take him back to his cell, he decided to intimate about his family.

He was especially proud of his daughter who was a final year medical student at the Louisiana State University Medical School, New Orleans, and followed that up by telling me why he was in Angola for a life sentence.

He said he had killed a man because of loyalty to his daughter. This man had raped his teenage daughter; and, in spite of repetitive appeals to the police, he walked free on the streets of Leesville to continue his acts of perversion.

According to this indignant but intelligent-sounding inmate, this pedophile told him in private that he would do it again and that there would be nothing he could do about it. In a fit of rage, this Angola inmate killed him and then reported himself to the police.

Even though incarcerated for life, this indignant inmate was unrepentant. He calmly told me he would do it again if a similar situation presented itself. He gave up his liberties that his daughter, now a medical doctor, could live in liberty. He forfeited his lifelong freedom that she may enjoy a lifetime of freedom.

*Until you learn to listen
to others, the world will
never listen to you!*

CHAPTER SEVENTEEN

LOYALTY TO THE CARRIER

"Honor thy father and mother; (which is the first commandment with promise:) That it may be well with thee, and thou mayest live long on the earth" (Ephesians 6:2-3).

Every person, alive or dead, was born from a carrier who is their parent. Parents serve as God's delivery vehicle through whom children come into the world. The Bible says, in Ecclesiastes 11:5, *"…thou knowest not what is the way of the spirit, nor how the bones do grow in the womb of her that is with child: even so thou knowest not the works of God who maketh all."*

Loyalty to one's parents, otherwise called carriers, signifies faithfulness to them and the child's intent to honor them forever. In Psalm 127:4-5, the Bible says, *"As arrows are in the hand of a mighty man; so are children of the youth. Happy is the man that hath his quiver full of them: they shall not be ashamed, but they shall speak with the enemies in the gate."*

It is a disloyal child that abandons the parents in their old age and leaves them moribund. The loyal child protects, provides, preserves, and promises cover for his or her parents at the decision points of life so the child is never ashamed.

With the increase in longevity in the USA, more grandparents are becoming burdened with caring for their following generations. Instead of children caring for their parents, it is the other way round. These generational doldrums in the American society has bankrupted the social security system and strangulated the older generation from financial solvency.

Statistics indicate that over 7.7 million children currently live with their grandparents. This figure is double the number in 1971 and represents a shifting demographic of where children are domiciled. A generational blessing is being aborted by disloyal children unaware of the power of legendary loyalty to the older generation because of an entitlement mentality.

These blessings include living well (Ephesians 6:3), longevity (Exodus 20:12), and increased light (Isaiah 58:8). These legends "...*hide not thyself from thine own flesh* (and so) *shall their light break forth as the morning,... their health spring forth speedily,...thy righteousness go before thee, the glory of the LORD...be thy reward* (and then) *shall thou call, and the LORD shall answer* (and when) *thou shalt cry,...he shall say, Here I am...*" (Isaiah 58:7-9).

ISAAC'S ILLEGITIMATE INSPIRATIONS!

The son of promise Isaac, was inherently loyal to his father Abraham. As a grown and energetic young man in Genesis 22, during which some commentators believe he was thirty plus years old, Isaac conceded to being placed on Mount Moriah's altar of sacrifice by Abraham who was at the time almost one hundred and forty years old.

In Genesis 22:9, the Bible says Abraham "...*bound Isaac his son, and laid him on the altar upon the wood.*" Isaac was loyal to his carrier and even agreed to be bound, knowing fully well there was no alternative sacrifice in sight (Genesis 22:1-8).

He did not dispute or despise his father's instructions but stayed aligned to God's instructions as espoused by his father. In Hebrews 11:17-19, the Bible says, "By *faith Abraham, when he was tried, offered up Isaac: and he that had received the promises offered up his only begotten son, Of whom it was said, That in Isaac shall thy seed be called. Accounting that God was able to raise him up, even from the dead; from whence also he received him in a figure.*"

Isaac could have rejected his father's instructions and jeopardized God's instructions to his father; but because of his loyalty to his father, he stayed the course and obtained a generational blessing. In Genesis 22:16-18, God told Abraham "...*for because thou hast done this thing and hast not withheld thy son, thine only son: That in blessing I will bless thee, and in multiplying I will multiply thy seed as the stars of the heaven, and as the sand which is upon the sea shore; and thy seed shall possess the gate of his enemies; And in thy seed shall all the nations of the earth be blessed.*"

Isaac's illegitimate inspirations were defeated by unalloyed loyalty to God and his carrier, Abraham, to create his inheritance in God. Without the laying down of his life in loyalty, this "...*seed* (through whom) *all the nations of the earth* (would) *be blessed*" (Genesis 22:18) may never have blossomed.

ARROWS OF THE LORD'S DELIVERANCE!

When a child is born, he or she is obligated to serve and honor that parent from which he or she came (Ephesians 6:3). Such loyalty is God-ordained, and anything contrary is alien to the gospel. Hebrews 12:9 describes this relationship further. It says, "...*we have had fathers of our flesh which corrected us, and we gave them reverence: shall we not much rather be in subjection unto the Father of spirits, and live?*"

The relationship between a child and his or her carrier is a covenant relationship shaped in reverence. Psalm 127:4 calls children "...*arrows...in the hand of a mighty man...*" that ensure "...*they...speak with* the (parents) *enemies in the gate*" (Psalm 127:5). Anything short of such reverence and honor for parents is an aberration.

Proverbs 23:22,24-25 says, "*Hearken unto thy father that begat thee, and despise not thy mother when she is old. The father of the righteous shall greatly rejoice: and he that begetteth a wise child shall have joy of him. Thy father and thy mother shall be glad, and she that bare thee shall rejoice.*"

Those who listen to their parents are rewarded, but those who loathe their parents' counsel will be destroyed. Proverbs 30:17 says, "*The eye that mocketh at his father, and despiseth to obey his mother, the ravens of the valley shall pick it out, and the young eagles shall eat it.*" Proverbs 20:20 adds, "*Whoso curseth his father or his mother, his lamp shall be put out in obscure darkness.*"

True legends learn to be loyal in life to parental instruction. Proverbs 15:5 says, "*A fool despiseth his father's instruction: but he that regardeth reproof is prudent.*" The word *prudent* in the original Hebrew means sensible or very cunning. Until a son or daughter becomes a loyalist who treasures, not tears down his or her parents, decisions will be full of folly, not wisdom.

Colossians 3:20 says, *"Children, obey your parents in all things: for this is well pleasing unto the Lord."* Children were created to be *"...arrows of the Lord's deliverance..."* (2 Kings 13:17) who are *"...sent out* (as) *arrows* (by the Lord)...(to) *scatter..."* (2 Samuel 22:15) enemies. How loyal these children are to their carriers or parents will determine how lethal they are against the enemies of theirs and their parents' souls.

THE LOYALTY OF BRIAN HOUSTON TO HIS DAD

Frank Houston had served as General Overseer of the New Zealand Assemblies of God and was a pioneer Pentecostal preacher in the Australasia region. He started Christian Life Center Church in Sydney, Australia; and in 1999, at the age of seventy seven, he handed the reins of the ministry to his son Brian Houston.

At the time, Brian Houston was already a well-known pastor in Australia. He had pioneered Hillsong Church, Sydney, and was leading the church into a worldwide outreach and television ministry. To the son, nothing could be greater than taking the reins from his father. He had sat under his father's ministry and considered him the greatest evangelical preacher he knew.

In a few weeks, however, the tables turned. Soon after taking the leadership of the churches superintended by his father, Brian Houston heard allegations of Pedophilia against his father. He accosted him; and to his utter disappointment, his father admitted to abusing a seven year old boy on one occasion. He denied any other allegations, but when eighth other boys came forward to accuse him of sexual abuse, Brian became incensed.

He suspended his father's being a licensed minister of the Assemblies of God. He also approached the families involved for an out-of-court settlement. He publicly reproved and rebuked his dad's actions, but in private he protected his dad from aspersions of the press and the police. Even though it was against the law, Brian Houston shielded his father from persecution by not reporting him to the police.

When Frank Houston died in 2004, Brian Houston celebrated his father with an eulogy. He said, describing him, *"He was a man who perhaps made some big mistakes a long time ago, but everyone here knows that he was a man who stood for what he believed in, and that in terms of preaching he was in a class of his own."*

Today, Brian Houston is still battling allegations of cover up. In November 2015, a Royal Commission investigating institutional responses to abuse accused him of failing to report allegations of pedophilia against his father to the appropriate quarters. In unalloyed loyalty to his carrier, he has fought derision, depression and now possible detention in defense of his father.

When you find your cause, it will unlock the King within you!

– Shane Warren
Lead Pastor, the Assembly
West Monroe, Louisiana

CHAPTER EIGHTEEN

LOYALTY TO THE CAUSE

"To subvert a man in his cause, the LORD approveth not. Who is he that saith, and it cometh to pass, when the Lord commandeth it not?" (Lamentations 3:36-37).

Your cause is why you were born. It is the purpose for your existence and your reason for living. It is the sum reality of your person and the total expression of your being. It is the call for which a believer was made!

Jesus said, in John 18:37, *"…To this end was I born, and for this cause came I into the world, that I should bear witness unto the truth…."* The loyalty-to-the-cause believer exhibits determination and fortitude in the midst of opposition. He or she pulverizes opposition and cripples any resistance on his or her path to greatness.

That is why in 1 John 3:8 John the Elder says, *"For this purpose the Son of God* (Jesus the Christ) *was manifested, that he might destroy the works of the devil."* Any where a people are vision driven, by their cause for living, they will always manifest in victory!

Gospel greats such as apostle Paul told King Agrippa in Acts 26:19, *"…I was not disobedient unto the heavenly vision."* This obedience resulted in his taking the gospel to the continents of Asia and Europe which revolutionized the world in his day.

In 1 Corinthians 9:25-27, he espoused his life philosophy saying *"… every man that striveth for the mastery is temperate in all things. Now they do it to obtain a corruptible crown; but we an incorruptible. I therefore so run,* not as uncertainly; so fight I, not as one that beateth the air but I keep under my body, and bring it into subjection…."

The legends of our time are not vagabonds but those with a cause. David told his older brother, when chastised for seeking Israel's vindication from Goliath, that "…*what have I now done? Is there not a cause?*" (1 Samuel 17:29). He went on to destroy Goliath, and is celebrated today as the greatest King Israel ever had. The Church is over due for glory and celebration, but it takes loyalty to a cause to become who God says she is.

THE ESAU EFFECT

Esau was not loyal to the cause that brought him to the world. He married strange women (Genesis 26:34-35), worshipped idols from his wives nations: worst of all, he despised his cause in life by selling his inheritance for a plate of pottage (see Genesis 25:30-34).

In Hebrews 12:16-17, God warns each member of His Church not to be a "…*profane person, as Esau, who for one morsel of meat sold his birthright. For ye know how that afterward, when he would have inherited the blessing, he was rejected for he found no place of repentance, though he sought it carefully with tears.*"

He lost his inheritance in a spate of crass materialism, and was condemned as a result (Genesis 25:30-34). After having given the blessing of the heir to Jacob, Isaac told Esau "…*I have made him thy lord, and all his brethren have I given to him for servants; and with corn and wine have I sustained him…*" (Genesis 27:37).

For his immediate needs, Esau forfeited a future laden with power and glory. He gave up his future to secure his today and was condemned to a rudimentary lifestyle, according to Genesis 27:40. Isaac prophesied to Esau, saying "*and by thy sword shall thou live and shall serve thy brother and it shall come to pass when thou shalt have the dominion, that thou shalt break his yoke from off thy neck.*"

JESUS – THE JEW WITH ONE JOB!

While on earth, Jesus was always focused on His assignment. He neither veered off nor detoured from his goal regardless of the opposition.

David prophesied about Him in Psalm 40:7, saying "Lo, *I come: in the volume of the book it is written of me, I delight to do thy will, O my God.*"

On one occasion, while en route from Galilee to Jerusalem, He "...*steadfastly set his face to go to Jerusalem, And sent messengers before his face. And they went, and entered into a village of the Samaritans, to make ready for him. And they did not receive him, because his face was as though he would go to Jerusalem*" (Luke 9:51-52).

The disapproval of the Samaritans' did not make Jesus redirect His journey. Rather, "...*they went to another village*" (Luke 9:56) and eventually arrived in Jerusalem where He was later crucified. His whole purpose in life was to carry out the plans of God for Him, irrespective of whose ox was gored, as written in the book.

In Hebrews 10:7-9, the Bible says of Jesus "...*I come (in the volume of the book as) it is written of me, to do thy will, O God. Above when he said, Sacrifice and offering and burnt offerings and offering for sin thou wouldest not, neither hadst pleasure therein; which are offered by the law; Then said he, Lo, I come to do thy will, O God....*"

He had only one job on earth: obeying His Father! He said in John 5:19, "...*The Son can do nothing of himself, but what he seeth the Father do: for what things soever he doeth, these also doeth the Son likewise.*" He did not pander to the crowd or attempt to please all-comers. He remained focused till the end.

In John 4:34, He told his disciples "*My meat is to do the will of him that sent me, and to finish his work.*" In Luke 12:49-50, he re-iterated his single-eyedness. He said, "*I am come to send fire on the earth; and what will I, if it be already kindled? But I have a baptism to be baptized with; and how am I straitened till it be accomplished!*"

No true legend becomes one without loyalty to a cause! The absence of a cause is the reason for the shortage of true legends in our time. Jesus is the greatest legend ever because he lived a life with a cause. He prayed to God in John 12:27, "...*for this cause came I unto this hour. Father, glorify thy name.*"

UNCLE CHUKA AND THE
SONS OF PERDITION!

I was in my final year of high school, and preparing for my graduation when my parents asked me to stay with my Uncle Chuka in order to adequately prepare for my final year exams.

Uncle Chuka was notorious for his party-going and womanizing. He was a nationally syndicated television host, and his home was always a beehive of activities for the societal elite in Lagos, Nigeria.

During the day, I was in the pre-varsity training program, and on my return I headed straight to my bedroom. I was, however, regularly assailed by provocative stares from his guests; and on several occasions I awoke to see sexually intimate couples having intercourse beside me.

As a newly born-again Christian, I found their conduct abhorrent. After a discussion with my father, I decided to relocate to another residence. I saw what I considered to be closest to perdition at Uncle Chuka's house. Consequently, I made up mind to stay as far away as I could from such environs in the future.

*Those who stop feeding
have stopped following, and
those who stop learning
have stopped leading!*

CHAPTER NINETEEN

LOYALTY TO THE CITIZENS

"The God of Israel said, the Rock of Israel spake to me, He that ruleth over men must be just, ruling in the fear of God" (2 Samuel 23:3).

The world is full of despots, demagogues, and even democratically elected leaders with no sense of loyalty to the citizens they are called to lead. They are their own alter-ego and everything revolves around them. They are *"...a generation, whose teeth are as swords, and their jaw teeth as knives, to devour the poor from off the earth, and the needy from among men"* (Proverbs 30:14).

The selfless and sacrificial leader has given way to the selfish and surreptitious leader who wants to taste power for the perks and privileges of office, and not to remove the burden of poverty overwhelming the needy. Proverbs 29:2 says, *"When the righteous are in authority, the people rejoice: but when the wicked beareth rule, the people mourn."*

The Christian leader or officeholder must be the very expression of Christ as he or she paints a picture of Jesus through that office. In 1 Thessalonians 5:12-13, Paul adjures the believer *"...to know them which labor among you, and are over you in the Lord, and admonish you; and to esteem them very highly in love for their work's sake...."*

It is unfortunate that many believers in office, as did David, have *"...given great occasion to the enemies of the Lord to blaspheme (His name)..."* (2 Samuel 12:14) and as a result deterred unbelievers from coming to the knowledge of Christ. God's advice to leaders of His church include, *"...*

Masters, give unto your servants that which is just and equal; knowing that you also have a Master in heaven" (Colossians 4:1).

If they do not treat their servants with justice, God promises to avenge on their behalf. He said in James 5:3-4 to the rich oppressors, *"...Ye have heaped treasure together for the last days. Behold, the hire of the laborers who have reaped down your fields, which is of you kept back for by fraud, crieth: and the cries of those which have reaped are entered into the ears of the Lord of sabaoth."*

THE TRYST OF TYRANNY!

The prophet Isaiah prophesied in Isaiah 10:1-2 on the outcome of a leader who rules like a tyrant. He said, *"Woe unto them that decree unrighteous decrees, and that write grievousness which they have prescribed; To turn aside the needy from judgment, and to take away the right from the poor of my people, that widows may be their prey, and that they may rob the fatherless!"*

Those who make evil decrees finally end in evil themselves, but those who rule justly and in the fear of the Lord become *"...as the light of the morning when the sun riseth, even a morning without clouds; as the tender grass springing out of the earth by clear shining after rain"* (2 Samuel 23:4).

Those leaders who are loyal to their citizenry become legends of their time. They become those God will *"... make... an everlasting covenant, ordered in all things, and sure..."* (2 Samuel 23:5). In Ephesians 6:7-9, the apostle Paul advises believers in authority *"With good will doing service, as to the Lord, and not to men: Knowing that whatsoever good thing any man doeth, the same shall he receive of the Lord, whether he be bond or free. And ye masters, do the same things unto them, forbearing threatening: knowing that your Master also is in heaven: neither is there respect of persons with him."* The way you treat others above or beneath you, will determine how God treats you!

Leadership is service, not the subjugation of others! It is loving people, not lording it over them. Jesus Christ, by example, demonstrated true leadership when He washed the disciples' feet. He said, in John 13:13-14, *"Ye call me Master and Lord; and ye say well; for so I am. If I then, your Lord and Master, have washed your feet; ye also ought to wash one another's feet."*

Tyrants run trysts around themselves, but servant leaders build sustainable legacies for generations following. In 1 Peter 5:2-4, the apostle Peter told those who were in leadership in the early church to "...*take the oversight thereof, not by constraint, but willingly; not for filthy lucre, but of a ready mind. Neither as being lords over God's heritage, but being examples to the flock. And when the chief Shepherd shall appear, ye shall receive a crown of glory that fadeth not away.*"

THE DOUBLE-HONOR LEADER

In 1 Timothy 5:17, apostle Paul adjures the church to "*Let the elders that rule well be counted worthy of double honor, especially those who labor in the word and doctrine.*" Not every ruler is worthy of double honor! It is the privilege of those who rule well or are perceived well as a result of the advantages they bring.

Too many leaders are whimsical instead of winsome! They take advantage of the people instead of creating advantages by which their followers can advance in life. The Christian leader is the one who will say, as did Paul, "...*and I will very gladly spend and be spent for you; though the more abundantly I love you, the less I be loved*" (2 Corinthians 12:15).

The double-honor or legendary leader's motive is not financial but futuristic. He chooses not to be "...*burdensome...for he seek(s) not yours but you (believing that)...children ought not to lay up for the parents, but the parents for the children*" (2 Corinthians 12:14). The greatest in the kingdom of God are not those who act as lords but those who see themselves as servants, even though they are lords over others (Matthew 23:11-12).

True leaders carry power and influence without exerting them. In Romans 13:4, Paul describes those who rule as "*ministers of God to thee for good. But if thou do that which is evil, be afraid; for he beareth not the sword in vain: for he is a minister of God, a revenger to execute wrath upon him that doeth evil.*"

They provide what the people need as God's ministers. When God wanted to bring Israel out of captivity, He gave her leaders and "... *pastors according to His heart, which shall feed you with knowledge and understanding*" (Jeremiah 3:15). They are called "...*they (that) watch for your souls as they that must give account...*" (Hebrews 13:17). True legendary leadership labors in the word of God, and watches over the people in order to give account for them appropriately.

They are not hirelings, but heirs of God. They are ready to give their lives for the sheep, unlike the hireling who "...*seeth the wolf coming, and leaveth the sheep and fleeth: and the wolf catcheth them and scattereth the sheep (and he) fleeth because he is an hireling and careth not for the sheep*" (John 10:12-13). In contrast, le1gendary leaders are loyal to their citizens or sheep and would willingly "...*lay down* (their) *lives for the brethren*" (1 John 3:16).

A CHANGE OF GUARDS!

Nigeria as a nation was at a major crossroads in 2015. The President Goodluck Jonathan had presided over a country that was teetering towards anarchy. His divisive policies had polarized the nation, isolated the intellectual middle class, impoverished the poor and unjustly made billionaires through corruption of nitwits unsuitable for their high-class society positions.

Worst of all, the *Al-Queda* clone, called *Boko-Haram*, was wrecking havoc across the country. The military were running away when challenged, and this once-giant-of-Africa was dovetailing into a speedy politically-sabotaged decline.

At this crossroads, the candidature of the opposition candidate General Muhammadu Buhari was gaining acceptance. In Nigeria, however, it was unheard of for sitting-government-officials to lose an election and so multiple political and religious leaders considered Goodluck Jonathan a shoo-in for the 2015 presidential election.

All that, however, changed when believers including myself began to pray! At the monthly Holy Ghost Nights and during personal times of prayer, the Holy Spirit told me that there was an imminent change of guard in the Nigerian political and religious hegemony.

He also told me General Buhari would win the upcoming election, against all odds, and fully confident in God's decision, I declared the word of the Lord to all and sundry. I was castigated and maligned but, alas, it manifested on May 2015.

General Buhari was sworn in as president of Nigeria on May 29 2015. Since then a sense of justice, accountability and zero tolerance for corruption has seized our nation. It has not augured well for the corrupt elite, Islamic fundamentalists and the irredentists; but for the poor and down trodden it has brought hope.

God is He who "...*changeth the times and the seasons...removeth kings and setteth up kings...*" (Daniel 2:21). He is the unchanging changer! Just as He changed guards politically in Nigeria, I believe a soon-coming "change of guards" is going to manifest in your marriage, finances, fortune, ministry and health soon in Jesus name.

The measure of a life,
after all, is not its
duration but its donation

- Corrie ten Boom (1892 -1983) 2nd
world war Holocaust survivor and
safe-haven provider for hundreds of
Jews in Nazi-controlled Netherlands.

CHAPTER TWENTY

LOYALTY TO CHRIST

"For to me to live is Christ, and to die is gain" (Philippians 1:21).

God has ways and thoughts that are higher than man's, but they are reserved for His arch-loyalists. In 1 Corinthians 2:9-10, Paul writes by the Spirit of God, *"...Eye hath not seen, nor ear heard, neither have entered into the heart of man, the things which God hath prepared for them that love him. But God hath revealed them unto us by his Spirit for the Spirit searcheth all things, yea, the deep things of God."*

There is a higher life available for believers, but it is found in deep places! True treasures are never shallow or found on the surface. They require going to deep depths to obtain the blessing. Jesus told Simon Peter, in Luke 5:4, *"Launch out into the deep, and let down your nets for a draught."*

Unfortunately, Peter let down only one net and almost lost his harvest as a result (Luke 5:5-7). The world believes in coincidence, convention and convenience but only confidence in God's word moves God. In Luke 18:8, Jesus asked *"...when the Son of man cometh, shall he find faith on the earth?"* Faith is the key rate-limiting-step to a person's deliverance, not fate, fame or familiarity.

Peter, like so many today had a secular humanistic world view, and was working with his instincts and reasoning faculties rather than with the mind of Christ. In Psalm 42:7-8, the Psalmist says, *"Deep calleth unto deep at the noise of thy waterspouts: all thy waves and thy billows are gone over me. Yet the LORD will command his lovingkindness in the day time, and in the night his song shall be with me, and my prayer unto the God of my life."*

A believer does not live a rudimentary or sedentary life, if their loyalty to Jesus Christ is deep. Such believers' become legends of their time because they unequivocally fear and love God passionately. They have only one earthly life to live and have decided to give it whole heartedly to the service of the kingdom of God. They believe in Christ's injunction to *"…seek… first the kingdom of God, and His righteousness and all these* (other) *things shall be added unto you"* (Matthew 6:33).

AS THE HEAD GOES…

It is a rule of thumb that blessings start from the head. Psalm 133:1-2 says, *"Behold, how good and how pleasant it is for brethren to dwell together in unity! It is like the precious ointment upon the head, that ran down upon the beard, even Aaron's beard: that went down to the skirts of his garment."*

If anything of virtue and value is to be achieved in this generation, it will start from the head of the church which is Jesus Christ. Ephesians 1:22-23 says, God *"…hath put all things under his feet, and gave him to be the head over all things to the church, Which is his body, the fullness of him that filleth all in all."*

Jesus is the Head of the church, and loyalty to His leadership attracts the largess of heaven to the body. In Colossians 2:19, the Bible says, *"… not holding the Head, from which all the body by joints and bands having nourishment ministered, and knit together, increaseth with the increase of God."*

When God's temple was being rebuilt, the word of the Lord was that Zerubbabel would *"…bring forth the headstone thereof with shoutings, crying, Grace, grace unto it"* (Zechariah 4:7). When the grace of God facilitates the headstone, which is Christ, prosperity and increase in the kingdom become inevitable.

In Haggai 2:18-19, the prophet Haggai said *"Consider now from this day and upward, from the four and twentieth day of the ninth month, even from the day that the foundation of the LORD's temple was laid, consider it. Is the seed yet in the barn? yea, as yet the vine, and the fig tree, and the pomegranate, and the olive tree, hath not brought forth: **from this day will I bless you**"* (emphasis added).

The church is not called to subsistence living, but to the supernatural life! This life is, however, buoyed by unalloyed and unflinching loyalty to our headstone and the head of our body Jesus Christ. Colossians 3:23-24 adjures believers as follows: "...*and whatsoever ye do, do it heartily, as to the Lord, and not unto men; Knowing that of the Lord ye shall receive the reward of the inheritance: for ye serve the Lord Christ.*"

STAKES IN BLOOD

In Philippians 2:20-21, apostle Paul says, "...*I have no man likeminded, who will naturally care for your state. For all seek their own, not the things which are Jesus Christ's.*" One of the proofs of stellar loyalty to Jesus Christ is selflessness or a life staked or established obedience to His word. His care for believers compels them to cast their cares on Him by humbling ourselves under His mighty hand, according to 1 Peter 5:6-7.

In Isaiah 33:20-22, the Bible says, "*Look upon Zion, the city of our solemnities: thine eyes shall see Jerusalem a quiet habitation, a tabernacle that shall not be taken down; not one of the stakes thereof shall ever be removed, neither shall any of the cords thereof be broken....For the LORD is our judge, the LORD is our lawgiver, the LORD is our king; he will save us.*"

The New Testament stake is placed in blood, not earth! The blood of Jesus was shed so that believers' lives are staked eternally in His name and for His cause, not theirs. In 2 Corinthians 5:14-15. The Bible says "...*the love of Christ constraineth us; because we thus judge, that if one died for all, then were all dead: And that he died for all, that they which live should not henceforth live unto themselves, but unto him which died for them, and rose again.*"

This gospel is a "blood sport" and it will take your life if you are to live it successfully. Our Lord and savior said, in Matthew 10:39, "*He that findeth his life shall lose it: and he that loseth his life for my sake shall find it.*" Until the church puts her stakes down in the covenant blood of Jesus, she cannot manifest as a loyalty legend.

The result of a staked, loyal or established life that is immoveable and based on the word of God is overflow and abundance. Isaiah 33:21 says, "*But there the glorious LORD will be unto us a place of broad rivers and streams; wherein shall go no galley with oars, neither shall gallant ship pass thereby.*"

THE COST OF DISCIPLESHIP

Corrie Ten Boon (1892-1983) was a Dutch Nazi-resistance fighter who emigrated to the United States of America in 1978. She was known for rescuing several hundred Jews who would have been killed by the Nazis in the Holocaust, but for her and her family's hospitality and labor of love.

Alongside her sister, she worked as the first female clock and watch repairer in the Netherlands. In her father's clock repair shop, that was located in the bottom floor of the family house, the Ten Boom family who were members of the Dutch Reformed Church started a Bible study in their home to propagate the love of Jesus to all-comers.

Even though they knew the possible repercussions of taking in Jews during the Nazi invasion of the Netherlands, Corrie and her family did not relent. They hid them in secret closets on the third floor of their town house, fed them and kept them warm and warned about any Nazi soldier's entry into their home.

Unfortunately after a few months of shepherding Jewish refugees to safety in collaboration with the underground resistance, she and her family were apprehended by the Nazis. They were taken to a German concentration camp in February 1944, during the Auschwitz-Holocaust era. It was during their incarceration that Corrie's father and sister died in March and September 1944 respectively.

Corrie Ten Boom was miraculously released in December 1944 as the allies neared Germany and, on her return home, she started a Christian rehabilitation program for those devastated by the war. During one of her talks in 1947, she came face-to-face with one of the guards responsible for torturing her and her sister in the German Ravensbruck Concentration Camp.

A whirlwind of emotions seized her: first hate then divine love and forgiveness. Eventually, she embraced him as he, the ex-Nazi officer, apologized for his past crimes toward her and her family and acknowledged Jesus Christ as his personal Lord and savior. Of that experience, Corrie testified in her daily journal *"I have never known God's love so intensely as I did then."*

Only a united church can heal a divided nation!

– Lou Engle (Coordinator, The Call Los Angeles USA)

CHAPTER TWENTY-ONE

LOYALTY TO THE CHURCH

"God hath tempered the body together…That there should be no schism in the body; but that the members should have the same care one for another. And whether one member suffer, all the members suffer with it; or one member be honored, all the members rejoice with it" (1 Corinthians 12:24-26).

A recent fad among the millennial generation is the rise of the "NONES." This group includes those who refuse allegiance to any religion and view church membership as a cult or fraternity. According to Barna 2012 research, about one third of young adults between 18 and 29 years of age are unaffiliated with any religious association (compared to 12% in 1979) and about 43% of these group drop out of church attendance by the age of adulthood[1].

In other statistics, a third of these adults under thirty have no religious affiliation (32%), compared with just one in ten who are 65 and older (9%). This connotes that young adults today are much more likely to be spiritually unaffiliated than previous generations were at a similar stage in their lives. Those "NONES" who claim they believe but refuse to be loyal to the church are going to be judged for their indecisiveness.

In Revelation 3:15, Jesus Christ said *"I wilt that ye were hot or cold but because you are lukewarm, I will spew you out of my mouth."* The two sons of Eli, Phinehas and Hophni, were disloyal to the law of Moses. They treated the women at the altar as whores, and on receipt of God's peoples' sacrifices, treated them sacrilegiously (see 1 Samuel 2:12-17). When Eli, their father and High priest, saw that "*...his sons made themselves vile, and he restrained them not*" (1 Samuel 3:13), and rather "*...honored his sons above God, to make themselves fat with the chiefest of all the offerings of Israel my people*" (1 Samuel 2:29) instead of judging them, God pulverized his whole lineage.

The outcome was devastating as the progeny of Eli was destroyed with a curse! His once-legendary family from which the priesthood arose became a beggarly tribe in Israel because of disloyalty to the Lord. In 1 Samuel 2:31,36 God says, "*Behold, the days come, that I will cut off thine arm, and the arm of thy father's house, that there shall not be an old man in thine house. And it shall come to pass that every one that is left in thine house shall come and crouch to him for a piece of silver and a morsel of bread, and shall say, Put me, I pray thee, into one of the priests' offices, that I may eat a piece of bread.*"

God takes the welfare of His church personally! He said, in Ezekiel 34:20-22, "*...I, will judge between the fat cattle and between the lean cattle. Because ye have thrust with side and with shoulder, and pushed all the diseased with your horns, till ye have scattered them abroad; Therefore will I save my flock, and they shall no more be a prey; and I will judge between cattle and cattle.*"

REHOBOAM'S REBUFF

Rehoboam, the son of King Solomon, had the world at his feet. He became King of Israel at the height of its wealth and power but, unfortunately, lost it all when he rebuffed the advice of the Israeli elders who ruled with his father. Instead, "*...he forsook the counsel which the old men gave him, and took counsel with the young men that were brought up with him...*" (2 Chronicles 10:8).

This act led to the loss of the Kingdom. In 2 Chronicles 10:15-16, the Bible says, "*So the king hearkened not unto the people...And when all Israel saw that the king would not hearken unto them, the people answered the king, saying, What portion have we in David; and we have none inheritance in the son of Jesse: every man to your tents, O Israel.*"

As an aftermath of Rehoboam's rebuff to the elders' advice, disunity arose between Judah and the other tribes of Israel leading to Jeroboam's breaking off and starting Samaria as a nation. In 2 Chronicles 10:19, the Bible says, "*...Israel rebelled against the house of David unto this day.*"

In 1 Timothy 5:1, Paul advises his protégé, Timothy, "*rebuke not an elder, but intreat him as a father; and the younger men as brethren.*" Church fights and splits are commonly the product of crass, rather than civil and composed, responses. Nothing engenders a church's legendary status like disunity and lack of civility.

In Acts 4:32-33, the Bible says, "*...the multitude of them that believed were of one heart and of one soul: neither said any of them that ought of the things which he possessed was his own; but they had all things common. And with great power gave the apostles witness of the resurrection of the Lord Jesus: and great grace was upon them all.*"

GOD'S GENERALS!

The rank of a general is not an overnight attainment. It takes years of experience (preferably war-time experience) and tested loyalty to the state and the army to become one. In the Kingdom of God, God's generals are those who have been attacked for their beliefs; but, in spite of their challenges, they still attest unalloyed loyalty to the Christ and His church.

They are not complacent warriors; but they are those of whom Jesus said, "*...the kingdom of heaven suffers violence, and the violent take it by force*" (Matthew 11:12). They don't break ranks, but stay their course for the cause of Christ! They are not of double heart, and as a result end up as experts (or legends) in their fields of expertise.

1 Chronicles 12:33 says, "*Of Zebulun, such as went forth to battle, expert in war, with all instruments of war, fifty thousand, which could keep rank: they were not of double heart.*" Those who break ranks, on the other hand, lose legend hood and forfeit their future.

In Joel 2:7, the prophet says, "*They shall run like mighty men; they shall climb the wall like men of war; and they shall march every one on his ways, and they shall not break their ranks.*"

The mark of a true general is unalloyed loyalty to his or her men. The prophet emphasizes this in Joel 2:8 when he says, "*Neither shall one thrust another; they shall walk every one in his path: and when they fall upon the sword, they shall not be wounded.*"

THE LOYAL CHURCH IS A CREATIVE CHURCH, NOT A CRISIS-RIDDEN CHURCH!

Kingsway International Christian Center (KICC), London, started with two hundred adult members in 1992 after its Senior Pastor, Matthew Ashimolowo, felt God's direction to leave the Foursquare denomination they were part of and start an independent charismatic church in the heart of the city.

He had been posted to London, United Kingdom, in 1984, to open a branch of the Foursquare denomination. After having served in that capacity for eight years he heard the voice of God telling him *the river I am about to give you is bigger than the one in which you are serving.*

He left the Foursquare denomination, but unlike several others prior and after him in the ministry, his departure was punctuated with goodwill, love and even rapprochement by some who initially had frayed nerves over his departure.

Today, KICC is easily one of the biggest churches in Western Europe and is at cutting edge of social, cultural, spiritual and political innovations in Great Britain. Recently voted the most influential Black Briton, Pastor Matthew continues to shape the culture rather than allow the culture shape him.

He has partnered with the sickle cell foundation in London to organize annual races and raise funds for Sickle cell, sponsored educational courses that encourage scholarship in the young black community and recently relocated the Church to their new 24 acre home in Buckmore Park, Chatham Kent near London, United Kingdom

His rise, amidst severe opposition, is a testimony of his legacy of service to the church. An author of over seventy books, he has ventured into the "miracle of the body and mind" ministry by opening KICC hospital and King's University in Ode-Emu, Oshun state Nigeria. Even though, he left the Foursquare denomination unceremoniously, Pastor Matthew still headlines several of that fellowships' evangelistic programs. He is an example of the loyal and serving, not libelous and strife-filled, church.

Choices change
actions, not chances!

CHAPTER TWENTY-TWO

LOYALTY TO THEIR CHOICES

"And if it seem evil unto you to serve the LORD, choose you this day whom ye will serve; whether the gods which your fathers served that were on the other side of the flood, or the gods of the Amorites, in whose land ye dwell: but as for me and my house, we will serve the LORD" (JOSHUA 24:15).

God does not fall off His throne because someone makes a mad or a bad decision. In spite of what people do, God remains God! He is loyal to loving the rebellious notwithstanding their choices. He said, in Jeremiah 31:3, *"...I have loved you with an everlasting love...."* In Romans 5:8, Paul adds that *"...God commendeth his love toward us, in that, while we were yet sinners, Christ died for us."*

Life is a product of choices, not chances. In his valedictory speech to the children of Israel, Joshua told the children of Israel *"...if it seem evil unto you to serve the LORD, choose you this day whom ye will serve; whether the gods which your fathers served that were on the other side of the flood, or the gods of the Amorites, in whose land ye dwell: but as for me and my house, we will serve the LORD"* (Joshua 24:15).

In a nutshell, Joshua told Israel that if they make the wrong decision he will be loyal to loving God and them nonetheless. Eventually, they did make their choice, and God was not part of it! In Judges 2:10-11, the Bible says *"...there arose another generation after them, which knew not the LORD, nor yet the works which he had done for Israel. And the children of Israel did evil in the sight of the LORD, and served Baalim."*

114

A similar scenario played itself out in Ephesus. Paul, after sojourning there for three years, told them, *"...of your own selves shall men arise, speaking perverse things, to draw away disciples after them. Therefore watch, and remember, that by the space of three years I ceased not to warn every one night and day with tears. And now, brethren, I commend you to God, and to the word of his grace, which is able to build you up, and to give you an inheritance among all them which are sanctified"* (Acts 20:30-32).

We are not responsible for other people's behavior. God did not abdicate the throne because of Adam and Eve's high treason, or the devil's seditions. He remains God, and His Word is infallible, notwithstanding the opportunities afforded or the opposition encountered. He lamented in Isaiah 42:19-21, *"Who is blind, but my servant? or deaf, as my messenger that I sent? who is blind as he that is perfect, and blind as the Lord's servant? Seeing many things, but thou observest not; opening the ears, but he heareth not. The Lord is well pleased for his righteousness' sake; he will magnify the law, and make it honorable"* (Isaiah 42:19-21).

Even though God's word had the ability to transform from blind to brilliant and from deaf to dumbfounding, the servant did not heed God's instructions to see and hear as stipulated in Isaiah 42:18. The result will be lives spoiled and stripped of glory according to Isaiah 42:22. His audacious Word, nonetheless, will remain honorable and magnified! God's word, like His Church, is loyal to men's choices and will not circumvent God's purpose because of their poor choices.

JUDAS, JOHN THE BAPTIST AND JOSEPH: LOST BUT LOVED!

Jesus knew Judas was stealing from the treasury (see John 12:5-8); yet He loved him. He told the disciples, after Judas had departed to fine tune his treacherous plans to betray Jesus, *"A new commandment I give unto you, That ye love one another; as I have loved you, that ye also love one another. By this shall all men know that ye are my disciples, if ye have love one to another"* (John 13:34-35).

Jesus prayed, anointed, washed, and prophesied over Judas Iscariot; but he had made a choice to be a traitor, notwithstanding. Even after admitting his wrongs, Judas *"...(seeing) that he was condemned, repented himself, and brought again the thirty pieces of silver to the chief priests and elders, saying, I have sinned in that I have betrayed the innocent blood…and went and hanged himself"* (Matthew 27:3-5).

John the Baptist died in prison for speaking truth to power in Mark 6:18. While in jail, he became offended at Jesus Christ (Matthew 11:6) and sent his disciples to ask Jesus, *"Art thou he that should come, or do we look for another?"* (Matthew 11:3). Jesus response was not to castigate or criticize John the Baptist because of his poor choice, but to be compassionate and consolatory toward him. He told his disciples, *"…among them that are born of women there hath not risen a greater than John the Baptist…"* (Matthew 11:11).

Love is always God's loyal response. He does not want a church that tries to take responsibility for other people's behavior. He wants a church that will love others' nonetheless. Jesus, in spite of his special relationship with John the Baptist and Judas, never took responsibility for their failings. He loved them in spite of them! He was loyal to Judas and John the Baptist's choices even if they were not what He wanted.

Joseph learned this lesson the hard way. A "go-getter" and a natural leader, he assumed responsibility even when it was not given to him (see Genesis 37:2 and 39:22). He stayed incarcerated till he learned the lesson of free choice, according to Psalm 105:17-22 . Instead of taking responsibility for the actions of others, God wanted Joseph to learn to take responsibility for his own actions and by so doing supernaturally serve the land of Egypt and the surrounding environs during the famine (see Genesis 47:13-26).

At the age of thirty, this revelation finally clicked in Joseph's mind. The word of the Lord set Joseph free from assuming other peoples' guilt and liabilities! In Psalm 105:17-22, the Bible says *"…Joseph,…whose feet they hurt with fetters…was laid in iron until the time that his word came* (for) *the word of the LORD tried him. The king sent and loosed him; even the ruler of the people, and let him go free* (and) *made him lord of his house, and ruler of all his substance to bind his princes at his pleasure; and teach his senators wisdom."*

This fact was exemplified by his response to the news of Pharaoh's summoning in Genesis 41:14. The Bible says *"…they brought him hastily out of the dungeon: and **he shaved himself**, and changed his raiment, and came in unto Pharaoh"* (emphasis added). Joseph stopped blaming others for his upheavals. Rather than be shaved by the king's courtiers as protocol demanded, he shaved and dressed himself without recourse to others' assistance. He chose to forgive Potiphar, his wife and his brothers and, instead, loved them in spite of their actions against him.

In Genesis 50:20-21, Joseph told his brothers "...*But as for you, ye thought evil against me; but God meant it unto good, to bring to pass, as it is this day, to save much people alive. Now therefore fear ye not: I will nourish you, and your little ones. And he comforted them, and spake kindly unto them.*" By not taking responsibility for others' actions and doing God's will regardless of their motives, Joseph changed his generation as a legend of his time.

THE MIRACLE OF A FREE SPIRIT!

Nothing communicates the gospel better than a free or unencumbered spirit. The Psalmist prayed in Psalm 51:12-13, "*Restore unto me the joy of thy salvation; and uphold me with thy free spirit. Then will I teach transgressors thy ways; and sinners shall be converted unto thee.*"

Whatever burden unwittingly weighs down believers eventually affects their testimony. Galatians 6:2-5 says, "B*ear ye one another's burdens, and so fulfil the law of Christ. For if a man think himself to be something, when he is nothing, he deceiveth himself. But let every man prove his own work, and then shall he have rejoicing in himself alone, and not in another. For every man shall bear his own burden.*"

The word *bear* as used in Galatians 6:2 means to carry away not carry upon. The mistake many good-meaning Christians make is to carry upon them a burden they should carry away by casting it upon the Lord. In Matthew 11:28-30, Jesus told his disciples, "*Come unto me, all ye that labor and are heavy laden, and I will give you rest. Take my yoke upon you, and learn of me; for I am meek and lowly in heart: and ye shall find rest unto your souls. For my yoke is easy, and my burden is light.*"

In Psalm 55:22, the Psalmist advices the church: "*Cast thy burden upon the* LORD, *and he shall sustain thee.*" In 1 peter 5:7, apostle Peter adjures the church to "*cast all your care upon him; for He* (God) *careth for you.*" The word used in the original Greek for care is the word distraction. In 1 Peter 5:8, it is no wonder, therefore, that apostle Peter warns the church "*Be sober, be vigilant; because your adversary the devil, as a roaring lion, walketh about, seeking whom he may devour."* A heart that is not distracted by cares will destroy the enemy, but one that is will be devoured.

Jesus remonstrated with his disciples in their afflictions telling them in John 14:1, *"Let not your heart be troubled: ye believe in God, believe also in me."* It is a choice on the believer's part, not some divine compulsion or God's obligation.

Moses chose to be troubled and, as a result, lost his mandate to take Israel to the promised land. In Numbers 11:11, *"...Moses said unto the LORD, Wherefore hast thou afflicted thy servant? and wherefore have I not found favor in thy sight, that thou layest the burden of all this people upon me?"* He shouldered the burdens of the Israelites, and it led him to make costly mistakes that stopped him from entering the promised Land (see Deuteronomy 1:12-13 and Numbers 20:10-11).

The believer is responsible for his or her actions, not the world's! The prophet Samuel told the children of Israel, after they had reneged on God by asking for a king, *"...as for me, God forbid that I should sin against the LORD in ceasing to pray for you: but I will teach you the good and the right way: Only fear the LORD, and serve him in truth with all your heart...But if ye shall still do wickedly, ye shall be consumed, both ye and your king"* (1 Samuel 12:23-25).

RESPONSIBILITY IS LIKE A RELAY RACE – HAND IT OFF WELL!

Kenneth Hagin (1917-2003) was once at the City of Faith Hospital mediplex, Oral Roberts University (ORU) praying for his grandson. As he prayed for his terribly ill grandchild, God told him he would not answer him on this occasion. When Kenneth Hagin enquired why, God told him *"It is time for your grandson to believe God and stand on God's Word for himself."*

Astounded, Kenneth Hagin ended his praying and went to inform his grandson who was in the Pediatric section of the hospital on his need to grow up spiritually and believe God's Word on healing. As he listened and applied God's healing principles from 1 Peter 2:24 and Matthew 8:17, the Leukemia he had been diagnosed with disappeared.

A generation that fails to hand off well will spoil the relay race for the incoming generation. An older generation's responsibility is to "*train up a child in the way he should go...*" (Proverbs 22:6) and "*...provoke (them) not...but bring them up in the nurture and admonition of the Lord*" (Ephesians 6:4).

Oral Robert (1918-2009) lived a life of faith and fidelity to God. In the process, he built the Oral Roberts Ministry and University as evidence to his great faith in God. His heir apparent and oldest son, Ronald Roberts (1945-1982), made a choice to use drugs and live a homosexual lifestyle. Finally, he committed suicide as a result.

At his funeral, his father said, "*Robert* (who spoke five languages and was near completion of his PHD in Linguistics) *would be remembered for the good things he did and, not for the wrong decisions he made around the end of his life.*" He loved him, notwithstanding his disloyalty.

David Yonggi-Cho, the pastor of the Yoido Full Gospel Church in South Korea, is reputed for a world-wide ministry and pastoring the largest Church in the world. As a result of lack of oversight, however, he fell prey to the corrupt wrangling of his oldest son ChoHee-Jun in a share-buying scandal worth $12 million.

When the judge asked him to indict his wayward son so that he would have no responsibilities in the case, he refused. Instead he said, "*My son can be unrighteous to me, but I cannot be unrighteous to my son.*" As a result, Pastor Cho was sentenced to a suspended sentence of three years and fined $5million.

PART V

TRAITS OF THE LOYAL

- THE LOYALTY OF THE AYES
- THE LOYALTY OF THE ARMOR BEARER
- THE LOYALTY OF THE ANGELS
- THE LOYALTY OF AXE
- THE LOYALTY OF THE ARK
- THE LOYALTY OF THE ASCETIC
- THE LOYALTY OF THE APERTURE
- THE LOYALTY OF THE ASSISTANT

God's ayes-men and ayes-women have no nays to God's ways!

CHAPTER TWENTY THREE

THE LOYALTY OF THE AYES

"But as God is true, our word toward you was not yea and nay. For the Son of God, Jesus Christ, who was preached among you by us, even by me and Silvanus and Timotheus, was not yea and nay, but in him was yea. For all the promises of God in him are yea, and in him Amen..." (2 Corinthians 1:18-20).

God has his yes-men and yes-women, otherwise called ayes-men and ayes-women! They are those who irrespective of what they are going through or what they will go through as a result of their decision, stand up to say yes in agreement to God's instructions. The promises of God are yes and amen (2 Corinthians 1:20), but until God finds a man or woman who will agree with Him, those promises are null and void.

Paul said, in 2 Corinthians 1:18, *"...our word toward you was not yea and nay."* As a result *"...all the promises of God in him are yea, and in him Amen...."* (2 Corinthians 1:20). The church, in agreement with God, becomes unassailable and undeniable! Eliphaz the Temanite agrees and says in Job 22:28, *"Agree with God, and be at peace there by good will come to you"* (RSV).

The promises of God are powerful, but without the church's understanding and implementing them through wisdom, they are mere words! In Hebrews 4:1-2, this truth is reemphasized. It says, *"Let us therefore fear, lest, a promise being left us of entering into his rest, any of you should seem to come short of it. For unto us was the gospel preached, as well as unto them: but the word preached did not profit them, not being mixed with faith in them that heard it."*

MIRACLE MIDWIVES

The Midwives, *Spiphrah* and *Pauh,* responsible for delivering the Hebrew women's children, stayed loyal to God and did not kill the Hebrew baby boys notwithstanding Pharaoh's instructions to do so. In Exodus 1:16-17, *"...he said, when ye do the office of a midwife to the Hebrew women, and see them upon the stools; if it be a son, then ye shall kill him: but if it be a daughter, then she shall live."*

They knew Pharaoh as the paramount ruler of the day who had power to terminate their contracts and possibly to kill them and end their careers, but they defied him nonetheless. Instead of hearkening to Pharaoh, they hearkened to the King of Kings, and He vindicated them.

In Exodus 1:17, the Bible says *"...the midwives feared God, and did not as the king of Egypt commanded them, but saved the men children alive."* They chose to be God's *yes-women.* In return God made them houses. In Exodus 1:21, the Bible says *"...it came to pass, because the midwives feared God, that he made them houses."*

The word interpreted for *houses* in the original Hebrew means *families* or *legacies.* One act of loyalty shattered a lifetime of infertility and fruitlessness that had pervaded their past generations. Their respective names, *Shiphrah* and *Puah,* mean beautiful and one who cries out and it demonstrates that any maestro who becomes a milestone in life starts with a mind that is beautiful and broken in prayer before God. They remained undeterred and unbroken in focus, and as a result, remain relevant for generations.

DIVIDED LOYALTY IS DISLOYALTY!

Jesus said in Luke 16:13, *"No servant can serve two masters: for either he will hate the one, and love the other; or else he will hold to the one, and despise the other. Ye cannot serve God and mammon."*

No loyalty is true that is divided! It is either all or none in God's kingdom. God has no place for no in his vocabulary. The rich man found this out fatally in Luke 16. When Abraham rejected his desire to have the dead preach to his living siblings, he told Father Abraham *"Nay, father*

Abraham: but if one went unto them from the dead, they will repent (Luke 16:30).

Those who get their prayers answered speedily understand this and follow God with a single and undivided eye. In Luke 11:34, Jesus said "*The light of the body is the eye: therefore when thine eye is single, thy whole body also is full of light;....*"

In 2 Samuel 12:3, the prophet Nathan tells the story of a poor man and his family who had one lamb, typifying the Lamb of God that took away the sins of the world called Jesus Christ (John 1:29), and to whom they gave unalloyed loyalty. He had access to everything they owned and embodied the family's growth and grace.

The poor man's loyalty to the lamb was impartial and impervious. The only way anyone could take it away from him was by secrecy and stealth. In 2 Samuel 12:12, the prophet Nathan told King David concerning his affair with Uriah's wife, "*...thou didst it secretly: but I will do this thing before all Israel, and before the sun.*"

Many have disguised divided loyalty as diplomatic, cultural or contemporary correctness when it is actually naked and barefaced disloyalty to God and His Word. If the devil can't destroy a man, he will distract him and if he can't distract him, he will deter him by stealthy euphemisms and New Age theories.

God is calling His church to complete commitment by a total takeover of the body by the Head called Jesus Christ. Intimidation, threats and naysayers will arise; but a determined church, like Jesus who "*...steadfastly set his face to go to Jerusalem*" (Luke 9:51), will overcome and bring revival to the nations.

FOREVER YES!

Carol and Jim Cymbala pastor the world-famous Brooklyn Tabernacle Church and Choir in Brooklyn, New York. Their daughter, Chrissy had always been a model child; but, to her parents' dismay at the age of sixteen she had a child out of wedlock. At eighteen, she moved out of the house and moved in with a man who was almost twice her age.

Her parents were distraught but not deterred. They maintained a testimony of faith with Carol Cymbala composing her famous hymn "He

Has Been Faithful to Me" in the throes of the two-and-a-half-year crises. Chrissie refused all their overtures, rejected counseling from seasoned Christian counselors and started using drugs and alcohol.

Then, one night during a church prayer meeting, a female church member sent Pastor Cymbala a note saying, "I feel impressed that we should stop the meeting and all pray for your daughter." Pastor Cymbala complied, and heaven rose up in attention as the whole church prayed for Chrissie.

Within forty-eight hours, Chrissy had reaffirmed her faith in Christ. She had had a dream that same Tuesday night of a deep abyss that never seemed to end and of God's protecting her from it. She literally ran to her parents' house, repented, and asked for their forgiveness. She entered the ministry thereafter, following Bible school, and is today a Pastor's wife and a mother of three lovely children.

Her story is chronicled in her recent book *Girl in the Song* as an inspiration to parents and teenagers of God's redeeming love. Her experience left an enduring lesson for Jim and Carol Cymbala which they have never forgotten. It is that with God all things are possible if persistent prayer is continually applied and faith always says, *"Yea and Amen."*

Until You Are Obsessed With Your Cause, You Cannot Possess It!

CHAPTER TWENTY-FOUR

THE LOYALTY OF THE ARMORBEARER

"And when his armor bearer saw that Saul was dead, he fell likewise upon his sword, and died with him" (1 Samuel 31:5).

In ancient Israel, the life of an armor bearer was tied to that of their master. Saul's armor bearer, for example, fell upon his sword in concordance with his master who had died earlier. Saul had *"...(in) battle...(being) hit... (and) was sore wounded of the archers. (And)...therefore Saul took a sword, and fell upon it"* (1 Samuel 31:3-4).

In 1 Samuel 25:28-29, Abigail made a statement to a wilderness-living and hand-out seeking David that embodies the mission statement and life philosophy of an armor bearer. She said, *"...the LORD will certainly make my lord a sure house; because my lord fighteth the battles of the LORD, and evil hath not been found in thee all thy days. Yet a man is risen to pursue thee, and to seek thy soul **but the soul of my lord shall be bound in the bundle of life with the LORD thy God** (emphasis added)."*

Those who become sure houses fight the Lord's battle and have their life bundled up with the Lord. An armor bearer seeks to fight his lord or master's battles and his life is worth living only when his master is alive. Failure to defend their master irks armor bearers so much that they take their life as a result!

The armor bearer's motto is "defend to the death." Jonathan, the son of King Saul, had such an armor bearer. In 1 Samuel 14:6, Jonathan told him *"...Come, and let us go over unto the garrison of these uncircumcised: it may be that the* LORD *will work for us: for there is no restraint to the* LORD *to save by many or by few."*

Even though it looked foolhardy and militarily unwise for two isolated soldiers, with no military backup according to 1 Samuel 14:1, to take on a garrison of possibly two thousand soldiers the armor bearer agreed to go with Jonathan. He said, *"...do all that is in thine heart: turn thee; behold, I am with thee according to thy heart."* (1 Samuel 14:7).

The loyalty of the armor bearer is total. They *"...love not their lives unto the death"* (Revelation 12:11) and are willing *"...to lay down (their)... lives for the brethren"* (1 John 3:16). This loyalty is a reflection of the New Testament ideals left for the church by Jesus Christ. He said, *"Greater love hath no man than this, that a man lay down his life for his friends"* (John 15:13). A person with true loyalty loves by giving up his or her life. As a result, God marks that person as a legend.

DAVID: THE ARMOR BEARER TO KING SAUL

David was appointed King Saul's armor bearer when the king was in dire straits. In 1 Samuel 16:21,23, the Bible says *"...David came to Saul, and stood before him: and he loved him greatly; and he became his armor bearer. And it came to pass, when the evil spirit from God was upon Saul, that David took an harp, and played with his hand: so Saul was refreshed, and was well, and the evil spirit departed from him."*

Like David, the armor bearer is at the service of the master with the only intention being to ward off evil from the master. They are there to protect, not pillage, and to help not harm them. The loyalty of the armor bearer was the reason, in spite of Saul's antagonisms towards David n his latter years, that he never rose up to harm him in any way.

In 1 Samuel 24, King Saul while seeking for David's life stayed in a cave where David and his men were already hidden. As a result of their advantageous position, David and his men could have killed Saul and his men. Instead, David chose to *"...cut off the skirt of Saul's robe privily"* (1 Samuel 24:4).

His loyalty to Saul, as his former armor bearer, riveted David's heart and *"...it came to pass afterward, that David's heart smote him, because he* had cut off Saul's skirt and he said unto his men, the LORD forbid that I should do this thing unto my master, the LORD's anointed, to stretch forth mine hand against him, seeing he is the anointed of the LORD" (1 SAMUEL 24:5-6).

David did not see the death of King Saul, his nemesis, as a credit to his murderer but as a debt for which the murderer must pay recompense. He was so determined to safeguard King Saul that at Saul's death by the hand of an Amalekite soldier, David commanded one of his young men who "...smote him that he died and David said unto him, thy blood be upon thy head; for thy mouth hath testified against thee, saying, I have slain the LORD's anointed" (2 Samuel 1:15-16).

David understood the loyalty of the armor bearer because he was one! He understood that true loyalty seeks not vengeance for self but victory for the Lord's army. His heart pangs were always to defend, not to destroy his master. Until his master's death he made that dedication the hallmark of his career.

In salute to the men of Jabesh-Gilead who rescued Saul and his sons' bodies from the Philistines' temple in 1 Samuel 31:8-13, David said, "... Blessed be ye of the LORD, that ye have shewed this kindness unto your lord, even unto Saul, and have buried him. And now the LORD shew kindness and truth unto you: and I also will requite you this kindness, because ye have done this thing" (2 Samuel 2:5-6). Loyalty legends bless those standing to protect the heritage of their master's heritage, but they curse those who seek to erode it.

THE ARMOR BEARERS OF JOAB!

When Absalom rebelled against his father, King David, in 2 Samuel 15, 16 and 17, it took the valiancy of Joab and his armor bearers to put him down. One of these armor bearers is listed among David's thirty mighty men. He is, "...Naharai the Berothite, the armor bearer of Joab the son of Zeruiah" (1 Chronicles 11:39).

As Absalom was dangling from an oak tree in 2 Samuel 18:9, and hanging "...between the heaven and the earth...", one of David's soldier's saw him. This man intimated Joab of his finding, and rather than do a carousel on the legitimacy and long term consequences of doing harm to Absalom with this well-intentioned soldier (see 2 Samuel 18:11-13), Joab put three darts through the heart of Absalom and his *"...young men that bare* (his) *Joab's armor compassed about* (Absalom) *and smote...and slew* (Absalom)"* (2 Samuel 18:14).

These armor bearers of Joab define loyalty. They saw their job as a service to their master and the nation, even if it went against the grain of David's instruction to their superiors. The erstwhile soldier who had earlier intimated Joab on the whereabouts of Absalom to the contrary was not an armor bearer. His objectives were long term, while those of the armor bearers were immediate.

The loyalty of the armor bearer is not about platitudes. It is about power! It is not about following a master about. It is faithfulness to act when called upon. The loyalty of the armor bearer does not seek to be a mere supporter of a cause. He or she is a servant to the cause for which they are called even if it costs them their livelihood, legacy and life. An armor bearer must *"endure hardness, as a good soldier of Jesus Christ* (for) *no man that warreth entangles himself with the affairs of this life; that he may please him who hath chosen him to be a soldier"* (2 Timothy 2:3-4).

KENT BRANTLEY: LOYAL EVEN UNTO DEATH

Kent Brantley is a family physician and current missions' medical adviser for Samaritan's purse, an arm of the Billy Graham Evangelistic Association (BGEA). He and his wife relocated their family in 2014 to the ELWA hospital, near Monrovia, Liberia, and became physician and home-school mom respectively to their two lovely daughters.

In the summer of 2014, however, the tranquility and serenity they had gotten accustomed to in Liberia changed with the outbreak of the ebola epidemic in Liberia. It killed more than 4,000 individuals from all walks of life, including several medical professionals.

As the situation gravely grew worse, with the Ebola virus doubling every twenty days in prevalence, Kent sent his wife and kids home to attend a family wedding. Within three days of their departure, Kent Brantley developed a fever and had to be quarantined while his colleagues tested his blood to ascertain if he had ebola or not.

The results came in fast and furious. He did have Ebola and would need the emergency *ZMapp* antiserum experimental drug to survive. The only problem was Nancy Writebol, another American missionary who worked with sterilization of surgical attires, had also developed ebola simultaneously and there was *ZMapp* sufficient for only one person.

While prayer was going on all over the world for Kent by family, friends and fellow brothers and sisters in Christ, he was making a decision that threatened his very existence. He told the leader of the ebola surveillance monitoring team in ELWA, *"give the ZMapp injection to Nancy."*

They, however, objected, and gave the *ZMapp* injection to him instead. Soon afterwards, both ebola victims were emergently evacuated by the United States Air force into the USA. Two weeks after their treatment commenced at American tertiary hospitals, they were discharged as clear of Ebola.

Dr. Kent Brantley went a step further. After three medical personnel in the USA contracted the disease from an ailing Liberian immigrant, he donated his serum to help save their lives. A missionary at heart, Kent Brantley, epitomizes what loyalty construes. It is not delicatessens, drudge reports or debunking other peoples' opinions. It is dedication to a cause - even in the face of death. Such ones', like Kent Brantley, live on as legends even after they are dead.

A loyalty decision makes
a legendary destiny!

CHAPTER TWENTY FIVE

THE LOYALTY OF THE ANGELS

"Bless the Lord, ye his angels, that excel in strength, that do his commandments, hearkening unto the voice of his word" (Psalms 103:20).

Angels are spiritual beings subject to the word of God. There are evil angels who were cast out of heaven for rebellion and are now set apart for perdition (see Revelation 12:7-12). Godly angels, on the other hand, are loyal to the Word of God and are set apart to minister to the saints.

The Bible says, in Hebrews 1:14, of these godly angels *"are they not all ministering spirits sent forth to minister for them who shall be heirs of salvation?"* In Psalm 103:21, they are also described as *"...ministers of His that do His pleasure."*

These Godly angels, in all their power and glory, are infinitely loyal to God's Word. As a result, they *"...excel in strength* (and)*...do his commandments, hearkening unto the voice of his word"* (Psalm 103:20).

One angel single-handedly *"...went out and smote in the camp of the Assyrians an hundred fourscore and five thousand..."* soldiers overnight (2 King 19:35). Jesus told his disciples, when the soldiers came to arrest him, *"...thinkest thou that I cannot now pray to my Father, and he shall presently give me more than twelve legions of angels"* (Matthew 26:53).

It took one slap from an angel to turn King Herod into a worm-ridden corpse in Tyre and Sidon (Acts 12:23). After twenty-one days of battle with the prince of Persia, Arch-angel Michael intervened and allowed for the delivery of God's answer to Daniel petition in Daniel 10:20.

134

These angels are a no-retreat-or-surrender army with unalloyed loyalty to God's Word. Their mission is unalienable and non-negotiable. They hearken only to the words of God's commands according to Psalm 103:20) and do not listen to men's opinions or what their environment or enemies say. As a result, their unwavering loyalty produces in them a legendary dimension called *excellence in strength.*

EXCEL IN STRENGTH!

Angels are described as those who "...*excel in strength...*" (Psalm 103:20). They touched Peter and his chains automatically fell off in an instant (see Acts 12:7). When they touched Jacob's ischio-pubis joint, he ended up with a limp for the rest of his life (Genesis 32:25,31-32).

Angels are legendary in strength because they stay loyal to the God who commands them. Before the fall of Adam, another crop of angels had attempted to "overthrow God" (see Revelation 12:7). Their leader, Lucifer, had resolved to "...*be like the most High...*" (Isaiah 14:14). In the end they were "...*cast out into the earth...*" (Revelation 12:9) and finally will be banished to everlasting fire in the lake of fire and brimstone (see Matthew 25:41 and Revelation 20:10).

These disloyal angels will suffer destruction but those who remain loyal to God will walk in authority. In Hebrews 2:2, the writer of Hebrews says, "...*the word spoken by angels was stedfast...*" and in 2 Peter 2:11, Peter further reminds the Church that "...*angels, which are **greater in power and might,** bring not railing accusation against them* (dignitaries*) before the Lord"* (emphasis added).

These angels of God follow strict divine guidelines and mandates, and as a result execute with dispatch divine assignments. They do not tolerate dissent. When the father of John the Baptist, Zechariah the priest, waned and disagreed with the words of the angel Gabriel, he was struck "...*dumb and not able to speak until the day that these things shall be performed because thou believest not my words, which shall be fulfilled in their season*" (Luke 1:20).

This type of loyalty, which is unperturbed by seemingly insurmountable obstacles, is what God requires of believers. The believer is going to "...

judge angels..." (1 Corinthians 6:3); therefore, the believer is expected to have an even higher standard of loyalty than the angels.

THE ANGEL OF ALACRITY

Angels are mono-syllablic! They answer in only one way - with God's Word. In other words, they answer with *alacrity* otherwise defined as *briskness* or *cheerful* readiness. This behavior is consistent with 1 Peter 5:2 that adjures leaders: *"Feed the flock of God which is among you, taking the oversight thereof, not by constraint,* **but willingly; not for filthy lucre, but of a ready mind;...**" (emphasis added).

The spirit of alacrity always follows the spirit of loyalty! When God sent the angels to Sodom and Gomorrah, they responded with alacrity. While Lot argued with the men of Sodom over their inflamed homosexual passions and its propriety, the angels *"...put forth their hand, and pulled Lot into the house to them, and shut the door. And they smote the men that were at the door of the house with blindness, both small and great..."* (Genesis 19:10-11). The next morning, while Lot *"...lingered, the men laid hold upon his hand, and upon the hand of his wife, and upon the hand of his two daughters; the LORD being merciful unto him: and they brought him forth, and set him without the city"* (Genesis 19:16).

Angels are duty-bound to do the word of God, in spite of any opposition they meet. They brook no dissent, as is evidenced by their violent reaction to Herod's blasphemy. In Acts 12:22-23, *"...the people gave a shout, saying, it is the voice of a god, and not of a man. And* **immediately the angel of the Lord smote him**, *because he gave not God the glory: and he was eaten of worms, and gave up the ghost"* (emphasis added).

The angel sent to bring the children of Israel into their promised land was described by God as one sent *"...to keep thee in the way, and to bring thee into the place which I have prepared. Beware of him, and obey his voice, provoke him not; for he will not pardon your transgressions: for my name is in him"* (Exodus 23:20-21).

Another angel was sent to deliver Jericho into the hands of the people of Israel. He refused to be distracted by human sentiments of primordial affiliations. When asked by Joshua if he was *"...for us, or for our adversaries?"*

(Joshua 5:13), he told Joshua, "...*as captain of the host of the* Lord *am I now come...*" (Joshua 5:14).

One of the attributes of loyalty is speed! It is not just obedience, but timely obedience that counts in the kingdom. The five foolish virgins did buy their oil (see Matthew 25:10); but because they did not operate with alacrity, they were locked out of the feast with the bridegroom (Matthew 25:10-12).

Angels are swift in obedience and swift to follow the Lord's instructions in execution. In 2 Kings 6:18, after Elisha gave the word to blind the army of the Syrians surrounding his complex in Dothan, the enemy soldiers were "...*smote with blindness according to the word of Elisha*" by the company of angels surrounding them. Tomorrow's legends are today's loyalists who pursue God's direction doggedly and with determination.

$5:80 PLEDGE

I was broke and actually in debt in 2006. I had less than $100.00 to my name, and I owed money on my brand-new car and home. As I neared the end of my contract as a surgical resident, I knew I needed a miracle to remain in America. Due to my surgical residency program's pyramidal scheme, I would be out-of-status if I accepted the offer of the chairman of General Surgery.

I had been a preliminary surgical resident for two years, and was delighted at the department's offer of a categorical surgical position but starting from year one again was fraught with risks as I had a seven year limit to complete my post-graduate medical training in America. Without another program opening their doors to me, I would be returning to my home country an unfinished product at post graduate medical education. I needed a miracle!

As I pondered on my future, I watched a television evangelist ask for a $58 seed-faith offering. I felt I could not participate as a result of my financial woes but the more I listened the stronger I was impressed on by the Holy Spirit to sow what ever seed I could afford. He said, "*why don't you give a $5:80 seed faith level for 12 months as an expression of your faith in God for a turn-around miracle?*"

I immediately complied with God's instructions. I called the Christian television network and pledged to give a seed faith of $5:80 for the next twelve months. In less than twelve months, my testimony manifested. I was accepted into a Family Medicine program with which God had given me favor and finished my residency successfully and in a timely manner as the best family resident in my class.

Today, I am the Medical Director of one of the largest Federally Qualified Health Centers in the state of Louisiana. I am also on the board of the Louisiana Academy of Family Physicians as well as a Louisiana State Medical society executive officer. I am a board-certified family physician fulfilling the call of God on my life to explore the vistas' of God's power to transform and excel in my generation, because I obeyed the voice of the Holy Spirit. Hallelujah!

*It's not the position
that makes the leader;
it's the leader that
makes the position*

– John Maxwell (Author, Leadership
expert, Pastor and founder of
Maxwell coaching team).

CHAPTER TWENTY SIX

THE LOYALTY OF THE AXE

"A man was famous according as he had lifted up axes upon the thick trees" (Psalm 74:5).

Every Christian is an axe in God's hand, but he or she must first be yielded to be used by the Maker. If they are going to become legends in their time, believers must first be as loyal as an axe is in the hand of its wielder. In Isaiah 10:15, God Almighty asks *"shall the axe boast itself against him that heweth therewith? or shall the saw magnify itself against him that shaketh it? as if the rod should shake itself against them that lift it up, or as if the staff should lift up itself, as if it were no wood."*

The propulsion and thrust of the person wielding the axe is what makes it effective. **Without a carrier, an axe is impotent.** In Jeremiah 51:20, God calls believers his battle axe. It is His power and presence, when yielded to, that shapes our lives into an unstoppable and unconquerable force. In Jeremiah 51:20-22, God declares *"Thou art my battle axe and weapons of war: for with thee will I break in pieces the nations; And with thee will I destroy kingdoms and with thee will I break in pieces the horse and his rider; and with thee will I break in pieces the chariot and his rider, With thee also will I break in pieces man and woman; and with thee will I break in pieces old and young; and with thee will I break in pieces the young man and the maid."*

The prophet Jeremiah saw himself several times as a broken record who was disenfranchised, mocked, imprisoned and victimized by Israel's leaders. In God's hands, however, he was a battle axe. He eventually

140

triumphed over his opposition because God revealed His word within him as "*...a hammer that breaketh the rock in pieces?*" (Jeremiah 23:29). The hammer or battle axe believer is too equipped with God's Word to be defeated by the world.

BATTLE-AXE BELIEVERS!

When God needs a job done, he employs spiritual warriors with a battle-axe mentality. These warriors see no opposition as insurmountable. They stand on the Rock of God's Word, of which Jesus said, "*...upon this rock I will build my church; and the gates of hell shall not prevail against it*" (Matthew 16:18).

The battleaxe believer refuses to allow the devil keep his or her stuff! These believers understand the "*...the kingdom of heaven suffereth violence; and the violent take it by force*" (Matthew 11:12). In this phrase, Jesus implies that to decisively obtain the prize the church must seize it by force or snatch it suddenly. Too many believers want a passive path to victory. In contrast, the battle axe believer understands that the path to the kingdom of God is riddled with violence!

In Matthew 3:8,10, John the Baptist warns the Sadducees and Pharisees: "*Bring forth therefore fruits meet for repentance. And now also **the axe** is laid unto the root of the trees: therefore every tree which bringeth not forth good fruit is hewn down, and cast into the fire*" (emphasis added).

The church is that axe that is laid at the root of trees and nothing corrupt or unfruitful is allowed to miss her wrath. Battleaxe believers are God's end-time destroyers. They carry their destroying weapons, the word of God, in their mouths and do not relent until their purpose is achieved. They are loyal to the end, and as a result they become legends of their time.

THE AXE OF THE LORD'S VENGEANCE!

In Ezekiel 9:1-2, six men were summoned by the Lord to execute divine vengeance on the city of Jerusalem and its inhabitants as a punishment for their sins. These men were not ordinary citizens but leading men who had "*...charge over the city...*" (Ezekiel 9:2).

Amongst these six men was one with an ink horn, and he went about placing a mark on the heads of those in "*...the midst of the city...of*

Jerusalem,…that sigh and that cry for all the abominations that be done in the midst thereof" (Ezekiel 9:4).

At the end of this assignment, the man with the inkhorn who had been followed by his five colleagues who *"…were told to slay utterly old and young, both maids, and little children, and women but… not near any man upon whom is the mark"* (Ezekiel 9:6), reported the matter saying *"…I have done as thou hast commanded me"* (Ezekiel 9:11).

Loyalty legends do what God asks them to do without alteration. As a result, they carve a niche for themselves in the sphere of world affairs. As did these six men, who had charge of the city of Jerusalem, men of loyalty command their generation.

In Psalm 74:5, the Bible says, *"A man was famous according as he had lifted up axes upon the thick trees."* Fame follows men willing to be wielded unwaveringly as an axe by their Maker. The dyed-in-the-wool and battle-scarred axes of the Lord go against the thickest and toughest oppositions (Psalm 74:5). As they do so, they become life's loyalty legends of their time.

GOD'S HOLY GHOST BULLDOZERS!

I was a marked man. I had reported the longest-serving professor of anatomy in my medical school to the authorities for conniving with his sons to divulge exam questions prior to exams. My intention was to abrogate the endless injustice meted out to the good, conscientious and hard-working medical students who refused to collude with some professors for preknowledge of the exam questions.

The day before the anatomy exam, my classmate accompanied by another friend walked up to me and said that the exam was on sale at a specific hotel for a certain sum by a brazen son of this professor of anatomy. I got into my car, picked an unidentified security apparatchik and headed for the hotel. All I had was my monthly allowance of fifty dollars, but I decided to spend it buying the questions set for the next day's exam.

At the risk of being recognized, I went into that hotel and bought the questions. It was about 10 P.M. at that time. By 5 A.M. the next morning, I handed the unopened exam script to the Provost of the College of Medicine and explained the circumstances under which I had obtained it.

My intervention saved the day for the honest students. The Provost ensured that the essay questions were changed, the multiple choice questions were cancelled and this anatomy professor dismissed after a thorough investigation was carried out.

Even though reporting this exam leakage brought death threats, denigration and my near dismissal from the medical school, I stood up as God's battleaxe and won. The long history of exam malpractice on my medical campus was broken, and those behind its operations were dismissed. I was God's change agent that day, and it signaled to me the power of uncompromised loyalty to bring change.

"The world has yet to see
what God will do with,
and for, and through, and
in, and by the man who
is fully consecrated to
Him...and by God's grace
may I be that man"

- D.L Moody (1837-1899)

CHAPTER TWENTY-SEVEN

THE LOYALTY OF THE ARK

"Now therefore arise, O LORD God, into thy resting place, thou, and the ark of thy strength: let thy priests, O LORD God, be clothed with salvation, and let thy saints rejoice in goodness" (2 Chronicles 6:41).

God's presence is akin to the loyalty of the ark. The ark which testifies of His presence, is promised to the believer till the end of the age. In Matthew 28:20, Jesus said, *"...I am with you alway, even unto the end of the world."* In Psalm 125:2, the Psalmist promises that *"as the mountains are round about Jerusalem, so the LORD is round about his people from henceforth even for ever."*

This theme of God being a loyal ark is manifested throughout scripture. The Lord Jesus is described as *"...a friend that sticketh closer than a brother"* (Proverbs 18:24) and even when *"...a woman forget her sucking child that she should not have compassion on the son of her womb? Yea, they may forget, yet will I* (God will) *not forget thee"* (Isaiah 49:15). He has promised *"I have graven thee upon the palms of my hands; thy walls are continually before me"* (Isaiah 49:16). These are the words of the faithful God to His people.

The ark of the Lord is described as the power of His presence. The ark is guaranteed to the believer as long as the matching conditions are met. In James 4:8, Elder James adjures believers: *"Draw nigh to God, and He will draw nigh to you. Cleanse your hands, ye sinners; and purify your hearts, ye double minded."* God is committed to believers; but first, they must draw near to Him and purify their hearts.

In Psalm 15:1-5, the Psalmist asks, "*Lord, who shall abide in thy tabernacle? who shall dwell in thy holy hill? He that walketh uprightly, and worketh righteousness, and speaketh the truth in his heart. He that backbiteth not with his tongue, nor doeth evil to his neighbour, nor taketh up a reproach against his neighbour. In whose eyes a vile person is contemned; but he honoreth them that fear the LORD. He that sweareth to his own hurt, and changeth not. He that putteth not out his money to usury, nor taketh reward against the innocent....*"

God's presence is the panacea for life's pains. It accords one a legendary status as a result of God's loyalty to His people who follow and fulfill His requisite conditions. Jesus, though the only begotten Son of God, said, "and He *that sent me is with me: the Father hath not left me alone; for I do always those things that please him*" (John 8:29). Even Jesus had to meet these requirements for divine presence in order to go "*...about doing good, and healing all that were oppressed of the devil; for God was with him*" (Acts 10:38).

THE FORCE OF HIS PRESENCE

In the wilderness journey to the promised land, "*when the ark set forward, that Moses said, Rise up, LORD, and let thine enemies be scattered; and let them that hate thee flee before thee. And when it rested, he said, Return, O LORD, unto the many thousands of Israel* (Numbers 10:35-36).

The Ark was the Israelites' guide and guard through the vagaries and violence in the wilderness. When it arrived in the camp of the Israelites, on one occasion, "*...all Israel shouted with a great shout, so that the earth rang again. And when the Philistines heard the noise of the shout, they said, what meaneth the noise of this great shout in the camp of the Hebrews? And they understood that the ark of the LORD was come into the camp*" (1 Samuel 4:5-6).

While "*...the Philistines were afraid, for they said, God is come into the camp. And they said, woe unto me! Who shall deliver us out of the hand of these mighty Gods? These are the gods that smote the Egyptians with all the plagues in the wilderness*" (1 Samuel 4:7-8). The Israelites rejoiced in the ark's presence unaware that the ark was about to be retaken and that God had departed from Israel because of the sins of Eli and his children. Although the ark had a reputation among the nations of destroying the Egyptian Empire with the twelve plagues, and its entry evoked fear in all comers, its presence did not translate into power because of sin in the camp.

In Joshua 3, when the priests baring the ark stood in the overflowing waves of the River Jordan, the waters receded so that the millions of Israelites could cross over (Joshua 3:1-12) on dry ground. The ark was always to go ahead of the people and not behind them. The scripture says, *"...When ye see the ark of the covenant of the LORD your God, and the priests the Levites bearing it, then ye shall remove from your place, and go after it. Yet there shall be a space between you and it, about two thousand cubits by measure:...that ye may know the way by which ye must go..."* (Joshua 3:3-4).

The Holy Spirit is the believer's modern-day ark of covenant *"for he dwelleth with you and shall be in you"* (John 14:17). He is come as *"...the Spirit of truth...(to) guide* (the church) *into all truth..."* (John 16:13). He cannot be bought, bullied or boxed in by circumstances, but will remain steadfastly present and loyal to the believer who pleases the father.

In John 14:12, Jesus said, *"He that believeth on me, the works that I do shall he do also; and greater works than these shall he do; because I go unto my Father."* The world of greater works is tied to the presence of the Holy Spirit. It was the same power of the Holy Spirit manifested at the River Jordan that turned a thirty-year-old minister of the gospel called Jesus of Nazareth into a global powerhouse in three and a half years.

That same power lives in the believer today and according to Romans 8:11, *"...if the Spirit of him that raised up Jesus from the dead dwell in you, he that raised up Christ from the dead shall also quicken your mortal bodies by his Spirit that dwelleth in you."*

THE ABIDING PRESENCE OF GOD!

It is not God's absence, but the presence of sin, that mitigates against the production of loyalty legends in our time. God is *"...of purer eyes than to behold evil, and canst not look on iniquity"* (Habakkuk 1:13). The ark of the Lord does not fail its people, but rather the people fail the ark. Its loyalty, as the ark of the Lord, is unassailable; but it will remain only where His presence is guaranteed by holiness.

Eli's family, for example, trifled with instead of treasured God's presence. Even though they were custodians of the ark, God asked them *"wherefore kick ye at my sacrifices and mine offering…and honorest thy sons above me, to make themselves fat with the chief of all the offerings of Israel my people?"* (1 Samuel 2:29).

As a result of this callous disobedience of God's ordinances, God said, *"I said indeed that thy house, and the house of thy father, should walk before me for ever: but now the LORD saith, Be it far from me; for them that honor me I will honor, and they that despise me shall be lightly esteemed"* (1 Samuel 2:30). They had a covenant of loyalty with the ark; but because of sin, they lost it and became beggars, bereaved and bastards, in God's house (1 Samuel 2:31-36).

God's presence is a *sine qua non* to those who seek Him with all their heart. The Prophet Jeremiah said, *"…ye call upon me, and ye shall go and pray unto me, and I will hearken unto you. And ye shall seek me, and find me, when ye shall search for me with all your heart"* (Jeremiah 29:12-13). God is not averse to the presence of His people; in fact he seeks their company. Songs of Solomon 2:4 says, *"He brought me to the banqueting house, and his banner over me was love."*

In Numbers 14:42-45, the following scenario explicitly portrays the necessity of God's presence. After failing to believe the report of Caleb and Joshua for which ten of the spies died, the leaders of Israel decided to go into the promised land, albeit without the presence of God. Moses told them, *"Go not up, for the LORD is not among you; that ye be not smitten before your enemies….Because ye are turned away from the LORD, therefore the LORD will not be with. But they presumed to go up unto the hill top: nevertheless the ark of the covenant of the LORD, and Moses, departed not out of the camp."*

If the people of Israel had been true to their covenant, God would have been true to them. He, who is a *"…God nigh unto them, as the Lord our God is in all things that we call upon him for,…*(needs believers to) *take heed to thyself, and keep thy soul diligently"* (Deuteronomy 4:7,9). God is unfailingly loyal. He says, in Jeremiah 31:3, that *"…I have loved thee with an everlasting love…."* His presence is from everlasting to everlasting, and for those who remain loyal to His covenant, he promises to make them innumerable and impregnable (see Numbers 23:9-10) such that *"…he hath as it were the strength of an unicorn...(and) no enchantment...(or) divination against"* them shall stand" (Numbers 23:22-23).

The children of Eli bequeathed an *Ichabod* generation to their progeny because they forfeited His presence. According to one of their wives, *"...the glory is departed from Israel because the ark of God was taken..."* (I Samuel 4:21). The ark is the believer's glory train, and when it is absent *Ichabod* or shameful living is inevitable.

T.L OSBORNE (1923-2013): CALL, COST AND CONSEQUENCES OF LOYALTY

T.L. Osborn, or T.L. as he was fondly called, was called by God to be an evangelist at fifteen years of age. He travelled across the continental United States with Evangelist E.M. Dillard. He later left for India as a foreign missionary with his wife at the age of twenty one.

T.L. and his wife, Daisy, dedicated themselves as missionaries to serve the people of India. Within a year, however, they departed from India in a critical state of spiritual and physical health. They took up a pastorate in Oregon, and decided to steer clear of missions in their immediate future due to their grim results they saw in India.

After listening to William Braham preach at a crusade, however, a desire for the exhibition of the power of God with signs following was lit in T.L. He heard God tell him, as he saw William Braham preach and demonstrate the power of God with signs following, *"You can do the same thing he is doing."*

In obedience to the voice of God, he left his fledgling congregation and returned to the mission fields of the world. He held crusades from Africa to Asia with attendance reaching as many as five hundred thousand in some crusades.

His crusades were characterized by epoch-making miracles such as lepers being healed, the blind seeing and cripples walking. After nearly seventy-five years of ministry, T.L. is widely regarded as the father of the mass evangelism movement to the nations of the world.

He pioneered mass-evangelism and open-air preaching in crusade settings all around the world. Through his ministry, more than 150,000 new Churches were planted and over 30,000 men and women were equipped with free Christian literature and tutelage to be full time missionaries to non-evangelized tribes and villages.

On his ministry desk in Tulsa, Oklahoma T.L. had a plaque that said *"Expect great things from God; Attempt great things for God."* He lived a life devoted to loving God, his family and the world and departed this world an eighty nine year old loyalty legend as a result.

Don't touch God's gold, the girls, or the glory of God

– Oral Roberts Mother's advise to her son before the commencement of his ministry.

CHAPTER TWENTY-EIGHTH

THE LOYALTY OF
THE ASCETIC

*"Thou therefore endure hardness, as a good soldier of Jesus Christ.
No man that warreth entangleth himself with the affairs of this
life; that he may please him who hath chosen him to be a soldier"*
(2 Timothy 2:3-4).

An *ascetic* is not an oft-used term in modern-day Christianity. In the days
of Paul the apostle, however, it was widely applicable to Christians. It is
defined as the practice of severe self-discipline and abstention from all
forms of indulgence, typically for religious reasons.

It is used in 2 Timothy 2:3, where Paul encourages Timothy to endure
hardness and suffer with him rather than to compromise with the world.
It is also implied in Philippians 4:12, where Paul says, *"I know both how
to be abased, and I know how to abound: every where and in all things I am
instructed both to be full and to be hungry, both to abound and to suffer need."*

The word interpreted in the Greek for *abase* is the Greek word *tapeinos*.
It is defined as humbling oneself by frugal living. A modern-church
movement hinged on luxury has eroded the ethos of loyalty by their
emphasis on luxury and diminishment of loyalty.

In the early church, *"Neither was there any among them that lacked:
for as many as were possessors of lands or houses sold them, and brought the
prices of the things that were sold, and laid them down at the apostles' feet:
and distribution was made unto every man according as he had need"* (Acts
4:34-35).

The result of this ascetic lifestyle was that among the early church, *"neither said any of them that ought of the things which he possessed was his own; but they had all things common. And with great power gave the apostles witness of the resurrection of the Lord Jesus: and great grace was upon them all"* (Acts 4:32-33).

The early Church rode on the loyalty of ascetics, as Jesus and His disciples typified, to become world changers and legends. In Luke 9:58, Jesus said *"...Foxes have holes, and birds of the air have nests; but the Son of man hath not where to lay his head."* In Romans 12:16, Paul advises the church: *"...Mind not high things, but condescend to men of low estate...."*

The ascetic's loyalty is not dependent on convenience or comfort, but in confidence to the word of the Lord. The life a believer lives is a life of commitment without any pre-requisite comforts! It is a life which, like Paul, *"...counts all things but loss for the excellency of the knowledge of Christ Jesus my Lord for whom I have suffered the loss of all things, and do count them but dung, that I may win Christ"* (Philippians 3:8).

THE LAST ENEMY CALLED COMFORT

One of the last enemies to be conquered before the Israelites entered their promised land was comfort. The Bible says, in Deuteronomy 3:11, *"... only Og king of Bashan remained of the remnant of giants; behold, his bedstead was a bedstead of iron...nine cubits...length, and four cubits breadth...after the cubit of a man."*

The final giant on the road to legendary loyalty is comfort! The iron bed belonging to *Og*, who was the last giant before Israel possessed the promised land, represents comfort. Until this generation makes Christ - not comfort - her priority, she can't enter her promised land.

Comfort is alien to the gospel! Too many modern-day believers believe this concept is an antiquated mentality, but to Jesus it is this archetypal lifestyle of benevolence and beneficence that will herald his return. The John the Baptist and Elijah (Malachi 4:5) generations that precede the Messiah's return to welcome Him back are not steeped in luxury, but loyalty.

In Matthew 11:11, Jesus speaking about John the Baptist said, *"But what went ye out for to see? A man clothed in soft raiment? Behold, they that wear soft clothing are in kings' houses. But what went ye out for to see? A prophet? yea, I say unto you, and more than a prophet."*

The luxury-seeking church is a puerile and placid church, but the church that walks in loyalty seeks Christ not comfort. They are a powerful church and like good soldiers, they "*...endure hardness...*" (2 Timothy 2:3) and become masters in their clime.

Jesus warned the church, "*...in the world ye shall have tribulation: but be of good cheer; I have overcome the world*" (John 16:33). Tribulation does not stop the overcoming church because though "*...troubled on every side, yet not distressed; we are perplexed, but not in despair; Persecuted, but not forsaken; cast down, but not destroyed; Always bearing about in the body the dying of the Lord Jesus, that the life also of Jesus might be made manifest in our body*" (2 Corinthians 4:8-10).

THE EXAMPLE OF THE GIBEONITES

Like the Gibeonites, many believers start off wrong in their race for life. They lie with vacillating truth, deceive and cheat. In Joshua 9, the Gibeonites heard of the conquest of Ai and lied to Joshua and the Israeli leadership claiming to be from a distant land (Joshua 9:9-14). As a result, the Israeli leadership made a covenant of peace with them without first seeking the Lord (Joshua 9:15).

The Gibeonites profession of faith, though later found to be false (Joshua 9:16-18), did not absolve the Israelites from the covenant they had entered into with the Gibeonites. The Gibeonites were, rather than destroyed, sentenced to an ascetic life of "*...be*(ing) *hewers of wood and drawers of water unto all the congregation...*" (Joshua 9:21).

God has entered into a covenant with the Church and our sin does not absolve Him of His covenant love for us. The covenant, however, demands a response from those who are loved. 1 John 4:19 says "*we love Him, because He first loved us.*"

The Gibeonites responded in love by keeping to the tenets of the covenant with Israel. During King Saul's reign, however, he oppressed and killed the Gibeonites with the intention of dispossessing them of their landed property (2 Samuel 21:1-2). This went against the requirements of the covenant Joshua had made with them (Joshua 9:13,23), and as a result

"...there was a famine in the days of David three years, year after year; and David enquired of the LORD. And the LORD answered, it is for Saul, and for his bloody house, because he slew the Gibeonites" (2 Samuel 21:1).

The *"...curse causeless shall not come"* (Proverbs 26:2), and many a time the cause of the curse in believer's lives may be disloyalty to the covenant because of greed. The Gibeonites, rather than breach their covenant of asceticism, told King David in response to his promise to ameliorate their situation that they *"...will have no silver nor gold of Saul, nor of his house; neither for us shalt thou kill any man in Israel"* (2 Samuel 21:4).

God is a God of covenant. The Gibeonites understood this fact. They had made a covenant in the presence of God to be allowed to live as long as they remained ascetic bondmen who drew water and fetched wood for the congregation of Israel. They were not going to compromise by asking for financial remuneration or the death of any Israeli man. Rather they asked for the *"...the man that consumed us, and that devised against us that we should be destroyed from remaining in any of the coasts of Israel. Let seven men of his sons be delivered unto us, and we will hang them up unto the LORD..."* (2 SAMUEL 21:5-6).

As a result of David's compliance with their request, the three-year famine ceased over the land of Israel for *"...after that God was in treated for the land"* (2 Samuel 21:14). God expects His church to operate with the same veracity on covenant as he does. Just as God *"...will not break His covenant, or alter the thing that is gone out of His lips"* (Psalm 89:34), God wants His body to go into covenants or agreements with the same loyalty and commitment irrespective of whatever perks disloyalty might offer.

The God of heaven halted the atmospheric changes of the earth and instituted famine in order to enforce the covenant rights of a loyal group of individuals called the Gibeonites (2 Samuel 21:1-3). How much more will God do same or more for today's believers who have a better and a more powerful covenant? According to Hebrews 8:6-8, Jesus *"...is the mediator of a better covenant, which was established upon better promises. For if that first covenant had been faultless, then should no place have been sought for the second. For finding fault with them, he saith, Behold, the days come, saith the Lord, when I will make a new covenant with the house of Israel and with the house of Judah."*

MIRACLE IN MORAVIA!

Count Zinzendorf (1700-1760) became a post reformation and pre-awakening giant in the faith through an ascetic lifestyle. Though from a privileged background and from one of the leading families of the 18th century, he gave up all his titles and trophies to fulfill God's call on his life.

He began in 1722 by letting some ten Moravians, led by Christian David, who had fled persecution in Modern-day Czech Republic take parts of his estate to set up a settlement. He called it "Herrnhut" meaning "under the Lord's watch." Within five years they were almost three hundred members of the Moravian Church in the settlement.

The settlement experienced a spiritual awakening in the summer of 1727. They covenanted to pray continually in groups of twenty-four men or women, and these prayers went on interrupted for one hundred years. Their lifestyle was one of commonality and their focus was sharing Jesus Christ with the poorest and most despised people of the world.

Within ten years of the common conclave in "Herrnhut," this group of six hundred ascetic Christians had sent out seventy missionaries to the ends of the earth. Sixty-five years after the first missionaries had been sent, they had sent three hundred missionaries throughout the world to such places as Algeria, Tanzania, South Africa, USA, Europe, South America and India. Since that time, they have established branches of the Church on every continent of the earth.

Loculation is Location minus Loyalty!

CHAPTER TWENTY NINE

THE LOYALTY OF THE APERTURE

"The Lord sent a word into Jacob, and it hath lighted upon Israel" (Isaiah 9:8).

An aperture is defined as an opening, hole or gap that is commonly used in photography or optical instruments to determine the amount of light passing through to a lens or onto a mirror. A believer can be the aperture through which the light of the gospel passes to his or her environment. Like Jacob, they accommodate the light and through loyalty to the chief Aperture, to whom they are called, they take their light to their surrounding communities.

Because Jesus arose as a daystar to light the nations, *"The people which sat in darkness saw the great light; and to them which sat in the region and shadow of death light is sprung up"* (Matthew 4:16). Without the loyalty of the chief Aperture, which in this case is Jesus Christ, the peoples of the land of Israel would have been enveloped and swallowed by darkness. Jesus said to the Church, "ye are the *light of the world. A city that is set on an hill* (that) *cannot be hid"* (Matthew 5:14).

This light has, however, been extinguished too many times to the detriment of the wider society because of the lack of loyalty from the light-bearers themselves. Matthew 5:15 says, *"Neither do men light a candle, and put it under a bushel, but on a candlestick; and it giveth light unto all that are in the house."*

According to Romans 14:7, "*...no man lives to himself, and no man dies to himself.*" The church, therefore, has a responsibility to be an aperture or light source through which the gospel can pierce the darkness. Matthew 5:16 says, "*Let your light so shine before men, that they may see your good works, and glorify your Father which is in heaven.*"

THE POWER OF LIGHT

The word of God is described as "*...a lamp unto my feet, and a light unto my path*" (Psalm 119:105). The only reason darkness still persists in the world is the absence of light. John 1:5 says, "*...the light shineth in darkness; and the darkness comprehended it not.*"

When light is present, peace is overwhelming. Psalm 76:3-4 says, "*There He broke the flashing arrows, the shields and the swords, the weapons of war. You are radiant with light....*" Since peace is an aftermath of light from God's word, there can be no greater load-lightener of life's burdens than the light of God's word. One word can change everything! The church is called to be that light the lightens up everything, and so leaves an aftermath of peace.

In 2 Peter 1:19, Apostle Peter describes this light. He says, "*we have also a more sure word of prophecy; whereunto ye do well that ye take heed, as unto a light that shineth in a dark place, until the day dawn, and the day star arise in your hearts.*" The aftermath of the light will be the dawning of a new day and the bringing of the morning star (otherwise called day star) in men's hearts. Those who receive this morning star also receive unparalleled authority over the nations.

Revelation 2:26-28 says, "*...he that overcometh, and keepeth my works unto the end, to him will I give power over the nations: And he shall rule them with a rod of iron; as the vessels of a potter shall they be broken to shivers: even as I received of my Father. **And I will give him the morning star**" (emphasis added).

DAVID: THE LIGHT OF ISRAEL!

David is recognized as one of the greatest kings that ever ruled Israel. He has Jerusalem, otherwise called the city of David, named in his memory. Even Jesus is affectionately called the *seed of David* in 2 Timothy 2:8. He

"*...served his own generation by the will of God, fell on sleep, and was laid unto his fathers...*" (Acts 13:36). He was abused, abandoned and left in abject want as a result of Saul's tirade of jealousy that took him all around the countries of Israel and Philistia, but he refused to stop shining his light.

In 2 Samuel 21:17, David's men called him "*...the light of Israel*" and adjured him not to go to battle with them anymore. In spite of his many shortcomings, David was still recognized as a "*...man after God's heart...*" (Acts 13:22) because he remained a light source for future generations. He was an aperture that brought the Messiah. For his loyalty to the aperture, he is today a legend! He had several opportunities to fold up and quit, but he didn't take them. He rummaged in caves (1 Samuel 22:1), associated with the enemies of Israel as a cover up (1 Samuel 29:3), but chose to remain God's aperture or window that today has reached future generations (1 Chronicles 17:24-27).

Christian's actions have ripple effects, and those actions can destabilize or distinguish generations that follow. In Psalm 54:6-7, David said, "*I will **freely** sacrifice unto thee: I will praise thy name, O Lord; for it is good. For he hath delivered me out of all trouble: and mine eye hath seen his desire upon mine enemies*" (emphasis added). Those who obey God with a free spirit, and allow God's light radiate through them, shine brightly for God and see deliverance from all trouble.

BONHOEFFER: A BURNING AND SHINING LIGHT TO NAZI GERMANY!

Dietrich Bonhoeffer (1906-1945) was a Lutheran minister, anti-Nazi German who strove to save multiplied German Jews Hitler had earmarked for destruction. At the age of twenty-one and with a Doctor of Theology-*Summa-Cum-Laude*-degree in-tow, Bonhoeffer travelled to New York's Union Theological Seminary for a post-graduate fellowship. A man of prodigious intellect, he taught Sunday School at Abyssinian Baptist Church, Harlem; and during his time in New York he grew to embrace social justice as a cause every Christian should uphold.

He returned to Germany thereafter and was ordained a Pastor with the German Prussian Church. He was offered a parish to pastor but rejected it on the basis of the Aryan paragraph, that made non-Aryan's ineligible for parish positions. He rejected Hitler's dominance of church affairs and led a minority of ministers to enact the *Barmen* declaration that emphasized Jesus as the head of the Church, and not the *Fuehrer*.

For his adamant opposition to Nazism, Bonhoeffer became a marked man. His newly formed *Confession Church* and its underground seminaries were repeatedly raided, and members were arrested. Several of its leading lights were dispersed all over Europe or incarcerated. In 1939, Bonhoeffer was hiding up in New York when Hitler invaded Europe and snowballed the world into a full scale war. Colleagues at Union Theological Seminary urged him to remain in the USA, but Bonhoeffer refused.

He said, "*I must live through this difficult period in our national history with the people of Germany. I will have no right to participate in the reconstruction of Christian life in Germany after the war if I do not share the trials of this time with my people.*" He returned on the last steamer from America to Germany and was immediately censored and persistently monitored by the Gestapo.

He developed an acquaintance with anti-Hitler forces in the German Army. Together they planned to assassinate Hitler and to press on with a more diplomatic faceoff with the Western World. His meticulously-designed plan, however, was exposed. As a result, on April 9th 1945, Bonhoeffer, alongside other conspirators, was hung to death. He paid the ultimate price for his faith and as he explained in his classic *The Cost of Discipleship*, "cheap grace is the mortal enemy of the Church and our greatest struggle will be for costly grace."

*The only place in life
where you start from
the top is the grave!*

CHAPTER THIRTY

THE LOYALTY OF
THE ASSISTANT

"But Jehoshaphat said, Is there not here a prophet of the Lord, that we enquire of the Lord by him? And one of the King of Israel's servants answered and said, Here is Elisha the son of Shaphat, which poured water on the hands of Elijah" (2 Kings 3:11).

In the Middle East, the assistant sat and watched his master eat and repeatedly poured water on his hands as needed. This was Elisha's task at the beginning of his ministry to Elijah. To some it was a demeaning and humiliating task, but to Elisha it was the mark of loyalty. A generation of overnight-success stories, with little apprenticeship, dot America's economic landscape and herald a departure from learning and loyalty to an emphasis on beauty and bravado in order to succeed. The word of God, however, cannot be broken (John 10:35).

Even the scriptures advocate for the time-tested principles of faith and patience to obtain His promises (Hebrews 6:12). Jesus waited thirty years to start His ministry. He became the center piece of all creation because *"...though He were a Son, yet learned he obedience by the things which he suffered"* (Hebrews 5:8).

Nothing will stay with you that does not first take from you and nothing lasts that grows too fast! Service, apprenticeship and loyalty are still the hallmarks of a life of honor in the kingdom of God. Proverbs 27:18 says, *"whose keepeth the fig tree shall eat the fruits thereof; so he that waiteth on his master shall be honored."*

It is step by step to obtain fruit in the kingdom, and those who wait receive its blessings. That is why in Mark 4:26-29, Jesus said "...*the kingdom of God as if a man should cast seed into the ground; And should sleep, and rise night and day, and the seed should spring and grow up, he knoweth not how. For the earth bringeth forth fruit of herself, first the blade, then the ear, after that the full corn in the ear. But when the fruit is brought forth, immediately he putteth in the sickle because the harvest is come."*

ELISHA: THE GILT-EDGED ASSISTANT!

Elisha was a gilt-edged prophet who shook kingdoms and territories. He oppressed kings by his spiritual-warfare tactics (2 Kings 6:1-8), healed incurable diseases (2 Kings 5:1-19), and manifested a double portion of the anointing on Elijah since he did twice as many miracles as Elijah but yet he started as a servant.

Forsaking a life of prestige and power, as connoted by the twelve yokes of oxen in his father's house (1 Kings 19:19), Elisha served as a servant through drudgery and deprivation until he received a double portion of the anointing upon Elijah.

He had unalloyed loyalty to Elijah. In spite of the shenanigans of the sons of the prophets, he chose to follow his master through easy and difficult times to Bethel, Gilgal and finally to Jordan (2 Kings 2:1-6) where he obtained the promised double portion anointing.

The servants who wait for and serve their master always desire to serve Him. They do not "...*seek their own*, (but) *the things which are Jesus Christ's*" (Philippians 2:20). Just as Bishop Timothy served the Apostle Paul, true loyalty serves "*... as a son with the father*, (who) *hath served with me in the gospel*" (Philippians 2:22).

Bishop Timothy went on to lead the Church after the first-generation leaders of the church, such as Elder John, Paul, and James the brother of Jesus had departed. His leadership, however, would never have happened without his first having served with Paul in the gospel.

It is a privilege, not just an opportunity, to be an assistant. When the disciples were looking for possible candidates to replace Judas, one of their criteria was "...*men which have companied with us all the time that the*

Lord Jesus went in and out among us, beginning from the baptism of John, unto the same day that he was taken away from us..." (Acts 1:21-22).

Leaders who become legends are not born, they are mentored, molded and made in the crucibles of assistantship. They rise through the ranks and do not have greatness thrown at them at their first squall. Even the Bible advocates a prospective appointee for the office of a bishop *"not* (to be) *a novice, lest being lifted up with pride he fall into the condemnation of the devil"* (1 Timothy 3:6).

THE POWER OF SERVANTHOOD

When a servant serves his or her master, he or she works in delegated authority. The Roman centurion exemplified this concept when he told Jesus, in respect to His offer to come to his house to heal his servant in Matthew 8:8-9, *"Lord, I am not worthy that thou shouldest come under my roof: but speak the word only, and my servant shall be healed. For I am a man under authority, having soldiers under me; and I say to this man, Go, and he goeth; and to another, Come, and he cometh; and to my servant, Do this, and he doeth it."*

He became a legendary centurion in his generation because of his sense of loyalty to his superiors. Jesus, speaking about this centurion said, *"Verily I say unto you, I have not found so great faith, no, not in Israel. And I say unto you, That many shall come from the east and west, and shall sit down with Abraham, and Isaac, and Jacob, in the kingdom of heaven"* (Matthew 8:10-11).

Those who attain legendary status in the kingdom start as servants, not lords! Jesus said, *"...whosoever will be great among you, let him be your minister; And whosoever will be chief among you, let him be your servant"* (Matthew 20:26-27). **Until you are under authority, you can never be in authority in the kingdom of God!**

It is the servant's heart that brings honor to life. Jesus said, in John 12:26, *"If any man serve me, let him follow me; and where I am, there shall also my servant be: if any man serve me, him will my Father honor."* The wise man added in Proverbs 27:18-19 *"Whoso keepeth the fig tree shall eat the fruit thereof: so he that waiteth on his master shall be honored. As in water face answereth to face, so the heart of man to man."*

Servants wield influence in the kingdom and can single-handedly realign acquaintances by his or her words. Proverbs 30:10 says *"accuse not a servant unto his master, lest he* (the servant*) curse thee, and thou be found guilty.*" It is the word of a servant that stands in the courts of public opinion.

Service is not mere acquiescence to those superior to you; if you serve approvingly, it can stamp you with authority and profitability in life. Hebrews 13:17 charges the believer, *"obey them that have the rule over you, and submit yourselves: for they watch for your souls, as they that must give account, that they may do it with joy, and not with grief: for that is unprofitable for you".*

THE MIRACLE OF MENTORSHIP

Milton Hershey founded the Hershey Chocolate company in 1894 at an industrial site in Lancaster, Pennsylvania. It has grown to become the largest chocolate company in North America. Out of it have come splinter companies producing alternate products such as Reese's Peanut Butter Cups.

The founder of the Reese Peanut Butter cup, Harry Burnett Reese, started work at Hershey in 1917 as a dairyman. By 1926, he had built his own factory which was later acquired by Hershey's chocolate company. The miracle of mentorship made this possible. Milton Hershey was a Mennonite Christian who believed in mentoring the younger generation.

Isaac Newton was once asked how he discovered and demonstrated the laws of gravity, motion, calculus and Newtonian mechanics. He answered *"If I have seen further, it is by standing on others' shoulders"* (February 1676). There is no need to reinvent the wheel when mentorship is in place.

Great gospel ministers like E.A Adeboye, Rod Parsley, Lester Sumrall, Kenneth Copeland, Craig Groeschel, Daniel Kolenda, Matthew Ashimolowo, David Oyedepo, Joel Osteen and others began as apprentices serving the likes of Joseph Akindayomi, Lester Sumrall, Oral Roberts, Bill Hybels, Reinhard Bonnke, Pastor Oyebanji, Archbishop Idahosa, and John Osteen respectively.

No matter how gifted a person is, they must first be subject to those in authority to walk in authority. Those who stop feeding have stopped following, and those who stop learning have stopped leading! Mentorship is just a makeover without the mistakes of the mentor!

PART VI

TEMPTATIONS OF THE (SUPPOSEDLY) LOYAL

- ELI: THE SIN OF NEGLIGENCE
- REUBEN: A ROAD SEVERALLY AND SEVERELY TRAVELLED
- DEMAS: THE DEAL OF A LIFE
- ELIAB: IN THE SHADOWS
- FIVE FOOLISH VIRGINS: SURREPTITIOUS AND SHUTTERED
- JUDAS: TREASURER, THIEF AND TRAITOR
- AARON: FROM VOICE TO VICE
- ESAU: ARROGANT, ALOOF AND ANTIQUATED

*Negligience Is Not
Neutrality; It Is
Negative Allegiance*

CHAPTER THIRTY-ONE

ELI: THE SIN OF NEGLIGENCE

"Wherefore kick ye at my sacrifice and at mine offering, which I have commanded in my habitation; and honourest thy sons above me, to make yourselves fat with the chiefest of all the offerings of Israel my people?" (1 Samuel 2:29).

Eli lived in the past glory of his office and so forfeited its future glory because of negligence and a nonchalant attitude toward the things of God. He told Samuel, after hearing from him that inevitable destruction awaited him and his family, *"...It is the LORD: let him do what seemeth him good"* (1 Samuel 3:18).

He was negligent and passive concerning spiritual events around him. When he saw Hannah praying without vocalization or verbalization but with her lips moving, he presumed her a drunken woman and said *"...How long wilt thou be drunken? put away thy wine from thee"* (1 Samuel 1:13-14).

He had served as high priest for forty years (1 Samuel 4:18) and was familiar with the rules and the role of the priesthood. Unfortunately, in his case **familiarity had bred contempt**. God asked him, through a man of God in 1 Samuel 2:29, *"Wherefore kick ye at my sacrifice and at mine offering, which I have commanded in my habitation;...?"*

In the Hebrew, the word used for *"to kick at my offerings and sacrifice"* means to be dissatisfied or to trample down and despise. Eli despised God and considered the opinion of his sons to be of more weight than God's instructions. In 1 Samuel 2:29b, the Lord asked him, *"...honourest thy sons above me, to make yourselves fat with the chiefest of all the offerings of Israel my people?"*

He lived in the past glories of his office. As a result, he forfeited his otherwise glorious future. He had the pedigree, position and prominence of his office; but internally he was puerile, powerless and passive.

RESTRAIN NOT REWARD!

Eli stood for nothing and so fell for anything (1 Samuel 4:18). He told his sons, in his customary passive and negligent tone, "...*I hear of your evil dealings by all these people. Nay, my sons; for it is no good report that I hear: ye make the LORD's people to transgress. If one man sin against another, the judge shall judge him: but if a man sin against the LORD, who shall intreat for him?"* (1 Samuel 2:23-25).

He rewarded them by keeping them in their office instead of remanding them into disciplinary confinement for breaking the law as God recommended. Rather, than Eli "...*restraining them...*" (1 Samuel 3:13), he rewarded them by "...*making themselves fat with the chiefest of all the offerings of Israel my people*" (1 Samuel 2:29).

Eli had no moral compunction to attack his sons' sins when he not only acknowledged it (1 Samuel 3:13), but also acquiesced and acquired spoils from their actions (1 Samuel 2:29). Instead of publicly reproving and removing them from office, he privately reasoned with them.

Paul told his protégés, Titus and Timothy respectively, to "*rebuke with all authority...*" (Titus 2:15) and to "*them that sin rebuke before all that others also may fear*" (1 Timothy 5:20) respectively. Jesus publicly rebuked Peter (see Mark 8:33), and was well regarded as one who spoke with authority (Luke 4:36) and without equivocation.

Eli failed because he wanted to please his sons more than he wanted to please God. He was a children-pleaser. As a result he lost his two children and the generations of children following because of negligence. His sons died in the battle with the Philistines (1 Samuel 4:11), his daughter-in-law died on the delivery table (1 Samuel 4:20), and he died at the gate of Israel (1 Samuel 4:18).

Ichabod or shame replaced glory in Eli's family because he neglected the word of God in his role as the high priest of Israel. In 1 Samuel 3:2-3, the Bible says "*...it came to pass at that time, when Eli was laid down in his place, and his eyes began to wax dim, that he could not see; And ere the lamp of God went out in the temple of the LORD, where the ark of God was....*"

He lost sight of the word as "*...the word of the LORD was precious in those days;* (and) *there was no open vision*" (1 Samuel 3:1). A bankruptcy of the word of God and a lack of divine vision were primarily responsible for the failure of Eli's ministry.

THE MINDSET OF A MEANDERER!

The man of God told Eli that God would destroy him and his family (1 Samuel 2:31-35). Yet he felt no compulsion to change his ways. He loved the wages of unrighteousness (1 Samuel 2:29), and had a *laissez-faire* mentality that did not aggressively set him on course to pursue an objective.

He was willing to follow anything that flickered as his light had earlier gone out (1 Samuel 3:3). He was unwilling to resist sin and followed the path of least resistance. Rather than confront sin, he conferred with it and lost his pride of place as a result.

Eli's non-confrontational stance was unlike the resolute stand the early fathers of the faith took who strove to resist sin and confront evil. Jesus Christ, for example, "*...resisted unto blood, striving against sin*" (Hebrews 12:4).

The failure of Eli was his desire for a soft lifestyle! While trying to please all and sundry, except God, he eventually "*...fell from off the seat backwards...and his neck brake and he died for he was an old man and heavy*" (1 Samuel 4:18). Those who stand for nothing fall for anything. Because he failed to confront sin, it eventually destroyed him.

LESTER SUMRALL: MAN WITH A MISSION

God draws patterns for lives of men and woman to instruct and direct them. He creates a special design for each rational being that is destined to live on this planet. If the individual wisely follows this divine blueprint, he will build a strong, successful, and happy character. Lester Sumrall (1913 – 1996) was one of such men.

After getting saved on his sick bed in 1929 New Orleans, Lester planted a church in Green Forest, Arkansas, in 1931 and was ordained by the Assembly of God. He began preaching itinerantly to the farmers in the area, but with no love for the people he was ministering to. It was at this juncture that God showed him a vision of multitudes dying and going to hell. Lester's heart was broken and he began to preach o his "farmers audience" with more compassion.

In 1934, God told Lester Sumrall to leave a revival in Oklahoma and go to Eureka springs, Arkansas to meet someone he intended to partner him with. Before he left Oklahoma, however, God had already instructed another minister – Howard Carter – to leave England, over four thousand miles away, for the same meeting. Unknown to both of them, God had commissioned their paths to collide at Eureka Springs, Arkansas.

Miraculously, after almost twelve months of no communication, Lester Sumrall arrived in Brisbane, Australia where he met Howard Carter. They started a two-year, fifty-thousand mile worldwide missionary journey that took them across Australia, to Singapore, Hong Kong, Java, the Dutch East Indies, Tibet, Manchuria, Japan, Korea, Germany, Brazil, Bolivia, France, Spain, Portugal, and England.

Lester Sumrall ended up setting up mega-churches in Manila, Philippines and Indiana, USA. He also founded universities, schools, television/radio stations and, in the 1960's, started the first worldwide faith-based relief organization. This great ministry still lives on today, into its third generation, with outstanding success

If you don't embarrass sin,
sin will embarrass you

– Dr. Jesse Duplantis
(Destreham, Louisiana)

CHAPTER THIRTY-TWO

REUBEN: A ROAD SEVERALLY AND SEVERELY TRAVELLED

> *"Reuben, thou art my firstborn, my might, and the beginning of my strength, the excellency of dignity, and the excellency of power: Unstable as water, thou shalt not excel; because thou wentest up to thy father's bed; then defiledst thou it: he went up to my couch"* (Genesis 49:3-4).

The tragedy of Reuben is the unfortunate outcome for several of God's chosen firstborns.' These ones are *"…the church of the firstborn…"* (Hebrews 12:23) and *"…those conformed to the image of His son that he might be the firstborn among many brethren"* (Romans 8:29). They are called to demonstrate His *"…might,…strength,…dignity and…excellency of power"* (Genesis 49:3) but regrettably they falter and fail at the footsteps of adultery.

He (Reuben) slept with his father's concubine and never repented. Genesis 35:22 says, *"…Reuben went and lay with Bilhah his father's concubine: and Israel heard it."* As a result, Reuben's blessings as firstborn were given to Joseph. Deuteronomy 33:16-17 says, *"…let the blessing come upon the head of Joseph, and upon the top of the head of him that was separated from his brethren. His glory is like the firstling of his bullock, and his horns are like the horns of unicorns: with them he shall push the people together to the ends of the earth…."*

Reuben's affair was an "open secret" and a sore to the purported integrity and loyalty a firstborn son owed his father. It cost Reuben the leadership of the family and nation, and left Reuben a near-failure.

About five hundred years after Jacob's pronunciation on Reuben for his surreptitious failings to the temptation of lust, Moses prayed for the tribe of Reuben saying, "*Let Reuben live, and not die…*" (Deuteronomy 33:6).

Sin will always take people further than they want to go, cost them more than they want to pay, and keep them longer that they want to stay! For Reuben's future generations, his failure that night was a permanent source of recrimination and regret that sounded the death knell on an otherwise promising genealogy.

WHAT YOU DO FOR ONE, DO FOR ALL!

Reuben was selective in his bid to protect Joseph from his siblings who wanted to kill him. In Genesis 37:21-22, he told them "*…let us not kill him…but cast him into this pit that is in the wilderness, and lay no hand upon him; that he might rid him out of their hands, to deliver him to his father again.*"

He wanted to look good to his brothers' without losing face with his father. He refused to "*…rebuke with all authority…*" (Titus 4:15) or "*…speak the truth in love…*" (Ephesians 4:15), as advocated in the Bible, but rather "*…compasseth…about with lies…*(and) *deceit*" (Hosea 11:12).

The Bible says, "*open rebuke is better than secret love*" (Proverbs 27:5). Jesus told his disciples, in Mark 13:37, "*…what I say unto you I say unto all…*" because God is not selective, but spiritual, in adjudication. He told Jeremiah, "*…gird up thy loins, and arise, and speak unto them all that I command thee: be not dismayed at their faces, lest I confound thee before them*" (Jeremiah 1:17).

Reuben, on the other hand, wanted to be in the good books of everybody but eventually ended nowhere in life. When he told his father, after Simeon was incarcerated in Egypt pending Benjamin's arrival, "*…deliver him into my hand, and I will bring him to thee again*" (Genesis 42:37) his suggestions were summarily dismissed.

He was a man-pleaser and, as a result, he became a restless soul without a foundation for his faith. Jesus asked the Jews of his day, who wanted him dead for sacrilege, "*How can ye believe, which receive honor one of another, and seek not the honor that cometh from God only?*" (John 5:44).

Those who seek man's honor never get God's honor or the God kind of faith! Reuben lost the honor and strength of the firstborn because he committed fornication and wanted honor from his brothers and not from God.

MOMENTUM: THE PRICE FOR A MOMENT'S MISTAKE

Sin builds momentum and must be nipped at inception. In Galatians 5:9, Paul said, "*a little leaven leaveneth the whole lump.*" Speaking more about the evil of a man's sleeping with his father's wife in 1 Corinthians 5:6-8, Paul buttresses this point further.

He said, "*….Your glorying is not good. Know ye not that a little leaven leaveneth the whole lump? Purge out therefore the old leaven, that ye may be a new lump, as ye are unleavened. For even Christ our passover is sacrificed for us. Therefore let us keep the feast, not with old leaven, neither with the leaven of malice and wickedness; but with the unleavened bread of sincerity and truth.*"

The gospel builds on momentum from sincerity and truth, not from selfishness and torment. Paul adjures the Ephesians to "N*either give place to the devil*" (Ephesians 4:27). He also advised believers "(to be) *wise unto that which is good, and simple concerning evil and the God of peace shall bruise Satan under your feet shortly….*" (Romans 16:19-20).

The battle plans of God do not give room for long drawn out battles of aggravation and collateral damages from enemy assaults. The outcome is decided quickly and decisively by the power of the Holy Ghost. Reuben was indecisive. His lack of decisiveness made him unstable (James 1:6-8) and eventually cost him the throne of glory earmarked for firstborn sons. It took him thirteen years, and only by affirmation of his brothers' guilt, to confess that the treatment of Joseph was wrong.

He told his brothers, after they had confessed to their sins against Joseph in Genesis 42:21, "…*Spake I not unto you, saying, Do not sin against the child; and ye would not hear? therefore, behold, also his blood is required*" (Genesis 42:22). Loyalty is not an evolving set of beliefs. It is a benchmark that irrespective of circumstances must not be breached. It lives on in legacies created out of conviction.

This slowness-to-respond-to-sin attitude cost Reuben his sanctification as well as his seniority in the family. His actions left vast implications for his progeny. Sin always starts as lust, but when uninterrupted and left to finish, it leaves death and destruction. James 1:14-15 says, *"…every man is tempted, when he is drawn away of his own lust, and enticed. Then when lust hath conceived, it bringeth forth sin: and sin, when it is finished, bringeth forth death."*

THE LIFE AND TIMES OF PASTOR ABEDINI

Pastor Abedini, an Iranian convert to Christianity, gave his life to Christ at the age of twenty. At the age of twenty-five, however, he had to flee Iran because of persecution and immigrated to the United States as an asylum seeker.

While in the USA, he met and fell in love with his wife – Naghmeh Abedini. The union has been blessed with two children, while Pastor Abedini's ministry continues to thrive as an associate minister at Calvary Church, Boise, Idaho.

In 2013, while trying to establish an orphanage in Iran, Pastor Abedini was arrested and imprisoned for proselytizing and refusing to renounce his faith in Christ. After three and a half years in some of the harshest jail conditions in the world, he was released amid some marital controversy.

His wife had, in November 2015, accused him of domestic assault, addiction to pornography and emotional abuse. In an Idaho court, she filed for marital separation. He refused to discuss his marital problems in public but sought for prayer through out this period of marital reconciliation.

Pastor Abedini denies the charges but confesses that he is not a perfect man. In his statement, he said *"I am a sinner, saved only by the wonderful grace of God. While I am far from perfect – as a man or a husband, I am seeking everyday to submit to God as He molds me into what He wants me to be."*

*It is not who you Tussle
with that Matters, it
is who you Trust!*

CHAPTER THIRTY THREE

DEMAS: THE DEAL OF A LIFE

"For Demas hath forsaken me, having loved this present world, and is departed unto Thessalonica…" (2 Timothy 4:10).

Demas had everything anyone could have ever wanted - the pedigree and business connections the city Thessalonica offered, the support and spiritual mentorship of fathers in the Lord such as Paul, and a robust work ethic and health that afforded him unlimited potential in the ministry.

In Philemon 1:24, Paul describes him as one of "…*my fellow laborers.*" The word used is a Greek word called *sungergos*. It implies one whom God employs as an assistant and as a fellow-worker with God. Demas was not a back-bencher, or a pew-warmer who fell off track from a poor social and spiritual network affiliation, but a "…*laborer together with God…*" (1 Corinthians 3:9) who had His core loyalties to God intact. Hosea 11:12 describes such ones as those who "…*rule with God, and* (are) *faithful with the saints.*"

Demas pitfall came, however, because he was a dealmaker. He wanted the fast lane to success and wealth, and became discontent with the ascetic and adversity-ridden life Paul lived in Rome as a prisoner. After years of loyalty, he left the faith and "…*forsook* (Paul) *having loved this present world and departed unto Thessalonica*" (2 Timothy 4:10). He is alleged to have come from Thessalonica, a city which had a reputation for commerce and industry as the center for Macedonian culture, and his departure for Thessalonica implies he forsook Paul to return to his trade and avoid the prying eyes of the Roman empire.

Demas wanted a security in the world that he opined apostle Paul's God could not give him. He had witnessed the beatings, starving, shipwrecks, hate speech and heinous crimes against humanity perpetrated against Paul (see 2 Corinthians 11:24-27), and wanted to broker one more deal with God. It was a deal that would eventually prove costly for his soul!

APART AWHILE TO ACQUIRE A FIRE!

Apparently, Demas did not maintain himself physically and spiritually. Eventually he became burned out in ministry. While he turned his back to the ministry and returned to Thessalonica, Paul requested Timothy to "... *bring with thee, and the books, but especially the parchments*" (2 Timothy 4:13).

Every month in America, 1500 pastors leave their ministries as a result of burnout, conflict or moral failure1. Forty-five per cent claim they have experienced depression and burnout to the extent they needed to take a leave of absence from the ministry.

Even Jesus told his disciples, "...*Come ye yourselves apart into a desert place, and rest a while: for there were many coming and going, and they had no leisure so much as to eat*" (Mark 6:31). This was soon after Herod had murdered John the Baptist by Herod and just before the feeding of the five thousand.

Many potential loyalty legends become bankrupt spiritually and eventually "...*faint in the day of adversity* (because their) *strength is small*" (Proverbs 24:10). That is why Paul advised his son in the Lord, Timothy, to "*take heed unto thyself, and unto the doctrine; continue in them: for in doing this thou shalt both save thyself, and them that hear thee*" (1 Timothy 4:16).

SUSTAINABILITY: THE KEY TO EVER-INCREASING FAITH

In the Old Testament, God required of the altar of incense and sacrifice that "*the fire shall ever be burning upon the altar; it shall never go out*" (Leviticus 6:13). It was not a fad. It was a fiery flame that depicted God's desire for His people.

He calls His ministers "...*a flame of fire*" (Hebrews 1:7) but without the wood these ministers, like Demas, will burn out. Proverbs 26:20 says, *"where no wood is, there the fire goeth out:...."* and in Haggai 1:8 God adjures Israel to *"go up to the mountain, and bring wood, and build the house...."*

The mountain represents the place of learning the word of God. Micah 4:2 says, *"...let us go up to the mountain of the LORD, and to the house of the God of Jacob; and He will teach us of his ways, and we will walk in his paths: for the law shall go forth of Zion, and the word of the LORD from Jerusalem."*

The word of God is the secret to a life of sustainable fire. This kind of fire is *"...unquenchable"* (Matthew 3:12) and impervious to burn out. It is akin to the fire that fell from heaven in the days of Elijah that *"...consumed the burnt sacrifice, and the wood, and the stones, and the dust, and licked up the water that was in the trench"* (1 Kings 18:38).

It is a fire that never goes out, no matter the adversity, attacks or antagonisms of the enemy. It is a fire anchored on the word of God. That fact is the reason the Psalmist advised, in Psalm 119:9, *"wherewithal shall a young man cleanse his way? By taking heed thereto according to thy word."*

There is a *bona fide* dimension of ever-increasing faith available to those who continually receive His word. Romans 10:17 says, *"...faith cometh by hearing, and hearing by the word of God."* Such ones never burnout, like Demas, but burn bright for eternity. In Daniel 12:3, the Bible says *"they that be wise shall shine as the brightness of the firmament;...."*

DAVID BRAINERD: TESTIMONY TO A LIFE OF FAITH!

David Brainerd (1718-1747) lost both parents at an early age. He was raised by his married older sister, Jerusha, and became the foremost evangelist to the Native Americans in 18th century North eastern America.

At the age of 21, he gained admission to study theology at Yale University and after three years, even though he was at the top of his class academically, he was expelled for bad language towards his faculty as concerning the awakening experience that was overcoming the campus.

The Yale campus had experienced an awakening similar to what the Americas' were experiencing, when George Whitfield and Jonathan Edwards visited their campus and stoked flames of revival in their midst.

David Brainerd was very vocal in his support of the awakening, and felt some of the theological faculty were insincere in their opposition. He voiced his concerns to some fellow students, and when the administration heard of his opposition they made him a scapegoat by expelling him with no recourse for re-admission.

David Brainerd was shattered; he left Yale disappointed, despondent and eventually depressed as he stated in his daily journal entries. He, however, resolved to focus on heaven's goal for his life and in pursuit of that, became a missionary to the Native American populations in North East USA.

Even though he was offered pastorates in East Hampton Long Island and in Millington, near his home town of Haddam, Connecticut, he chose rather to focus on his heavenly journey and fulfill the call of God for his life. He once prayed, in one of his daily journal entries that became the best-selling book titled *The Life of David Brainerd*, saying "may I never loiter on my heavenly journey."

While alive he reached hundreds of Native Americans with the gospel. His body was, however, wracked by pain with all the traveling and arduous travelling circumstances he had to endure. He died in 1747 at the age of 29 years from tuberculosis but lives on today as a loyalty legend in the hearts of those his writings and actions have impacted.

His journal entries were published by Jonathan Edwards as *The Life of David Brainerd* and it has impacted missionaries from William Carey to Jim Elliot for centuries. His rejection at Yale also spurred the establishment of alternative institutions of higher learning, like Brown, Princeton and Dartmouth universities by the Baptist, Presbyterian and missions board to the Native Americans, that were more sympathetic to the awakening.

Small-thinking Eliab's of this world are threatened by the cause-identifying David's of their time!

– Shane Warren
(Lead Pastor The Assembly
West Monroe, Louisiana)

CHAPTER THIRTY FOUR

ELIAB: IN THE SHADOWS

"Furthermore over the tribes of Israel: the ruler of…Judah, Elihu, one of the brethren of David…" (1 Chronicles 27:16,18).

Eliab had grown accustomed to being in the shadows of David, when as King of Israel, David appointed him governor over Judah (see 1 Chronicles 27:18). As the first son of Jesse, and the heir to the "Jesse enterprises", he had secretly felt David was subtly trying to take his position.

He had told David, when Goliath came down from Gath threatening the armies of Israel with obscenities, *"why camest thou down hither and with whom hast thou left those few sheep in the wilderness? I know thy pride, and the naughtiness of thine heart; for thou art come down that thou mightest see the battle"* (1 Samuel 17:28).

This episode highlights a major chink in Eliab's armor – lack of self-esteem. He had always felt eclipsed by David, and his reaction to David's bravado and *camaraderie* with the Israeli soldiers was just a self-projection of his lack of courage and confidence when facing life's battles.

Eventually, when he and his families' lives were in danger from King Saul's assault, they ran to David for protection. 1 Samuel 22:1 says, *"David therefore departed thence, and escaped to the cave Adullam: and when his brethren and all his father's house heard it, they went down thither to him."*

THE GOVERNOR WHO FACED HIS GOLIATHS!

At the anointing of Saul's successor, Samuel the prophet saw Eliab and exclaimed *"…surely the Lord's anointed…"* (1 Samuel 17:6). In a sharp rebuttal, however, God told him *"...look not on his countenance or on the height of his stature; because I have refused him for the* LORD *seeth not as man seeth for man looketh on the outward appearance, but the* LORD *looketh on the heart"* (1 Samuel 17:7).

Eliab met the physical requirements for kingship, but he was not spiritually qualified for the position. He was supposedly loyal to the God of Jesse; but God, who searches the heart, rejected him for his small-mindedness, pride, pettiness and lack of self-esteem and courage.

The grace of God will raise you only where it can keep you! The temptation of Eliab is to live a lie by doing what you are spiritually ill-equipped for by using your physical attributes. In the process you over extend and out reach yourself to the detriment of your spirit man. Solomon, the wisest man in his time, said *"...the prosperity of fools shall destroy them..."* (Proverbs 1:32) and *"...the labor of the foolish wearieth every one of them, because he knoweth not how to go to the* city" (Ecclesiastes 10:15).

God, however, intervened and saved Eliab from a mammoth conspiracy! He became Governor of Judah (1 Chronicles 27:18) under the leadership of king David and thrived in that position. He was never supposed to be on the platform, as was David his brother who was serenaded for killing Goliath (1 Samuel 18:7). He was a behind-the-stage operator who was designed to stay in the shadow of his younger brother.

Even though Goliath was a terror to Israel in Eliab's time, the real goliaths that stifled Eliab and kept his legendhood locked up were his small thinking, aptitude for strife and keenness to be a sight-only participator in the battles of life (see 1 Samuel 17:28). This supposedly loyal "king-material" was living a lie by taking kingly positions he couldn't handle. The appointment as governor saved him from inevitable failure, and kept his legacy intact because he chose to be loyal to his brother, King David.

FIRSTBORN IS NOT A FREEHOLD!

Many firstborns' are given positions of authority because of their positions in the family, and not because of God's calling upon their lives. They occupy the *status-quo* allotted to them as a result of their place as first-borns' in the family, and as a result, miss out on their spiritual destinies in God.

The family freehold is not necessarily the portion of the family firstborn, but the lot of God's spiritual firstborns'. Roman 8:29-30 says *"whom he did foreknow, he also did predestinate to be conformed to the image of his Son, that he might be the firstborn among many brethren. Moreover whom he did predestinate, them he also called: and whom he called, them he also justified: and whom he justified, them he also glorified."*

A freehold is something glorious that is bequeathed to generations following. It is the lot of God's firstborns, and not family firstborns' who are stuck on their titles but who are oblivious of their destiny. David, though the last born, had a higher spiritual aptitude and attitude than his eldest brother Eliab and assertively asked him *"...is there not a cause?"* (1 Samuel 17:29) when Eliab challenged his effrontery for coming to the battle.

God has always used so-called minnows to accomplish His liberation agenda for mankind. He chose Joseph not Reuben, Moses not Aaron, Jacob not Esau, Abel not Cain, and Gideon who called himself *"...the least in my father's house"* (1 Samuel 6:15) over his older siblings. These ones were younger than their siblings, like David was to Eliab, but they were called to bring the glory of God to their generation because of their unalloyed loyalty.

In 1 Corinthians 1:27-29, the Bible says *"...God hath chosen the foolish things of the world to confound the wise and God hath chosen the weak things of the world to confound the things which are mighty and base things of the world, and things which are despised, hath God chosen, yea, and things which are not, to bring to nought things that are that no flesh should glory in his presence."*

TRIUMPHING THROUGH THE TOIL

Paul Osteen was a well-known and well-liked General surgeon in Little Rock, Arkansas when his father died in 1999. His father had founded Lakewood Church Houston in 1959, and from its small beginnings, had seen it rise to become one of the largest charismatic congregations in the nation.

Unlike Paul, Joel was well known in the Houston mega Church, having worked side-by-side with his father in a behind-the-scenes role as a TV programmer. He was not the firstborn, but he was father's choice as successor.

Since the appointment of Joel as senior Pastor of Lakewood Church, the Church has grown more than fivefold to become the largest congregation in the continental United States and Canada. It averages more than 50,000 congregants, attending six services every weekend, at its one hundred million dollars Compaq center facility.

This success would not have been possible without Paul staying in the shadows of Joel as head of pastoral ministry and teaching minister at the Church. Rather than compete with his brother for stage time, Paul remains in the background pulling the necessary strings to make Lakewood a success.

He has combined his executive pastor role with a successful medical missions ministry that has metamorphosed into mobilizing medical personnel for missions. He and his wife now spend 4-6 months annually on the missions field as medical missionaries and the rest of the year as teaching pastors at Lakewood Church when in the Houston, Texas area.

God does not want borrowed vessels; He wants broken vessels!

CHAPTER THIRTY-FIVE

FIVE FOOLISH VIRGINS: SURREPTITIOUS AND SHUTTERED

"Afterward came also the other (foolish) *virgins, saying, Lord, Lord, open to us. But he answered and said, Verily I say unto you, I know you not. Watch therefore, for ye know neither the day nor the hour wherein the Son of man cometh"* (Matthew 25:11-13).

To be surreptitious means to do something clandestinely or covertly. Many saints have lost their covenant relationship with God to the covert dealings of the enemy. These five foolish virgins are pick of the bunch.

These five foolish virgins were seemingly sacred, but in reality they were surreptitious. At the outset of their journey, these foolish virgins "… *took their lamps, and took no oil with them; But the wise took oil in their vessels with their lamps"* (Matthew 25:3-4).

Even though complacent, for *"while the bridegroom tarried, they all slumbered and slept"* (Matthew 25:4), the virgins were not marked as loyal or disloyal based on their slumbering or prayer less attitude. The action that determined the loyalty of the virgins, and marked them as wise or foolish, was the presence or absence of (spiritual) oil in their lives respectively.

In Ephesians 4:30, Paul says, "…*grieve not the holy Spirit of God, whereby ye are sealed unto the day of redemption."* The foolish and wise virgins were both saved, sanctified and serving in the Church, but only the wise virgins carried oil which is a symbol of the Holy Spirit (see Isaiah

61:3). Without the Holy Spirit, even believers are surreptitiously or by stealth easily deceived.

That is the reason Elder John in 1 John 2:27-28 said, "...*the anointing which ye have received of him abideth in you, and ye need not that any man teach you: but as the same anointing teacheth you of all things, and is truth, and is no lie, and even as it hath taught you, ye shall abide in him. And now, little children, abide in him that, when He shall appear, we may have confidence, and not be ashamed before him at his coming.*"

THE BORROWED LIFE!

The five foolish virgins lived a life of deceit. Everybody who met them considered them the epitome of humility and godliness, but inside they were hypocritical and in gruesome spiritual condition.

Jesus told the leading Jews of His day, "*Woe unto you, scribes and Pharisees, hypocrites! for ye are like unto whited sepulchres, which indeed appear beautiful outward, but are within full of dead men's bones, and of all uncleanness. Even so ye also outwardly appear righteous unto men, but within ye are full of hypocrisy and iniquity*" (Matthew 23:27-28).

These five foolish virgins were locked out of the marriage supper with the bridegroom because of their deceitful double standards. They told the wise virgins, when the announcement of the bridegroom's imminent arrival was made, "...*Give us of your oil; for our lamps are gone out*" (Matthew 25:8).

They were willing to live a borrowed life rather than to be a broken and built-up vessel of the Lord. They talked the talk but never walked the walk. It was only when the bridegroom came, and made the foolish virgins accountable to Him and other believers' that the true status of their lamps as empty and without oil, was known.

This self-deceit cost them. In James 1:22, James, the son of Mary and biological half-brother of Jesus, said "...*be ye doers of the word, and not hearers only, deceiving your own selves.*" Those who live borrowed lives are not known by the Master, regardless how often they call him Lord (Matthew 25:11-12). The truth is a believer is either full of the Holy Spirit or empty of Him! It is either they dwell in His presence or meet perdition in His absence.

THE TRIAL OF YOUR FAITH

Every faith will be tried. In 1 Peter 1:7, Peter the apostle said "*...the trial of your faith, being much more precious than of gold that perisheth, though it be tried with fire, might be found unto praise and honor and glory at the appearing of Jesus Christ.*"

It is the trial of faith that determines the quality of the life lived. 1 Corinthians 3:13 says, "*Every man's work shall be made manifest: for the day shall declare it, because it shall be revealed by fire; and the fire shall try every man's work of what sort it is.*"

Those who have "*...spoken words and swearing falsely in making a covenant; this judgment springeth up as hemlock in the furrows of the field*" (Hosea 10:4). Shame is the consequence for a life of deceit, but glory is the result when sincerity, truth and transparency are lived.

The church is called to transparency and sincerity, not trickery and subterfuge. In 2 Corinthians 3:2-3, the Apostle Paul tells the church in Corinth that they "*...are our epistle written in our hearts, known and read of all men:... manifestly declared to be the epistle of Christ ministered by us, written not with ink, but with the Spirit of the living God....*"

A life full of faith is the solution to the foolishness of self-deceit. Until a man or woman believes the word of God, it is impossible to live above the lies of man. The foolish virgins went to purchase oil not on the directive and impulse of God's word but on the pressures placed on them by others (Matthew 25:10). They went to buy the oil, but because their actions were not done in faith, it was considered sin in their lives (Romans 14:23).

In Hosea 10:12-13, the prophet Hosea said, "*...Sow to yourselves in righteousness, reap in mercy; break up your fallow ground: for it is time to seek the LORD, till he come and rain righteousness upon you. Ye have plowed wickedness, ye have reaped iniquity; ye have eaten the fruit of lies: because thou didst trust in thy way, in the multitude of thy mighty men.*"

LIVING A LIFE OF PRAISE

In my fifth year of medical school, I was living mostly in my father's hotel for logistic purposes. In that hotel was a young man who worked part-time as a steward in the hotel, but was a full time student at the Institute of Metallurgical Technology (IMT), Enugu Nigeria.

He had had a beleaguered childhood; his parents were divorced, siblings abandoned and he was practically paying his and his siblings way through school. He was dogged, determined, driven and in me he saw a mentor of sorts for his aspirations.

I always pointed him to Jesus Christ, and told him *"He can do all things through Christ that strengthens him"* (Philippians 4:13). Right before his eyes, I was serving God full throttle, and maintaining decent grades in medical school. I never brought any girls to the hotel, and I never indulged in any vices such as smoking or alcohol. Rather, I was always out praying in the hotel courts or preaching to guests and staff alike.

He was amazed, but more was to come. After my last exam in medical school, termed the 5th MBBS, I returned to Abuja (my parents' city of domicile) to celebrate prior to the release of the results. The city my medical school is domiciled in was abuzz with the news of the impending release of the results of the most difficult exam in our state. Yet I was 600 miles away cooling my heels in my dad's house. He was perplexed and, if only to prove if my God was really who I had said Him to be, this young man went and stood for hours on the line just to check the results of my exam.

Before his very eyes, he saw men and women break down in tears of disappointment or jubilation. He looked keenly for my result. To his utter shock, I had passed with flying colors. His pupils expanded as he called me explaining why he why he had gone to my medical school and what he had seen and why he now believed in the God of all possibilities. He was so awestruck by my story of fidelity, faithfulness and fruitful Christian living, that it motivated him to pursue his academics even more strenuously and to make a success of them.

Today, he is a Business graduate with a successful business and family. He learned from my life the power of living a life of praise. Even though he grew up without a father, I was able to reflect the role of a father-figure to him through my life, and today he is living what some consider a successful life.

I Am Not Just A Song;
I Am A Storm Causing
Satanic Disruption!

CHAPTER THIRTY-SIX

JUDAS: TREASURER, THIEF AND TRAITOR!

"Yea, mine own familiar friend, in whom I trusted, which did eat of my bread, hath lifted up his heel against me" (Psalm 41:9).

Judas Iscariot was the treasurer of the *Jesus Christ of Nazareth Ministries* (John 12:6). He was in charge of the purse, and his peers trusted him (see Psalm 41:9). Judas was so trusted that even though Jesus told His disciples that he *"...whom I shall give a sop, when I have dipped it* (shall betray me), *and when he had dipped the sop, he gave it to Judas Iscariot, the son of Simon"* they still did not believe the betrayer was Judas Iscariot.

They, instead, thought *"...that Jesus had said unto him, Buy those things that we have need of against the feast; or, that he should give something to the poor* (after) *he had...received the sop..."* (John 13:29-30). The disciples could not imagine Judas as a traitor or thief. To them, he was their trusted treasure who had portrayed loyalty and fidelity.

To the world, he was apostle Judas and the treasurer of the greatest ministry ever in Israel but inwards Judas was a thief and a traitor. His failures started from within, and eventually manifested outwardly as disloyalty.

JUDAS LACKED DIVINE REVERENCE!

To reverence means to show honor or respect. In spiritual parlance, it represents the believer's awe at being in God's presence. Judas, to the contrary, felt no *gravitas* towards God. While at the home of Simon the Leper, Mary had broken a bottle of spikenard perfume valued at a year's wages or 300 pence and wiped Jesus feet with the anointing from the perfume (see John 12:3).

In response to this generous gesture, Judas asked, "*Why was not this ointment sold for three hundred pence, and given to the poor?*" (John 12:5). He was a thief, according to John 12:6, and was more interested in the physical things of life than the spiritual. To this tardy response, Jesus said "*let her alone: against the day of my burying hath she kept this. For the poor always ye have with you; but me ye have not always*" (John 12:7-8). **Judas did not regard Jesus' presence as much as the presents** He could bring into the ministry.

It was his lack of divine reverence that drove Judas toward avarice and eventual betrayal of Jesus. He left the house of Simon the leper, and "... *went unto…(the) chief priests* (saying) *what will ye give me, and I will deliver him* (Jesus) *unto you? And they covenanted with him for thirty pieces of silver and from that time he sought opportunity to betray him*" (Matthew 26:14-16).

Thirty pieces of silver, according to Genesis 37:28 and 1 Kings 20:29, was the value of a half-year's wages and nearly equivalent to a slave's life according to Leviticus 27:3. It, thus, shows what value Judas placed on Jesus! Judas did not revere Jesus Christ, or see Him as a rewarder in the light of Hebrews 11:6, but rather saw Him as a rogue-leader who was nothing better than a foreign slave in value.

Not for Judas the sense of majesty Isaiah felt in God's presence in Isaiah 6:5, or the power that threw John the Elder and Ezekiel down on their faces at His presence in Revelation 1:17 and Ezekiel 3:23 respectively. He was more interested in the carnal things of life which were temporal than the spiritual things of life which are eternal (2 Corinthians 4:18).

His lack of divine reverence drove him further and further from Jesus. While Peter strove to encounter Jesus after the triple denial in John 21:7, Judas "...*which had betrayed him* (Jesus), *when he saw that he was condemned, repented himself, and brought again the thirty pieces of silver to the chief priests and elders, saying, I have sinned in that I have betrayed the innocent blood*" (Matthew 27:3-4). He went to man, and not to God, and in futility lost his life via suicide (Matthew 27:5) as a result.

THE LIFTER OF THE HEEL

Judas lifted his heel to the Lord (Psalm 41:9). In the Hebrew culture, this action is magnified supplanting of a trusted friend. It was more than just the act. It was the vulgarity and violence employed in its execution that marked Judas's act of betrayal as both sordid and symbolic. To lift up the heel was the *sine-qua-non* of a traitor and represented the highest level of betrayal.

He suffered from an inundated sense of condemnation (Matthew 27:3). As a result, he lived out the script of his accusers which included betrayal and suicide. Rather than believe God's report, he believed the evil report of his enemies and consequently, lost his apostleship (Acts 1:17-20).

In 2 Timothy 3:1-4, Paul warns the last day church about the spirit of those last days. He said, *"This know also, that in the last days perilous times shall come. For men shall be lovers of their own selves, covetous, boasters, proud, blasphemers, disobedient to parents, unthankful, unholy, without natural affection,* **trucebreakers, false accusers**, *incontinent, fierce,* **despisers of those that are good***, traitors, heady, high minded, lovers of pleasures more than lovers of God"* (emphasis added).

Paul was attempting to call attention to the strong correlation between trucebreakers and false accusers, and between traitors and those that despise those that are good. Jesus did not come into the world to condemn it, but to save it (John 3:17). Only a life lived in celebration, not condemnation, of the saving acts of Jesus can be truly loyal. No wonder then that in Titus 2:15, Paul advises his protégé saying *"these things speak, and exhort and rebuke with all authority. Let no man despise thee."*

You cannot work in condemnation when you walk in the Spirit. Romans 8:1 says *"there is therefore now no condemnation to them which are in Christ Jesus, who walk not after the flesh, but after the Spirit for the law of the Spirit of life in Christ Jesus hath made me free from the law of sin and death."* It is the Holy Spirit that evokes celebration! The *"...kingdom of God is not meat and drink but righteousness and peace and joy in the Holy Ghost"* (Romans 14:17) and the Holy Spirit is *"...wine that maketh glad the heart of man, and oil to make his face to shine..."* (Psalm 104:15). The spirit of condemnation is the enemy that creates destruction, but the spirit of celebration augments creativity.

PHIL ROBERTSON: A REBEL WITH A CAUSE

Phil Robertson left college at the age of twenty-one with a degree in physical education from the famed Louisiana Tech, Ruston, Louisiana, where he played as a quarter back on a football scholarship. He opted not to play on the Louisiana Tech team of 1968 and turned down an offer from the Washington Redskins to focus on duck hunting.

As graduation drew closer, Phil Robertson and his classmates discussed their future aspirations. Most of them were heading to graduate school, or blue chip firms in the Gulf Coast. Phil, on the other hand, opted to teach high school sports while working on his Masters so that he could continue duck hunting.

Because Phil stuck to his vision in life, he is worth conservatively over $15 million today! He started making duck calls called Duck Commander; and as the interest in duck calls grew, so did Phil's popularity and finances. He, as the patriarch of the family, masterminded the move of the Duck Commander brand to television.

He and his family currently host the number one television reality show *Duck Dynasty* in television on A and E television. Their programs, which are seen in over one hundred countries grossed the largest ever opening-day viewing on U.S. television with thirteen million viewers in October 2013.

A devout Christian, Phil also caught the attention of the world with his frank and forthright discussions on faith and family. Not ashamed of the name of Christ, he has not been afraid to stand alone, if need be, to make Christ known. He stood strong when the secular media called for his television show to be axed, for supposedly offensive remarks made about the gay and Lesbian culture, and prevailed.

Just as he jettisoned his classmates appeal to join the corporate or pro-world of football, Phil has stood alone in matters of faith also and prevailed. He has become a celebrated voice in Christian media and has branched into book publications and motivational speaking. He arrived at this juncture, not by depending on man's affirmation, but by depending on and looking unto Jesus Christ – the author and finisher of his faith.

You cannot reason with unreasonable people!

CHAPTER THIRTY SEVEN

AARON: FROM VOICE TO VICE

"And no man taketh this honor unto himself, but he that is called of God, as was Aaron" (Hebrews 5:4).

Aaron was called to be a voice for Moses to the people. His role was to amplify God's word as delivered through Moses for the listening audience. In Exodus 7:1-2, God told Moses, *"See, I have made thee a god to Pharaoh: and Aaron thy brother shall be thy prophet. Thou shalt speak all that I command thee: and Aaron thy brother shall speak unto Pharaoh,...."*

Aaron's singular qualification for the ministry was his voice. When God looked with disapproval on Moses protestations to leading the Israelites out of Egypt, He said, *"Is not Aaron the Levite thy brother? I know that he can speak well....And thou shalt speak unto him, and put words in his mouth and I will be with thy mouth, and with his mouth, and will teach you what ye shall do. And he shall be thy spokesman unto the people: and he shall be, even he shall be to thee instead of a mouth, and thou shalt be to him instead of God"* (Exodus 4:14-16).

After fulfilling this role for a couple of years, God elevated Aaron and his genealogy to be priests unto Him in the temple (Exodus 28:1). This opportunity raised Aaron's profile in Israel to the extent that some of the Levites murmured against him in envy (Numbers 16:11). His voice was respected and revered as high priest, but his singular ministry was still to be a voice for Moses.

This celebrated voice of Aaron soon became a vice to Moses' ministry, because of misplaced priorities. In Numbers 12:1-2, the Bible says, *"and Miriam and Aaron spake against Moses because of the Ethiopian woman whom he had married: for he had married an Ethiopian woman. And they said, Hath the LORD indeed spoken only by Moses? hath he not spoken also by us? And the LORD heard it."*

Aaron's voice had become a vice, due to his misplaced loyalties. He was called to be a voice, and was sharply rebuked by God for attempting to smear Moses reputation. God told him and Miriam, *"my servant Moses is not so, who is faithful in all mine house. With him will I speak mouth to mouth, even apparently, and not in dark speeches; and the similitude of the LORD shall he behold: wherefore then were ye not afraid to speak against my servant Moses? And the anger of the LORD was kindled against them; and he departed"* (Numbers 12:7-9).

Aaron's temptation is one that is regularly seen in today's world. It is the power of broken focus after having been given additional responsibilities. This added responsibility robs people of their destiny by multiplying their perspective, to the point that they lose their original purpose for living. Aaron's primary assignment was to be a voice for Moses. Even after his ordination for the High priesthood, Aaron's role was to augment and amplify Moses not attack him. He lost the notion of being only a voice for Moses, as his notoriety grew, and eventually that attitude became his vice!

THE MISTAKE THAT MARRED MIRIAM, BUT ANNOUNCED AARON

Next to crossing the Red Sea and bringing Israel out, the healing of Miriam's leprosy was another sign and wonder that stupefied the Israeli world. She was the first identifiable leper healed and God committed her to the mandatory seven days outside the camp statute (Numbers 12:14-15), before her healing.

The reason for Miriam's miracle was to put a consciousness of the fear of God in Israel for his word. Deuteronomy 24:8-9 says, *"take heed in the plague of leprosy, that thou observe diligently, and do according to all that the priests the Levites shall teach you…. Remember what the LORD thy God did unto Miriam by the way, after that ye were come forth out of Egypt."*

You must follow rules in spite of who is involved. John 10:35 says, "... *the scripture cannot be broken*". Aaron identified Miriam's leprosy, according to Leviticus 13, and in accordance with scripture he was required to put her away for a time. Instead he cried out, "*Let her not be as one dead, of whom the flesh is half consumed when he cometh out of his mother's womb*" (Numbers 12:12).

Aaron and Miriam had made the mistake of castigating God's prophet, Moses, but Aaron escaped punishment because the law says the priest is instrumental in bringing healing to lepers and so can't be a leper himself! In Leviticus 13:3, the Bible says, "and *the priest shall look on the plague in the skin of the flesh: and when the hair in the plague is turned white, and the plague in sight be deeper than the skin of his flesh, it is a plague of leprosy: and the priest shall look on him, and pronounce him unclean.*"

Aaron's high priestly credentials were never more highlighted than on this occasion. He demonstrated divine immunity and God's special judgment for the priesthood. Notwithstanding his current role, Aaron's first love was never to be forsaken. If it did, it would have arduous results. In Revelation 2:4-5, Jesus told the Church in Ephesus, "*Nevertheless I have somewhat against thee, because thou hast left thy first love. Remember therefore from whence thou art fallen, and repent, and do the first works; or else I will come unto thee quickly, and will remove thy candlestick out of his place, except thou repent.*"

FROM MINISTRY TO MONSTROSITY

Aaron was designed to be a voice for Moses. Rather he became a voice for the reprobate and corrupt side of Israel. He was to be subsumed in Moses anointing, but as he struggled for the stage with Moses, he lost the anointing.

After Moses had spent days on the mountain seeking God's face for Israel, the people turned to Aaron and said, "*...Up, make us gods, which shall go before us; for as for this Moses, the man that brought us up out of the land of Egypt, we wot not what is become of him*" (Exodus 32:1).

Aaron at this time had just been anointed alongside his family genealogy as high priest and priests unto the Lord God Almighty respectively (see Exodus 28:1-2). He wielded immense influence in Israel;

and under pressure to please the grumbling multitudes, he erected a calf for the people to worship.

He told them, *"These be thy gods, O Israel, which brought thee up out of the land of Egypt….tomorrow is a feast to the LORD And they rose up early on the morrow, and offered burnt offerings, and brought peace offerings; and the people sat down to eat and to drink, and rose up to play"* (Exodus 32:4-6).

The erection of that calf took Aaron from ministry to monstrosity! Years later, as Moses reminisced that occasion, he said *"…and the LORD was very angry with Aaron to have destroyed him: and I prayed for Aaron also the same time and I took your sin, the calf which ye had made, and burnt it with fire, and stamped it, and ground it very small, even until it was as small as dust: and I cast the dust thereof into the brook…"* (Deuteronomy 9:20-21).

The monstrosity of that idolatrous calf etched itself on the psyche of the Israelites and cost Aaron his legendary status as high priest and elder in Israel. His ministry never recovered, following this ugly scene of idolatry at the foot of Mount Sinai. Afterward, he veered from following God as he joined Moses to hit the rock at the waters of Meribah, an act for which God denied them entry into the promised land (Numbers 20:10-13).

Aaron's purpose was not to be a voice for the people to God but to be the voice of God to the people! He misconstrued his assignment as high priest, and as a result, forfeited his role as God's voice to the people.

WILLIAM SEYMOUR: GOD'S APOSTOLIC PIONEER

William Seymour (1870-1922) was born in Centerville, Louisiana to African American freed slaves. After stints as a waiter in Indianapolis, his ministry started in 1902 as an ordained minister of the Church of God in Cincinnati, Ohio. While sitting in the back room of a Bible school in Houston Texas, on one occasion, he heard the minister (Rev. Parham) teach about the baptism of the Holy Spirit for the first time in 1905 and his heart was stirred to receive that gift.

In alliance with a woman called Neeley Terry, William Seymour moved to Los Angeles to experience the revival that was going on in the city at the time. After being locked out of some churches in Los Angeles for preaching *glossolalia* or speaking in tongues, he started the Azusa street mission in 1906.

Initially, it was a family Bible study but as news of the outpouring of the Holy Spirit spread more and more people came and got filled with the Holy Spirit with the evidence of speaking in tongues. People came from all over the world, newspaper headlines were made and signs, wonders and miracles occurred amongst the members.

One of the cardinal aspects of William Seymour's ministry was the inter-racial harmony between all races. The meetings continued thrice a day daily for three years continually with thousands saved, healed and filled with the Holy Spirit. Through the Azusa street mission, South America and Europe received the baptism of the Holy Spirit and a multi-cultural and inter-racial church like had never been seen on the earth was born.

After three years of continuous and unabated revival, the spirit of sectarianism and racism reared its head in the Azusa street mission. A group of Caucasians, led by William Durham, led about six hundred members away from William Seymour's congregation citing racial inter-relationships as the cause.

In spite of setbacks from a hostile media who labeled his followers eccentric and outlandish, plus white supremacy groups in the church who were against racial integration, William Seymour ploughed ahead with the message of Pentecost. He died in 1922, but left a faith movement that pioneered Pentecost in the 20th century and shaped the fastest growing demographic of the church world today with over nine hundred million spirit filled believers in the world today.

*If your memories are bigger
than your dreams, you are
living in the past and the
past never sees the future!*

… Dr. Jesse Duplantis
(Destrehan, Louisiana)

CHAPTER THIRTY-EIGHT

ESAU: ARROGANT, ALOOF, AND ANTIQUATED

*"Lest there be any fornicator, or profane person, as Esau, who for one morsel of meat sold his birthright for ye know how that afterward, when he would have inherited the blessing, he was **rejected**: for he found no place of repentance, though he sought it carefully with tears"* (Hebrews 12:16-17).

Esau was antiquated. He lived in the past and for the present. In the process, he missed out on an otherwise glorious future. After forfeiting his inheritance for a morsel of meat (Genesis 25:29-34), he wept sore (Genesis 27:38) and vowed to kill his brother Jacob for stealing his birthright (see Genesis 27:41-42).

He lived the rest of his life in regret of that one ill-fated moment of momentary pleasure that relegated him to a second class citizen in his brother's presence. According to Genesis 33:4 and Hebrews 12:17, even though Esau forgave Jacob who was his chief protagonist in the pursuit of the blessings, he never forgave himself! It says *"...he found no place of repentance, though he sought it carefully with tears"* (Hebrews 12:17).

The purpose of the gospel of the Kingdom of God is to give man a hope and a future. The gospel absolves man of the mistakes of the past and gives him a new beginning and a fresh start. In Jeremiah 29:11, God says, *"For I know the thoughts that I think toward you, saith the LORD, thoughts of peace, and not of evil, to give you an expected end."* In 2 Corinthians 5:21, the Bible says God "...*hath made him* (Jesus) *to be sin for us, who knew no sin; that we might be made the righteousness of God in him.*"

THE BLANKET BAN!

Esau could have had a legacy of generational spiritual success. According to Hebrews 12:15, he was poised to inherit the blessing but was disqualified by a blanket ban for being profane and despising his birthright. In Hebrews 12:16, the Bible says "*lest there be* (a)...*profane person, as Esau, who for one morsel of meat sold his birthright,...(and who) when he would have inherited the blessing, he was rejected.*"

It adds in Genesis 25:33-34, concerning Esau, "He *sold his birthright unto Jacob. Then Jacob gave Esau bread and pottage of lentiles; and he did eat and drink, and rose up, and went his way: thus Esau despised his birthright.*"

The word *profane* (as used in Hebrews 12:16) is the Greek word *Bebelos* which means unfit for access or crossing the threshold through unauthorized or improper access. Esau did not revere or respect the birthright, and was arrogant and aloof in the manner he cast it off for a morsel of meat.

Esau fell prey to the "big-man's syndrome." The word used in Genesis 25:34 for despise is a Hebrew word that means to raise one's head contemptuously, or disdainfully. His perks, privileges and position as firstborn made him proud and as a result he lost the inheritance.

In 1 Peter 5:5, Peter adjures believers to "...*be clothed with humility: for God resisteth the proud, and giveth grace to the humble. Humble yourselves therefore under the mighty hand of God, that he may exalt you in due time.*"

The blanket ban that turns a seemingly loyal believer to a byword in the covenant is pride. It may not be immediately obvious to all onlookers but it is the one sin that causes God to resist a believer.

Jesus said, in John 15:5-6, "*I am the vine, ye are the branches: He that abideth in me, and I in him, the same bringeth forth much fruit: for without me ye can do nothing. If a man abide not in me, he is cast forth as a branch, and is withered; and men gather them, and cast them into the fire, and they are burned.*"

Nothing of worth has ever been produced separate from God. **It takes abiding in the vine to abound in life.** In John 15:7, Jesus said "*if ye abide* *in me, and my words abide in you, ye shall ask what ye will, and it shall be done unto you."*

THE SECRET TO BURNOUT!

The temptation of Esau was the flesh! He did not crucify his flesh, and it eventually cost him the inheritance he so desired. He told Jacob, at the point of famishment, *"…I am at the point to die: and what profit shall this birthright do to me?"* (Genesis 27:32).

He had an unbridled passion that cost him his passion for the inheritance! In Hebrews 12:16, the Bible likens him to a fornicator or those who *"…takes fire in his bosom,…goes upon hot coals,…*(by) *going in to his neighbor's wife…"* (Proverbs 6:27-29).

The number one cause of burn out is the flesh! If a believer does not crucify the flesh, it will cause him or her to make a shipwreck of their faith. Paul said, in 1 Corinthians 9:27, *"I keep under my body, and bring it into subjection: lest that by any means, when I have preached to others, I myself should be a castaway."*

Only a life that is alive to sin can experience burn out. If a believer is dead to sin, as described to in Romans 6:6-7 and Galatians 2:20, he is alive spiritually and so can't burn out. Rather, he or she has the eternal life of God that can never be consumed.

In John 6:63, Jesus said, *"It is the spirit that quickeneth; the flesh profiteth nothing…."* The Holy Spirit is the secret to a life without burnout. It quickens and replenishes, while the flesh only wastes away and brings the physical and the second death (Romans 8:5-11).

THE MYSTERY OF THE FIRSTBORN

Scientists have for years debated back and forth the importance of family position in life attainments. To secular humanistic sociologists and scientists, the firstborn is the *Primus inter pares* with privileges and power to go with their position.

They have greater ambition and acquire higher educational degrees than their younger siblings. They are more accomplished and have a higher tendency to develop a higher intelligence quotient (I.Q) than their siblings.

Examples of high achieving first born children include Hilary Clinton, Angela Merkel, Winston Churchill, John Wayne and Sylvester Stallone.

The firstborns' in the Bible were, however, not as successful. Most of them were overshadowed by younger siblings or, having made the wrong decisions, evaporated off the scene. For example David overshadowed Eliab, Jacob trumped Esau, Joseph overtook Reuben and Samson was buried in the dust of the philistines with his enemies.

The Bible says first borns are the father's "...*might, beginning of strength and the excellency of* (his)...*dignity and* ...*power*" (Genesis 49:3). They are entitled to a "...*double portion of all that he hath*..." (Deuteronomy 21:17) as the firstborn and wields enormous influence and power in getting things done (see Exodus 11:1-5).

As the "...*church of the firstborn*..." (Hebrews 12:23), however, New Testament believers have no need of family position to trump their opposition. All they need is God, who has made them "...*to be conformed to the image of His son that He might be the firstborn among many brethren*" (Romans 8:29) to make them take their rightful place in dominion and greatness.

PART VII

TRIUMPH OF THE LOYAL

- › **ELEVATION**
- › **EMPATHY**
- › **EXCELLENCE**
- › **ENLIGHTENMENT**
- › **EMPOWERMENT**
- › **EXCESS**
- › **ENTHUSIASM**

Take time to analyze the life of a good man, and see that it was not achieved by accident or good fortune, but was a life in submission to the will of God

- Lester Sumrall (1913-1966)

CHAPTER THIRTY NINE

ELEVATION

"I have planted, Apollos watered; but God gave the increase. So then neither is he that planteth any thing, neither he that watereth; but God that giveth the increase" (1 Corinthians 3:6-7).

Paul understood the principle of increase. He knew that true increase was of the Lord and not based on Apollo's oratorical skills (Acts 18:24) or a superior intellect such as he possessed (see Philippians 3:4-6 and Acts 22:3).

He told the Church in Corinth that *"…my speech and my preaching was not with enticing words of man's wisdom, but in demonstration of the Spirit and of power"* (1 Corinthians 2:4). He added, when communicating with the Thessalonica Church, *"…our gospel came not unto you in word only, but also in power, and in the Holy Ghost, and in much assurance"* (1 Thessalonians 1:5).

God, as a covenant-keeping partner, will always elevate the loyal who put their trust in Him, and not in man. The Psalmist said, *"Trust in the Lord, and do good; so shalt thou dwell in the land, and verily thou shalt be fed. Delight thyself also in the Lord: and he shall give thee the desires of thine heart. Commit thy way unto the Lord; trust also in him; and he shall bring it to pass"* (Psalm 37:3-5).

On the contrary, those who look to man never see increase. In Jeremiah 17:5-6, God says, *"…Cursed be the man that trusteth in man, and maketh flesh his arm, and whose heart departeth from the Lord. For he shall be like the heath in the desert, and shall not see when good cometh; but shall inhabit the parched places in the wilderness, in a salt land and not inhabited."*

Those who lean on man die in the desert, but the believer who trusts in God thrives in the most unfavorable circumstances. In Jeremiah 17:6-8, God adds, *"Blessed is the man that trusteth in the LORD, and whose hope the LORD is. For he shall be as a tree planted by the waters, and that spreadeth out her roots by the river, and shall not see when heat cometh, but her leaf shall be green; and shall not be careful in the year of drought, neither shall cease from yielding fruit."*

TODAY'S LOYALISTS ARE TOMORROW'S LIFTED

Paul epitomized a life of loyalty during his sojourn here on earth. He said, in Galatians 2:20, *"I am crucified with Christ: nevertheless I live; yet not I, but Christ liveth in me: and the life which I now live in the flesh I live by the faith of the Son of God, who loved me, and gave himself for me."*

He considered his qualifications, attainments and spiritual accomplishments as *"...the loss of all things, and do count them but dung, that I may win Christ. And be found in him, not having mine own righteousness, which is of the law, but that which is through the faith of Christ, the righteousness which is of God by faith: That I may know him, and the power of his resurrection..."* (Philippians 3:8-10).

Paul wanted to increase, to elevate and to taste the power of Christ, but he understood that loyalty was the only trusted route to this experience. He forsook all the trappings of his legal background that were steeped in climbing the pedestals of the Pharisees and became a voice for the New Testament Church instead.

He took the gospel to the Asian continent and wrote two-thirds of the New Testament. He founded Churches in as far flung as Rome and Thessalonica and upturned whole hedonistic and pagan cultures for Christ (Acts 17:16-22). It was, however, predicated on a selfless gospel that had Christ at the center.

He told beleivers' in Philippians 2:4-5, *"look not every man on his own things, but every man also on the things of others. Let this mind be in you, which was also in Christ Jesus."* He stood for Christ, and as a result he stood out in life and ministry!

STRIVING FOR THE MASTERY!

Paul never settled for mediocrity or average but continually strove for excellence. He said in 1 Corinthians 9:24-25, *"Know ye not that they which run in a race run all, but one receiveth the prize? So run, that ye may obtain. And every man that striveth for the mastery is temperate in all things."*

The word used for temperate is the Greek word *egkrates* which means to exercise self-control or to be continent. Paul followed Christ at the expense of self in all things. As a result, he obtained the mastery.

He describes himself as a *"...wise master builder..."* (1 Corinthians 3:10) who builds on the foundation *"...no man...laid which is Jesus Christ"* (1 Corinthians 3:11). Those who become masters in life stop building on self and start building on God instead!

Such believers' do not live for self anymore but rather *"...die daily..."* (1 Corinthians 15:31). Their God is not their belly, as those Paul described in Philippians 3:19 were, but their God is the God of the Bible. These believers worship God not for what He can give them, but for who He is.

These believers become masters in all climes and spheres because of from selfless living. They forsake all and become all-around fruitful believers. Even before he declared self-control as the key to mastery in life and ministry (1 Corinthians 9:25), Paul made himself an example for the brethren to emulate.

He said, *"...I made myself servant unto all, that I might gain the more. And unto the Jews I became as a Jew, that I might gain the Jews; to them that are under the law, as under the law, that I might gain them that are under the law; To them that are without law, as without law, (being not without law to God, but under the law to Christ,) that I might gain them that are without law. To the weak became I as weak, that I might gain the weak: I am made all things to all men, that I might by all means save some"* (1 Corinthians 9:19-22).

Because of His altruistic and alchemistic mindset that strove to turn men to the mind of Christ, Paul became a jewel in his generation. He exemplified those described in Malachi 3:16-17; it says, *"...a book of remembrance was written before Him for them that feared the LORD, and that thought upon his name. In that day when I (God) make up my jewels I will spare them, as a man spareth his own son that serveth him."*

TRUETT CATHY: TESTED, TRUTHFUL, AND TRUSTWORTHY!

Truett Cathy (1921-2014) built the chicken chain Chick-Fil A into a 6.2 billion-dollar business with over 1,900 chains in 42 states of America. It is currently the largest family- owned-service restaurant in the world and has the highest same store sales in the U.S. it is currently the largest quick-service-chicken restaurant in the country.

Truett Cathy's biblical values have shaped the company and revolutionized how Christians do business. He makes sure all his restaurants are closed on Sundays and has awarded more than thirty million dollars in scholarship to deserving staff to forward their education.

At the time of death, he was still teaching weekly Sunday school at the local Baptist Church, in Jonesboro Georgia, he worshipped at. He also testified that the Bible has been his investment guide throughout his life. The motto of his company is "Glorify God by being faithful with what has been entrusted in our hands."

In the face of a changing world view on marriage, eternity, and the inerrancy of scriptures, Truett has stood strong and tall. He was married to his wife, Jeanette, of more than seventy years and all three of their children work for the business and are still married to their first spouses.

After sixty seven years of business, Chick Fil A remains one of the few major companies that are family-owned, family-operated and still successful in its third generation. Truett Cathy has left a legendary status that still lives on today in the family and financial empire he bequeathed to his children.

Life is too tough to do alone!

– SHANE WARREN (Lead Pastor –
The Assembly West Monroe Louisiana)

CHAPTER FORTY

EMPATHY

"Blessed be God, even the Father of our Lord Jesus Christ, the Father of mercies, and the God of all comfort; Who comforteth us in all our tribulation, that we may be able to comfort them which are in any trouble, by the comfort wherewith we ourselves are comforted of God" (2 Corinthians 1:3-4).

Empathy is the ability to feel what others are feeling. It is the ability to walk in other people's shoes as a result of the spirit of compassion in one's own heart. In 2 Corinthians 1:3-4, Paul says a believer is able to comfort others because of the comfort he or she has received from the Lord. That is divine empathy.

Those who stay loyal to God and become legends in their time are those who have at one time been afflicted but now receive comfort and healing from the Holy Spirit. For example, amidst all the threatening and vituperations of the Sanhedrin against the early Church, they *"...were edified; and walking in the fear of the Lord, and in the comfort of the Holy Ghost, were multiplied"* (Acts 9:31).

To walk in the fear of the Lord connotes loyalty, and it was this attribute in the early Church that caused edification and comfort that spurred their divine empathy in Acts 4:33-35. The Bible asks the believer to *"bear ye one another's burdens, and so fulfill the law of Christ"* (Galatians 6:2). In the preceding verse, however, Paul warns that *"if a man be overtaken in a fault, ye which are spiritual, restore such an one in the spirit of meekness; considering thyself, lest thou also be tempted."*

It means, therefore, that the only people who can truly bear others' burdens are the spiritual or the unalloyed and loyal believers! **True compassion starts with spiritual conviction**, not just comforting words. When loyalty to God abounds, empathy is readily available. Paul said, "*...I seek not yours but you: for the children ought not to lay up for the parents, but the parents for the children. And I will very gladly spend and be spent for you; though the more abundantly I love you, the less I be loved*" (2 Corinthians 12:14-15).

RUTH: THE POWER OF EMPATHY

In the Bible, the life of Ruth epitomizes loyalty and empathy. As a widow who had suffered the loss of her husband, brother-in-law and father-in-law in a space of ten years (Ruth 1:2-5), she could have wallowed in self-pity. Rather, because she had a spirit of loyalty that engendered empathy, she set out to help and heal a mother-in-law who was hurt and wounded from life's bruises (see Ruth 1:20-21).

When Naomi, Ruth's mother-in-law, prevailed on Ruth to jettison her as her fellow Moabite daughter-in-law had done earlier, "*...Ruth said, Intreat me not to leave thee, or to return from following after thee: for whither thou goest, I will go; and where thou lodgest, I will lodge: thy people shall be my people, and thy God my God: Where thou diest, will I die, and there will I be buried: the LORD do so to me, and more also, if ought but death part thee and me*" (Ruth 1:16-17).

Ruth defied all reason to stay with her Jewish mother-in-law. Even though a Moabite, which was a tribe considered outcasts in Israel and ostracized to their tenth generation from the temple (see Deuteronomy 23:3), and with slim prospects of raising a family in a foreign culture, she persisted and prospered.

The Bible says, in Ruth 1:18, that Noami "*...saw that she was stedfastly minded to go with her....*" It was that steadfastness or loyalty to God's people and God's word that made Ruth a woman of empathy. She refused to use her hurt as an excuse to hurt others. Instead, she used it to be a healing balm to comfort Naomi.

When Ruth's future husband Boaz met her for the first time, he referred to this loyalty and empathy in her. He said, "*...It hath fully been*

217

shewed me, all that thou hast done unto thy mother in law since the death
of thine husband: and how thou hast left thy father and thy mother, and
the land of thy nativity, and art come unto a people which thou knewest not
heretofore. The LORD recompense thy work, and a full reward be given thee of
the LORD God of Israel, under whose wings thou art come to trust" (Ruth 2:11).

Eventually, Ruth was rewarded! She married Boaz, a wealthy
businessman who was also Naomi and her kinsman redeemer. Later, she
bore a son (Ruth 4:13), called Obed who became the grandfather of King
David. Out of that genealogy, came Jesus Christ the Savior of the world
(Mark 1:1-16) and the church of the firstborn (Hebrews 12:23).

Ruth was a woman of empathy and loyalty. Her mother-in-law's friends
described her to Naomi as *"...thy daughter in law, which loveth thee, which
is better to thee than seven sons,..."* (Ruth 4:15). Love is the proof of loyalty,
and empathy is its byproduct! Legends, like Ruth, are celebrated today
because they refused to let life stifle their empathy quotient.

JESUS: MOVED BY COMPASSION, NOT CRITICISM

Jesus Christ had just suffered a major loss. The man who announced
His ministry and heralded His coming, John the Baptist, had just been
killed by beheading. The Bible says, in Mark 6:27-28, *"...the king sent
an executioner, and commanded his head to be brought, and he went and
beheaded him in the prison, And brought his head in a charger,...."*

Prior to that, however, John the Baptist had renegade on his loyalty
to Christ. He had questioned whether Jesus was really the Christ and so
had sent his disciples to ask *"...art thou he that should come, or do we look
for another?"* (Matthew 11:3). He had become a "closet critic" of Jesus
ministry while he was in jail for criticizing King Herod (Mark 6:17-18),
and according to Jesus was offended at Him (Matthew 11:3).

Rather than wallow in self pity and animosity against Herod, or
abrasively blame John for the critical spirit that brought his ministry to an
end, Jesus positioned himself to challenge the *status-quo* around Him with
compassion. After the beheading of John the Baptist, Jesus *"...saw much
people, and was moved with compassion toward them, because they were as*

sheep not having a shepherd: and he began to teach them many things" (Mark 6:34).

The phrase *moved with compassion*, as used in Mark 6:34, is akin to empathy. It means Jesus felt the people's pain, poverty and perpetual desolation even though He had just suffered an even greater personal loss. In loyalty to this cause for which God had sent Him to the earth and in demonstration of His spirit of empathy, Jesus "...*went forth, and saw a great multitude, and was moved with compassion toward them, and He healed their sick*" (Matthew 14:14).

Jesus Christ was not just a wayfaring preacher. He was a way making pastor! He was so moved with compassion for His sheep that He set out to make a way for them. His unalloyed loyalty to the will of God (Hebrews 10:7) spurred His compassion for the corrupt and His love for the lost. He did not come just to do His Father's job, but He came to "...*bring many sons unto glory...*" (Hebrews 2:10).

THE BIRDS OF ONE NEST

When eagles are renewing their strength, they lose their wings and beat their beaks into the surrounding rock. Their plumage withers and so they can't fly during this season of their life. As a result of their wings deterioration, they are restricted in their nests and their fellow eagles come to their aid during this time.

The eagles that nourish their fledgling colleagues are not novices, however, but those that have gone through the mottling process themselves. At some stage of the molting process, these older and more mature eagles, who have experienced molting before, drop meat to replenish the molting eagle's energy, because its oily fat stores are used to stimulate the growth of new feathers.

Similarly, the believers who remain loyal through the process of pruning and persecution end up more compassionate and sympathetic than others who haven't seen similar trials and situations. They fly high, but look low at the travails of others in order to help them develop into full maturity. Their expert eyes catch the writhing eyes of their colleagues and they provide succor for them in their times of trials and temptation.

Tobe Momah

In Job 39:27-29, the Bible says *"Doth the eagle mount up at thy command, and make her nest on high? She dwelleth and abideth on the rock, upon the crag of the rock, and the strong place. From thence she seeketh the prey, and her eyes behold afar off."*

Similarity maintains the status quo, but difference marks one out for distinction!

CHAPTER FORTY-ONE

EXCELLENCE

"And over these three presidents; of whom Daniel was first: that the princes might give accounts unto them, and the king should have no damage. Then this Daniel was preferred above the presidents and princes, because an excellent spirit was in him; and the king thought to set him over the whole realm" (Daniel 6:2-3).

One of the brightest lights in Bible chronicles is Daniel. A gifted administrator, he ruled over several climes of government because of his unalloyed loyalty to God. He never failed to acknowledge God as His source, but he also stayed loyal to his political superiors.

While serving during the reign of King Nebuchadnezzar, Daniel *"... purposed in his heart that he would not defile himself with the portion of the king's meat, nor with the wine which he drank:"* (Daniel 1:8). As a result of this divine loyalty, God set him over the kingdom as *"...a great man, and gave him many great gifts, and made him ruler over the whole province of Babylon, and chief of the governors over all the wise men of Babylon"* (Daniel 2:48).

In King Belshazzer's reign, he *"...clothed Daniel with scarlet, and put a chain of gold about his neck, and made a proclamation concerning him, that he should be the third ruler in the kingdom"* (Daniel 5:29).

He was elevated further during the reign of King Darius who had established one hundred and twenty princes in his realm. He then set *"... over these* (princes) *three presidents; of whom Daniel was first: that the princes might give accounts...and the king should have no damage" (Daniel 6:2).*

Daniel was not a wayfaring follower who only served the Kings in his domain when it was convenient. He was a covenant-keeping servant who served with steadfast loyalty, as seen by his faithfulness to ensure the king had no damage. As a result of this unalloyed loyalty, he had an excellent spirit that pervaded everything he did (Daniel 6:4).

THE PRODIGIOUS PRESIDENT WHO UNDERSTOOD PURPOSE

Daniel was a prodigy in his time. He was described as "...*ten times better than all the magicians and astrologers that were in all his realm*" (Daniel 1:20). He also had special "...*understanding in all visions and dreams*" (Daniel 1:17).

It was this understanding of his times that set him above his peers! The Bible says, "...*the children of Issachar, which were men that had understanding of the times, to know what Israel ought to do; the heads of them were two hundred; and all their brethren were at their commandment*" (1 Chronicles 12:32).

Those who lead and become legends as a result of their leadership skills have understanding of their purpose that births excellence in their life and ministry. They stick to God's plans for their lives and exemplify excellence as a result.

Proverbs 17:27 says "...*a man of understanding is of an excellent spirit*" and in Proverbs 13:15, the wise man said "*good understanding giveth favor but the way of transgressors is hard.*" Daniel had favor (Daniel 1:9) and was fruitful in a foreign land because he understood his purpose.

Daniel did not become great because he belonged to any clique or cult in Babylon. He became great because he stuck to divine purpose amid peer and palace pressure. He spoke truth to power (see Daniel 5:18-23) and obeyed God notwithstanding the consequences (Daniel 6:10).

At the end of his nearly fifty-year reign in Babylon, King Darius attested to Daniel's loyalty. He asked, "*O Daniel, servant of the living God, is thy God, whom thou servest continually, able to deliver thee from the lions?*" (Daniel 6:20). When believers serve God continually, it is an attestation of their loyalty, and this brings them excellence in life and ministry.

DANIEL: EUNUCH, EERIE AND EXCELLENT

Excellence is not extremism, but normal Christian living. It is what every believer is called to. In Philippians 1:10, the Bible says believers should "...*approve things that are excellent; that ye may be sincere and without offence till the day of Christ.*"

Daniel had an excellent spirit which resulted in his "interpreting dreams, showing of hard sentences and dissolving of doubts" (Daniel 5:12). His secret was divine salesmanship! God raised him because he revered God, and notwithstanding whose ox was gored, he "...*believed in his God*" (Daniel 6:23).

Daniel was castrated thus making him a eunuch. His spiritual and physical affections were, as a result, directed toward no one else but his Maker. He was akin to "...*a glorious church, not having spot, or wrinkle, or any such thing; but that it should be holy and without blemish*" (Ephesians 5:27).

The excellent Church serve no one but the Lord. They live a life of commitment and manifest uncommon greatness as a result. In Proverbs 12:26, the Bible says "*the righteous is more excellent than his neighbor*" (emphasis added). A person cannot recover excellence if he or she does not sell out to God in righteousness.

Another sell-out attribute of Daniel that marked him out as a loyalty legend, was his eeriness. He was unique, uncanny and considered weird by some of his contemporaries. He refused the luxurious food of king Nebuchadnezzar's table, and instead asked for water and vegetables (Daniel 1: 12).

He refused to stop praying when king Darius signed an edict banning prayer in Daniel 6:1-10. He broke rank with the other wise men and prophets telling King Belshazzar "...*thou has not humbled thine heart...But has lifted up thyself against the Lord of heaven...and ...hast praised the gods of silver, and gold, of brass, iron, wood, and stone, which see not, nor hear, nor know: and the God in whose hand thy breath is, and whose are all thy ways, hast thou not glorified*" (Daniel 5: 22-23). As a result, King Belshazzar was killed that same night (Daniel 5:30)!

Your similarity makes for the status-quo, but your difference makes for your distinction in life and ministry. Daniel was different and unique, and to some eerie but he stood for what God had called him to be. At the end of his four-king trans-generational reign, Daniel left a legacy that was unequalled. Even God used him as a benchmark for righteousness (see Ezekiel 14:14), and in Hebrews 11:32-33 Daniel is celebrated as one the heroes in the Hall of fame of faith.

THE FIREPROOF BROTHERS WITH A COURAGEOUS FLYWHEEL THAT WEREN'T AFRAID TO FACE GIANTS

Alex and Stephen Kendricks have revolutionized the world of Christian film making. Before their advent, most Christian films were looked at as amateurish, low-budget and poor-quality pictures but since the launch of their maiden project, *Flywheel*, in 2003 they have raised the bar on what to expect from the Christian film industry.

Born to the home of a gospel minister and school teacher, the Kendrick brothers went to Seminary and worked as media pastors at Sherwood Baptist Church Albany, Georgia between 2003 and 2013. The vision of Alex Kendrick at his job interview with Michael Catt, senior pastor of Sherwood Baptist Church, was to *"make a low-budget, full length movie as an outreach to the community."*

The Kendrick's vision of excellence spurred the making of *Flywheel*, *Facing the giants, Fireproof, Courageous* and *War room films* and made their accompanying DVD and book sales best sellers. Their maiden film sold more than a million copies while their latest project, War room, was the number one film in America on its release.

Using a cast of mostly volunteers, and sourcing funds from church contributions they have upturned records and set spiraling statistics of born-again conversions, DVD sales and increased run of their movies among movie goers. Their second film, *Facing the Giants*, garnered $10.1 million. Their third film, *Fireproof*, brought in $33.4 million in sales while their fourth film, *Courageous*, brought in $34.5 million.

As a result of the success of the Kendrick brothers' films, new Christian movie-makers have emerged having been spurred to pursue excellence in full-length feature films by their success. They are pace-setters and trail-blazers in the Christian film industry and are living legends today because of their loyalty.

Obey God and leave the consequences to Him.

- Charles Stanley (1932-)
Senior Pastor First Baptist
Church Atlanta Georgia USA

CHAPTER FORTY TWO

ENLIGHTENMENT

"Trust in the LORD *with all thine heart; and lean not unto thine own understanding. In all thy ways acknowledge him, and he shall direct thy paths. Be not wise in thine own eyes: fear the* LORD, *and depart from evil"* (Proverbs 3:5-7).

The word "acknowledge" as used in Proverbs 3:5, is the Hebrew word *Yada.* It means to know with certainty or be enlightened. **Those who know God with certainty are never left in the dark in life.**

The psalmist prayed to God in Psalm 74:20 saying, "H*ave respect unto the covenant: for the dark places of the earth are full of the habitations of cruelty."* Those who are faithful to the covenant and remain loyal to God never inhabit the dark places of cruelty. They stay enlightened.

The word of God is described as "*...a lamp unto my feet, and a light unto my path* (because) *I have sworn, and I will perform it, that I will keep thy righteous judgments"* (Psalm 119:105-106). It takes loyalty to God's word to shed light on one's ways.

When God sees a man or woman who is loyal to the call of God on his or her life, He shines and enlightens his or her path. After telling Jeremiah he was "*...ordained...a prophet unto the nations"* (Jeremiah 1:5), He told him not to be afraid. God told him further, "*...Thou hast well seen: for I will hasten my word to perform it"* (Jeremiah 1:13).

MARY: LOYALIST, LIGHTBEARER AND LIFTER OF MEN

Mary, the mother of Jesus, was a Galilean teenage hand maiden betrothed to Joseph the carpenter when angel Gabriel appeared to her saying, *"…Hail, thou that art highly favored, the Lord is with thee: blessed art thou among women"* (Luke 1:28).

Rather than argue with the angel, as Zechariah the father of John the Baptist, had done in Luke 1:18-23, Mary said to the angel, *"…Behold the handmaid of the Lord; be it unto me according to thy word"* (Luke 1:38). This, in spite of the fact, she was a virgin who had never been with a man.

It was that loyalty streak that enlightened Mary. Her cousin, Elizabeth, prophesied that because of Mary's faith *"…there shall be a performance of those things which were told her from the Lord"* (Luke 1:45). Rather than bemoan her novel situation, Mary exploded in praise (see Luke 1:46-55).

Light always follows loyalty. Zechariah, the father of John the Baptist, after being released from dumbness celebrated his son saying *"…thou, child, shalt be called the prophet of the Highest: for thou shalt go before the face of the Lord to prepare his ways…to give light to them that sit in darkness and in the shadow of death, to guide our feet into the way of peace"* (Luke 1:76,79).

THE BIGGER THEY COME, THE HARDER THEY FALL!

In Habakkuk 3:11, the Bible says *"The sun and moon stood still in the heavens at the glint of your flying arrows, at the lightning of your flashing spear"* (NIV). The glint or flash from arrows or spears in the above scripture typifies enlightenment and revelation.

It took only one glint from God's arrow and light from His flashing spears to stop the sun and the moon. According to 1 Corinthians 15:41, these stars occupy various realms of glory, but one revelatory word from God stopped them in their tracks.

It is not the greatness of the enemies, but the greatness of God's word that matters. In Isaiah 42:21, the prophet of God said, *"The LORD is well pleased for his righteousness' sake; He will magnify the law, and make it honorable."*

When "...*the light shineth in darkness...the darkness comprehended it not*" (John 1:5) and must disappear irrevocably. What wins life's battles is the availability of light regardless of how gross the darkness is.

In Isaiah 60:1-3, the Bible says "*arise, shine; for thy light is come, and the glory of the* LORD *is risen upon thee. For, behold, the darkness shall cover the earth, and gross darkness the people: but the* LORD *shall arise upon thee, and his glory shall be seen upon thee. And the Gentiles shall come to thy light, and kings to the brightness of thy rising.*"

In the battle of the wilderness, Jesus Christ only spoke the word of God and conquered the devil in Matthew 4:1-10. As a testament to the power of the revealed word of God, Jesus Christ said in Matthew 4:4, "...*Man shall not live by bread alone, but by every word that proceedeth out of the mouth of God.*"

Real life victories are won on the platform of the proceeding Word. It is not a mundane religious exercise or a routine familiarity with the word that births the *Zoe* life of God. It is the word that proceeds actively from the mouth of God. Such words are *Rhema*, from the original Greek word for *revelation*, not logos in the Bible according to 2 Corinthians 3:6.

It is when God's revelation is mixed with faith that the word's inherent ability is activated. In Hebrews 4:2-3, 12 the writer of Hebrews says "...*the word preached did not profit them, not being mixed with faith in them that heard it. For we which have believed do enter into rest (as)...the word of God is quick, and powerful, and sharper than any two edged sword, piercing even to the dividing asunder of soul and spirit, and of the joints and marrow, and is a discerner of the thoughts and intents of the heart.*"

HOWARD CARTER: A LIFE OF TRUTH, TENACITY AND TRIUMPH

Howard Carter (1891-1971) was born in Birmingham, England UK to a British soldier father and French noble mother. He was born with a speech impediment and suffered taunting from fellow students growing up.

Though born into a nominal Anglican family, Howard Carter did not become a believer until 1911. He received the baptism of the Holy Spirit while actively involved in the Crown Mission Christian ministry in

Birmingham and in 1916, he quit his secular job to pioneer two Pentecostal churches in Great Britain.

In 1921, he was appointed as the president of the Hempstead Bible school, the first Pentecostal Bible school in England, and rose to become the chairman of the Assemblies of God in Great Britain and Ireland between 1934 and 1945.

He, famously, went to prison in 1919 as a conscientious objector to being drafted as a soldier in the first Word war. During his incarceration, Howard Carter served as a mentor to delinquent and incarcerated youths and wrote his revolutionary manual titled "Questions and answers on spiritual gifts."

After serving for twenty seven years at Hempstead Bible school, and exploring the frontiers of missions with Lester Sumrall, Howard Carter re-located to the United States of America. He married an American minister, Ruth Steelberg, in 1952 and spent his last 23 years criss-crossing America as a leader of the Assemblies of God in America.

His legacy lives on in the lives of the hundreds of student pastors he mentored and taught. His legacy also continues in the fields of missions he visited with Lester Sumrall and Smith Wigglesworth, and continued to support throughout his lif

His spirit of discernment is exemplified by the spiritual bond cemented in prayer between him and Lester Sumrall. Though they met for the first time in 1932 at Eureka Springs, Arkansas, Howard Carter had been told in 1930 through a God-inspired vision, that He would send him a travelling companion from afar to minister alongside him and to support the work worldwide.

When he met Lester Sumrall in 1932, on the first day of the conference in Eureka Springs, Arkansas, he spoke verbatim those words God had spoken to Howard Carter[1] eighteen months earlier. They re-connected twelve months later in New Zealand and from there went on a 50,000 miles, twenty nation tour that pioneered multiple churches in Asia and East Europe.

How loyal you are to God,
determines how lethal
you are to the enemy!

CHAPTER FORTY-THREE

EMPOWERMENT

"I have suffered the loss of all things, and do count them but dung, that I may win Christ, and be found in him, not having mine own righteousness, which is of the law, but that which is through the faith of Christ, the righteousness which is of God by faith: That I may know him, and the power of his resurrection,..." (Philippians 3:8-10).

Empowered believers live as the righteousness of God by the faith of Christ, and not by man's opinions! According to Philippians 3:10, these ones taste of *"...the power of his resurrection, and the fellowship of his sufferings, being made conformable unto his death."*

Paul, who authored the book of Philippians, tasted the resurrection power of God. He said *"I count all things but loss for the excellency of the knowledge of Christ Jesus my Lord for whom I have suffered the loss of all things, and do count them but dung, that I may win Christ"* (Philippians 3:8).

The empowered believer loses his or her life in the fight for the God kind of faith. In Isaiah 53:12, the Bible says *"therefore will I divide him a portion with the great, and he shall divide the spoil with the strong; because he hath poured out his soul unto death...."*

The greatness of the gospel is hinged on the gruesome death to the flesh of believers'. **It is those who kill the flesh that live in the power of the Spirit**. In Galatians 5:24-25, Paul says, *"...and they that are Christ's have crucified the flesh with the affections and lusts. If we live in the Spirit, let us also walk in the Spirit."*

THE THREE HEBREW BOYS

God went with the three Hebrew boys, Meschach, Shadrach and Abednego into the furnace of affliction after King Nebuchadnezzar commanded them to be thrown into it for disobeying his orders to bow to an idolatrous statue he had erected.

Daniel 3:19-20 says, *"Then was Nebuchadnezzar full of fury, and the form of his visage was changed against Shadrach, Meshach, and Abednego,... and commanded that they should heat the furnace one seven times more than it was wont to be heated. And he commanded the most mighty men that were in his army to bind Shadrach, Meshach, and Abednego, and to cast them into the burning fiery furnace."*

These three Hebrew boys stood for the Lord. In Daniel 3:16-18, they said, *"O Nebuchadnezzar, we are not careful to answer thee in this matter. If it be so, our God whom we serve is able to deliver us from the burning fiery furnace, and he will deliver us out of thine hand, O king. But if not, be it known unto thee, O king, that we will not serve thy gods, nor worship the golden image which thou hast set up."*

Even though they went against the grain of public opinion in Babylon, and against the authoritarian Nebuchadnezzar's decree, they refused to buckle. They remained loyal to God, and Jesus became their "fourth man in the fire" (Daniel 3:25). An astonished King Nebuchadnezzar exclaimed *"...I see four men loose, walking in the midst of the fire, and they have no hurt; and the form of the fourth is like the Son of God."*

They were not afraid to speak truth to power; and as a result, God vindicated them. In all their discussions, they acknowledged the Lordship and supremacy of God; consequently, he made them legends in their time for their unalloyed loyalty to Him.

After they were brought out of the furnace with no smell of smoke or singed attire found on them, Nebuchadnezzar made a decree saying, *"Blessed be the God of Shadrach, Meshach, and Abednego, who hath sent his angel, and delivered his servants that trusted in him, and have changed the king's word, and yielded their bodies, that they might not serve nor worship any god, except their own God"* (Daniel 3:28).

When God empowers you, those who mocked you will make you! Those who railed at you will raise you because of your loyalty to God. In

Daniel 3:30, the Bible says, *"then the king promoted Shadrach, Meshach, and Abednego, in the province of Babylon."*

LOYALTY IS A LIFETIME OATH!

An oath is a testament of one's loyalty. In Ecclesiastes 5:4-6, the Bible says, *"When thou vowest a vow unto God, defer not to pay it; for he hath no pleasure in fools: pay that which thou hast vowed. Better is it that thou shouldest not vow, than that thou shouldest vow and not pay. Suffer not thy mouth to cause thy flesh to sin; neither say thou before the angel, that it was an error: wherefore should God be angry at thy voice, and destroy the work of thine hands?"*

The oath, if maintained for life, becomes a testimony of a life of loyalty that God will bless with His excess and power. If, on the the other hand, that oath is repeatedly and flimsily broken it will bring poverty and a destruction of the works of your hands. In 2 Samuel 21:1-5, for example, Saul broke the covenant Joshua had entered into with the Gibeonites and caused an unmitigated famine in the land.

It takes a life oath of loyalty to bring God's largess to pass. In Psalm 50:14-15, the psalmist adjures believers to *"...pay thy vows unto the most High: And call upon me in the day of trouble: I will deliver thee, and thou shalt glorify me."* Those who operate in God's deliverance and glorifying power keep their vows. They do not break them.

MY WIFE'S EUNUCHISTIC VOW!

My wife, Rita Momah, gave her life to Christ as a teenager. She got saved through the outreach ministry of the Full Gospel Business Men's Fellowship International (FGBMFI) in the early 1980's and became a fervent prayer and praise worship leader.

She relinquished positions in high school (including social prefect) because she did not want a position that may compromise her Christian values and ethics. She rose to the leadership of the student fellowship (Students Christian Movement and Gospel Youth Ministries International), and through these avenues experienced God to the hilt.

As she pursued God ardently, she wanted nothing to do with the cares of the world. She even made a "eunuchistic" vow stating to God that she will be dedicated to God and not marry for the rest of her life. She did this in sincere love for the Lord and when she got into college, maintained her eunuchistic vow.

In her second year of medical school, however, I met her while preaching to my classmates before the morning lecture. I had asked her if she was willing to sing as a prelude to my sermon, and amazingly she said yes.

Every other person I had asked prior to her had jettisoned my idea, as though it were a lunatic's idea and made me feel as though I were born "out of season." Rita was like an oasis in a desert and I began to align with her as a singer for my sermons.

In 1993, as a young and sturdy 20 year old medical student, God revealed her to me as my future wife. I did not, however, propose until after graduating from medical school seven years later. We were both leaders in the campus Christian community, and in order to maintain our integrity as a couple and in obedience to God's timing, delayed any real acquaintance till after graduation.

In 2003, we got married and it was only two years after we got married that she revealed she had made an eunuch's vow. I was stunned, and after some introspection and prayer, prayed for that vow to be broken over her life and for her full expression as a wife and mother.

God answered our prayer and as a family we are abounding physically, spiritually and materially. She has since learnt to make vows that are righteous, and avoid rash or impetuous decisions. Hallelujah

There is no pit so deep, that God's love is not deeper still!

…Betsie Ten Boom (1885-1944).

CHAPTER FORTY-FOUR

EXCESS

"Honor the LORD with thy substance, and with the first fruits of all thine increase: So shall thy barns be filled with plenty, and thy presses shall burst out with new wine" (Proverbs 3:9-10).

It is a covenant of excess that we have in the body of Christ. Christ came and became poor on the earth so that *"...though he was rich, yet for your sakes he became poor, that ye through his poverty might be rich"* (2 Corinthians 8:9).

To exemplify his commitment to excess, Jesus made a promise while here on earth. He said, *"I am the vine, ye are the branches: He that abideth in me, and I in him, the same bringeth forth much fruit: for without me ye can do nothing"* (John 15:5).

In the kingdom of God, excess is standard! In fact, Jesus said the mark of a disciple is the excess or much fruit they brought forth. In John 15:8, he said *"Herein is my Father glorified, that ye bear much fruit; so shall ye be my disciples."*

For example, in Matthew 14:15-21 Jesus touched a boy's brunch meal of five loaves and two fish, and fed upwards of ten thousand people with twelve baskets full of fish and bread left over.

In Joel 2:13-14, the prophet exclaims to Israel *"...rend your heart, and not your garments, and turn unto the LORD your God for he is gracious and merciful, slow to anger, and of great kindness, and repenteth him of the evil. Who knoweth if he will return and repent, and leave a blessing behind him."* The God of excess does not leave his people broken and busted but if they show adequate remorse he always leaves behind a blessing.

The God of the New Testament believer is not a God of scarcity, but a God of abundance. When He appeared to Isaiah in Isaiah 6:1, His *"... train filled the temple"* as He sat high and lifted up on the throne. God is characterized by excess, and a loyal church will be filled with His largess!

ABRAHAM: ACCESSING THE ABUNDANT GOD

Abraham is considered our patriarch in the Christian faith. According to Romans 4:16, because of his stellar principles of faith, he offered up Isaac *"...accounting that God was able to raise him up, even from the dead; from whence also he received him in a figure"* (Hebrews 11:19).

It was through faith that *"Abraham, when he was called to go out into a place which he should after receive for an inheritance, obeyed; and he went out, not knowing whither he went* (for) *by faith he sojourned in the land of promise, as in a strange country, dwelling in tabernacles with Isaac and Jacob, the heirs with him of the same promise: For he looked for a city which hath foundations, whose builder and maker is God"* (Hebrews 11:8-10).

Abraham's avenue to accessing the abundance of God was faith. He was *"...very rich in cattle, in silver, and in gold"* (Genesis 13:2) and through *"Christ* (who) *hath redeemed us from the curse of the law, being made a curse for us...* (the church has received) *the blessing of Abraham...on the Gentiles through Jesus Christ"* (Galatians 3:13-14).

Faith opens doors that are seemingly impossible. Even though a stranger in Gerar, Abraham believed God and rose to such pedestals that even generals and presidents of nations were intimidated by his wealth (see Genesis 21:22-23). The Bible says, *"the effectual fervent prayer of a righteous man availeth much"* (James 5:16), not little!

Abraham's life of excess was, however, paved with sacrificial obedience. His wealth was a divine reward for unalloyed loyalty and complete obedience to God's word. The Bible says in Psalm 112:1-3 *"Blessed is the man that feareth the LORD, that delighteth greatly in his commandments. His seed shall be mighty upon earth: the generation of the upright shall be blessed. Wealth and riches shall be in his house: and his righteousness endureth for ever."*

REPAIRING THE BREACH AND RESTORING THE PATHS TO DWELL IN!

The devil has made a breach on our modern day world. He has escalated poverty, worsened sicknesses, and made the gap between the haves' and have-nots' even wider. The loyalty legends of our time are those who stand with God to repair that breach and restore the paths to dwell in for others in society (see Isaiah 58:12).

The world is looking for saviors from the church, which is the modern day Mount Zion (see Hebrews 12:22)! In Obadiah 1:21, the Bible says *"...saviors shall come up on mount Zion to judge the mount of Esau; and the kingdom shall be the* LORD's.*"*

In these last days, God is raising up a church of saviors to repair the breach and restore the paths for humanity to dwell in. These paths are no ordinary paths, but *"...the way of holiness* (for) *the unclean shall not pass over it but it shall be for those: the wayfaring men, though fools,* (who) *shall not err therein. No lion shall be there, nor any ravenous beast shall go up thereon... but the redeemed shall walk there"* (Isaiah 35:8-9).

These paths consist of, not only purity, but also prosperity! There is a generation called to bring holiness and health, purity and power and wealth and wellness spiritually back to the body of Christ and it is this generation. Abraham showed that it is possible to be blessed and still be burning for the kingdom with passion.

These ones, who restore the paths to dwell in and repair the breach, don't "play dead" while everything around them is in danger but rather *"...loose the bands of wickedness,...undo the heavy burdens,...let the oppressed go free,...break every yoke,...deal thy bread to the hungry,...bring the poor that are cast out to thy house* (and) *when thou seest the naked, that thou cover him; and that thou hide not thyself from thine own flesh"* (Isaiah 58:6-7).

The outcome of such dangerous faith and powerful prayers is a life of excess. In Isaiah 58:11, the Bible says these ones *"...satisfy their souls in drought, and make fat thy bones:* (so that) *thou...be like a watered garden, and like a spring of water, whose waters fail not."*

THE GOD OF "TOO MUCH"

Mart green is the Oklahoma based billionaire and Chairman/chief executive of MARDEL and Hobby lobby group of companies. A born again Christian, he has been in the fore front of fulfilling the gospel's message by film, media and book format. He has single handedly sponsored crusades to the third world, produced films from a Christian viewpoint and supported causes that have made him a bundle of life for institutions like Oral Roberts University (ORU).

Through the Green family, the Obama administration's American Care Act (ACA) injunction to make all American employers comply with ACA's abortion laws, was overturned by the Supreme court of America1. They took on the greatest power in the world, and won!

As a result of this landmark judgment, several companies who were going against their conscience to prescribe abortion medications in order to comply with A.C.A were free to continue serving their community without an infraction on their conscience.

Today, this family owned companies - Hobby Lobby and MARDEL - have more than 600 branches worldwide with greater than four billion dollars in turnover annually. The Green family are faithful members of their local Assemblies of God Church, and fast upwards of thirty days in a year.

Their love for the Lord and their loyalty in promoting His "...*righteous cause...*" (Psalm 35:27) have marked them out as legends of their day. From a living room business, with a budget of $600.00, the Green family has expanded their business frontiers to all over the United States of America with outstanding success.

It takes loyalty, not labor,
to receive legendary status
in the kingdom of God!

CHAPTER FORTY FIVE

ENTHUSIASM

"I have set the LORD always before me: because he is at my right hand, I shall not be moved. Therefore my heart is glad, and my glory rejoiceth: my flesh also shall rest in hope" (Psalm 16:8-9).

The believer who stays loyal stays excited. In Psalm 16, David acknowledges the presence of God as his cause for glorying, rejoicing and resting in hope (see Psalm 16:8-9). The proof of loyalty to God and abiding in His presence is not sorrow, worry and loss of laughter. It is the fullness of joy.

In Roman 14:17, Paul says, *"...the kingdom of God is not meat and drink; but righteousness, and peace, and joy in the Holy Ghost."* It takes joy to operate in the kingdom, but it takes loyalty to the king to have true joy.

When God's kingdom is present, it makes all men rejoice! That is the reason, in Romans 14:18, Paul adds *"...he that in these things* (righteousness, peace and joy) *serveth Christ is acceptable to God, and approved of men."*

His Church is called to be *"...the joy of the whole earth..."* (Psalm 48:2) and the source of men's rejoicing. It (joy) is the harbinger of salvation, for*"...with joy shall ye draw water out of the wells of salvation"* (Isaiah 12:3).

Without joy Christianity is dull and dour. This enthusiasm or joy is however provoked by an unalloyed loyalty and holiness in the individual that stirs up God to fight on their behalf. In Nehemiah 8:10, the Bible says *"...this day is holy unto our LORD: neither be ye sorry; for the joy of the LORD is your strength."*

ABIGAIL: NABAL'S PLEASANTNESS, DAVID'S PRESERVATIVE!

Abigail is celebrated as the wife of King David, according to 2 Samuel 3:2. For years prior, however, she had suffered in pain and pity as the wife of Nabal. Though a wealthy man, Nabal was widely recognized as a "...*man (who) was churlish and evil in his doings...*" (1 Samuel 25:3). The interpretation of the words *churlish* and *evil* in the original Hebrew is cruel and affliction respectively. This nature was what Abigail had lived with for years without complaining.

The Bible describes her as "...*a woman of good understanding, and of a beautiful countenance...*" (1 Samuel 25:3). In spite of her adversity and oppressive home surroundings, she maintained a pleasant visage that attracted people to her and her husband. She had an enthusiastic personality, buoyed by a sense of loyalty to God, her husband and family.

When Nabal railed at David's men for asking for some sheep as fair compensation for protecting his sheep (1 Samuel 25:14-15), Abigail stood up to defend his foolishness and imperfect disposition to strangers (see 1 Samuel 25:23-31). Abigail was Nabal's pleasantness. She enthusiastically pleaded with David for Nabal, and after much pleading David replied saying "...*I have hearkened to thy voice, and have accepted thy person*" (1 Samuel 25:35).

Just as she was Nabal's pleasantness, Abigail was also David's preservative. She stopped David from shedding unnecessary blood. After Nabal fell dead from a sudden stroke in 1 Samuel 25:39, David asked for her hand in marriage. Abigail had never betrayed her covenant of marriage to Nabal, notwithstanding his incorrigibility. It was this loyalty that made her a source of enthusiasm to thousands around her. She was not a fair-weather friend or sleek spouse who stood only for the good times, but she fulfilled her vows as unto the Lord.

Even as David's wife, Abigail remained loyal to the crown. Despite the fact that she was David's senior most wife (see 1 Samuel 25:39), she never tried to enthrone her son born to David – Daniel (see 1 Chronicles 3:1) – as the heir to the throne of David. She never complained when Daniel's younger siblings – Absalom and Adonijah – attempted to usurp the throne (2 Samuel 12:15 and 1 Kings 1:5-9), but remained loyal to the palace as a silent supporter of King David. She described herself as David's "*...handmaid* (called to) *be a servant to wash the feet of the servants of my lord*" (1 Samuel 25:41), even though she was a queen. Such loyalty cannot but spur enthusiasm!

LOYALTY: A RECIPE FOR EXCITEMENT

Too many believers lose their passion for living by consistently changing their "loyalty quotient." Rather than stay loyal to the leading of the Holy Spirit, they innovate falsely and, as a result, lose their inspiration from the Holy Spirit that births excitement (see).

Elihu, in Job 32:18-20, said, "*...the spirit within me constraineth me. Behold, my belly is as wine which hath no vent; it is ready to burst like new bottles. I will speak, that I may be refreshed....*"

Until a believer stays loyal to the Holy Spirit, he or she cannot be refreshed spiritually! There must be spiritual influence to birth inspiration spiritually, physically and emotionally. In Job 32:8, Elihu says "*...there is a spirit in man: and the inspiration of the Almighty giveth them understanding.*"

Gideon was living a dull, dour and despondent existence (Judges 6:5-15), until he broke free from the cacophony of idols in his father's house (Judges 6:25-29). He exchanged fear for faith and emptiness for excitement by remaining loyal to God (Judges 7:2-7), notwithstanding the odds.

The panacea to a lackadaisical existence in Christ is loyalty. Those who hold on to the horns of the altar are those who stay excited and enthusiastic in life. In Isaiah 64:7, the prophet said, "*...there is none that calleth upon thy name, that stirreth up himself to take hold of thee....*"

If a believer fails to take hold of God in loyal living, he or she cannot stir up the gift of God in them. These *stirred-up* ones are the enthusiastic believers who abolish a dour and dull Christian existence. They live the power of a passionate life as a result of their unalloyed loyalty to God.

JESSE DUPLANTIS: PROPHET OF JOY TO HIS GENERATION

Dr. Jesse Duplantis (1949 -) is an apostle of joy to the nations. He epitomizes Christ's admonition to believers to be "*...of good cheer; (for) I have overcome the world,*" (John 16:33).

Jesse Duplantis got born-again listening to Billy Graham, in a Philadelphia bathroom in 1974, and started full time ministry in 1976. he is the president of Jesse Duplantis Ministries (JDM) and founder of Covenant Church New Orleans, Louisiana USA.

These ministries have traversed the nations with a global Television ministry and impacted millions of people in several ministry crusades and evangelistic campaigns. He started as a youth evangelist, and has brought men and women from across international and denominational lines to the knowledge of Christ.

Prior to Jesse Duplantis ministry, ministers were accustomed to keeping dour demeanors and among Christian leaders they seemed to see the work of the Lord as a burden and not a blessing. The joy of the Lord had become a job for the Lord, and these ministers resonated misery, mechanical worship and a mundane ministry.

Jesse Duplantis, however, has continued to be a breath of fresh air in ministry. His ministry has cross-cultural, trans-generational and even inter-denominational appeal because of its inspirational and joy giving attitude.

Notwithstanding circumstances, like Katrina, sickness or recession, Jesse Duplantis has continued to play the joy card in loyalty to the word of God. He believes, like Paul, to *"Rejoice in the Lord always: and again I say, Rejoice"* (Philippians 4:4).

In a world assaulted by daily media blitz highlighting doom, danger and disaster, Jesse Duplantis has brought the good news of the gospel with hope and joy that is contagious, if not downright Christian!

PART VIII

TOOLS FOR LOYALTY

- GUARD YOUR SPIRIT
- GRACE FOR SUCCESS
- GRIT OF A SOLDIER
- GATHER FOR STRENGTH
- GIVING IN SIMPLICITY
- GREATNESS OF THE SCRIPTURES
- GLORY FOR THE SUPERNATURAL

*If you take care of
the anointing within,
God will take care of
the attacks without!*

– Shane Warren
(Lead Pastor the Assembly
West Monroe Louisiana)

Chapter Forty Six

Guard Your Spirit

"...the Lord, the God of Israel, saith that he hateth putting away: for one covereth violence with his garment, saith the Lord of hosts: therefore take heed to your spirit, that ye deal not treacherously" (Malachi 2:16).

Those who guard their hearts increase in loyalty! The wise man said in Proverbs 4:23, *"Keep thy heart with all diligence; for out of it are the issues of life."* These issues of life connote deliverance, prosperity and security, but only a guarded heart can take advantage.

Paul told his protégé, Timothy, *"Take heed unto thyself, and unto the doctrine; continue in them: for in doing this thou shalt both save thyself, and them that hear thee"* (1 Timothy 4:16). Those who bring salvation to their hearers take heed, first and foremost, to themselves by guarding their spirit and continuing in the Word of God.

An unguarded spirit is like a city without walls. It can be extremely vulnerable and penetrated at will by all and sundry, as a result. In Proverbs 25:28, the wise man said *"He that hath no rule over his own spirit is like a city that is broken down, and without walls."*

The writer of Malachi put the blame of disloyalty between spouses to their not guarding their spirit. In Malachi 2:14-15, the Bible says *"...the Lord hath been witness between thee and the wife of thy youth, against whom thou hast dealt treacherously: yet is she thy companion, and the wife of thy covenant....Therefore take heed to your spirit, and let none deal treacherously against the wife of his youth."*

An unguarded spirit will be run over by enemy fire, but a life on guard continually will be delivered. In 2 Corinthians 2:11, Paul says *"Lest Satan should get an advantage of us: for we are not ignorant of his devices,"* and Proverbs 22:3 and 27:12 adds *"A prudent man foreseeth the evil, and hideth himself: but the simple pass on, and are punished."*

THE TRAGEDY OF SELF-DECEPTION!

An unguarded spirit is a loose canon. It doesn't guard or garrison itself but allows all-comers to enter and dwell within. Worst of all, a loose spirit deceives itself. In Galatians 6:3, the Bible says *"...if a man think himself to be something, when he is nothing, he deceiveth himself."* Those who deceive themselves are full of pride and are empty inside. These are those who fail to hear God's word and do it!

Elder James in James 1:22-25 prays that believers *"...be ye doers of the word, and not hearers only, deceiving your own selves for if any be a hearer of the word, and not a doer, he is like unto a man beholding his natural face in a glass: For he beholdeth himself, and goeth his way, and straightway forgetteth what manner of man he was."*

The person who does not understand or know him-or herself is a vagrant spirit. Such individuals live life out of course and end tragically. According to the Psalmist, *"they know not, neither will they understand; they walk on in darkness: all the foundations of the earth are out of course...* (and so) *ye shall die like men, and fall like one of the princes"* (Psalm 82:5,7).

It is one thing to deceive another person, but when a person deceives him or herself it is a tragedy of monumental proportions. God's will for His Church is not to be cursed, but to be blessed. He said, in James 1:25, *"But whoso looketh into the perfect law of liberty, and continueth therein, he being not a forgetful hearer, but a doer of the work, this man shall be blessed in his deed."*

Failure to keep guard over one's spirit is tantamount to deceiving oneself and leads to a cursed existence. Apostle Paul, in 2 Corinthians 13:5, says, *"Examine yourselves, whether ye be in the faith; prove your own selves. Know ye not your own selves, how that Jesus Christ is in you, except ye be reprobates?"*

BALAAM: A CASE OF INNOCUOS INSANITY

When the Bible describes a man as having the "madness of the prophet" because of his actions, it illustrates the impracticability of that man's actions. Balaam, though wearing the toga and having the paraphernalia of a prophet, acted more as a parasite!

In 2 Peter 2:15-17, the Bible describes him thus: it says *"which have forsaken the right way, and are gone astray, following the way of Balaam the son of Bosor, who loved the wages of unrighteousness; But was rebuked for his iniquity: the dumb ass speaking with man's voice forbad the madness of the prophet. These are wells without water, clouds that are carried with a tempest; to whom the mist of darkness is reserved for ever."*

Balaam's actions did not align with his words. He eulogized God greatly (Numbers 22:18) but exploited the weakness of the Israelites for the Midianite women to introduce sin and corruption in their camp. In Revelation 2:14, Jesus tells the Church in Pergamos, *"But I have a few things against thee, because thou hast there them that hold the doctrine of Balaam,who taught Balac to cast a stumbling block before the children of Israel, to eat things sacrificed unto idols, and to commit fornication."*

Though he began as a loyalty buff, Balaam's legacy was tainted by avarice, corruption and desire for filthy lucre. His outer clout and coverings were a camouflage for his inner-soul struggles that eventually eclipsed an otherwise envious destiny. He failed at the footsteps of success because he failed to guard his spirit from the vituperations of the flesh. As a result, he lives on today in perfidy instead of praise.

THE POWER OF A MADE UP MIND

Masiyiwa Strive (1961 -) is the founder and president of Econet wireless, a multinational telecommunications company with offices in Nigeria, New Zealand, England, Canada, Zimbabwe, South Africa and South America. It was founded in 1994, after Masiyiwa - then a recent graduate of the University of Wales -, left the security of his job with the nationalized telecommunications company to start his own company.

His vision was to develop the first wireless network in Zimbabwe. Unfortunately, his former employers balked at the idea and ensured the government of the day never licensed Econet. Rather, a state formed company, with foreign technical partners, was given the first wireless license in Zimbabwe.

Rather than be discouraged, Masiyiwa persisted with his vision. As a devout Christian, Masiyiwa was opposed to paying bribes and kickbacks to government officials. He decided to pursue his case through the courts. He took the government to the Supreme Court of Zimbabwe and after a four-year protracted battle that nearly bankrupted Masiyiwa, Econet finally won. A license to provide cell phone service in Zimbabwe was given to them, as the court declared that the government monopoly on telecommunications had violated the constitution's guarantee of free speech. Econet's first cell phone subscriber was connected to the new network in 1998.

While Masiyiwa waited to gain the government's approval for operations in Zimbabwe, he was able to start a cell phone network in neighboring Botswana. Econet Wireless Holdings then established a presence in over 15 countries, including other African nations, New Zealand, and the United Kingdom. The company also diversified into satellite communications, fixed-line telephone services, and Internet service.

Since then Econet has increased in leaps and bounds. Masiyiwa Strive has a majority stake in Econet and is currently estimated to be worth over $1.4 billion. Masiyiwa attributed his success in part to the ethical integrity he developed through the devotional practice of reading the Bible for an hour every morning. He served on the boards of such international development agencies as the Southern African Enterprise Development Fund and the Rockefeller Foundation.

In line with its Christian-based vision and mission, Econet has a broad strategy for social and community investment, and through these programs, Econet supports a diverse range of charitable causes including children orphaned by AIDS/HIV, religious and church organizations, as well as an annual scholarship program that provides financial assistance. Masiyiwa and his wife, Tsitsi, currently have over 30,000 orphans on their scholarships for school enrollment from elementary to University education.

His friends, including Norman Nyazema the erstwhile chairman of Econet Wireless Zimbabwe, attest to Masiyiwa's sense of purpose. He said, in an interview with the Financial Mail, that *"Strive is driven by focus,*

*determination and passion and for him failure is not an option, no matter
how many obstacles are thrown in his way."*

A classical case in point is when he bought the majority shares of the
dominant opposition Newspaper. Its contents irked the government of
Robert Mugabe and it was shut down for several years but yet Masiyiwa
stuck with his investment. Today, this newspaper - the *Daily News*
Newspaper - is fully operational and redefining newspaper publications
in Zimbabwe.

Grace is not for Minnows,
but for Masters!

CHAPTER FORTY SEVEN

GRACE FOR SUCCESS

"Ye therefore, beloved, seeing ye know these things before, beware lest ye also, being led away with the error of the wicked, fall from your own stedfastness. But grow in grace, and in the knowledge of our Lord and Savior Jesus Christ..." (2 Peter 3:17-18).

Grace means *charis* in the Greek. It is defined as divine enablement or influence on a believer's heart. Where there is grace, dominion and triumph are inevitable! Grace provokes divine triumph and an unfailing never-say-die mentality. It stirs up an incorrigibly unconquerable spirit that never stops regardless of how intimidating the circumstances may be.

When Zerubbabel looked incapable of finishing the temple in his lifetime, the word of the Lord came to him saying *"...Not by might, nor by power, but by my spirit, saith the LORD of hosts. Who art thou, O great mountain? before Zerubbabel thou shalt become a plain: and he shall bring forth the headstone thereof with shoutings, crying, Grace, grace unto it. Moreover the word of the LORD came unto me, saying, the hands of Zerubbabel have laid the foundation of this house; his hands shall also finish it;..."* (Zechariah 4:6-9).

That temple was eventually rebuilt (see Ezra 6:15), and its eventual completion was not a product of human chances, connections or cash but divine *Charis* or grace. True grace is independent on human effort, but fully dependent on God's influence and will. When grace is available, the believer does not just pontificate. Rather, they become proof-producers of the God-kind of evidence.

In 2 Corinthians 9:8,11, Apostle Paul speaking by the Spirit of

God says, "*...God is able to make all grace abound toward you; that ye, always having all sufficiency in all things, may abound to every good work... Being enriched in every thing to all bountifulness, which causeth through us thanksgivings unto God.*"

If they don't walk in His grace, however, they are discarded and abandoned to destruction by the climes of the enemy. In Hebrews 12:15, believers are adjured to "(look) *diligently lest any man fail of the grace of God* (and) *any root of bitterness springing up trouble you, and thereby many be defiled.*" A lack of grace not only troubles one's destiny. It can also destroy one's progeny and all that come in contact with such a one.

GRACE FOR GREATNESS

Nehemiah was facing great odds as he stood before King Artaxerxes in Nehemiah 2. He had just been informed about the broken down walls of Jerusalem, and his sad countenance attracted the attention of the King.

Grace, however, came to his rescue. In Nehemiah 2:18, the Bible says Nehemiah told "*... them of the hand of my God which was good upon me; as also the king's words that he had spoken unto me. And they said, Let us rise up and build. So they strengthened their hands for this good work.*"

The aphorism "hand of God" represents the grace and power of God upon a man's or woman's life. In 1 Kings 18:46, the Bible says, "*the hand of the LORD was on Elijah; and he girded up his loins, and ran before Ahab to the entrance of Jezreel.*"

Grace makes the impossible possible. When the hand of God came upon Elijah, he outran the chariots of King Ahab. When the hand of the Lord came upon Nehemiah, the King gave him more than he needed. Grace makes for greatness, no matter the odds. It turns situations that went awry into abundance and sets the captives free.

When the apostles were being intimidated and persecuted by the Sanhedrin and Roman authorities, the Bible says "*...with great power gave the apostles witness of the resurrection of the Lord Jesus: and great grace was upon them all. Neither was there any among them that lacked...*" (Acts 4:33-34).

Believers who have grown in success and steadfastness started with the grace of God. In 2 Peter 3:17-18, Apostle Peter says "*...beloved seeing* *ye know these things before, beware lest ye also, being led away with the error of the wicked, fall from your own stedfastness. But grow in grace, and in the knowledge of our Lord and Savior Jesus Christ.*" God's grace unlocks an uncanny and unwavering loyalty that money, men or material possessions can't overthrow.

GRACE TO REIGN

Those who reign in life have definitely tasted of the grace of God. In Romans 5:17, Apostle Paul asserts "*...if by one man's offence death reigned by one; much more they which* **receive abundance of grace and of the gift of righteousness shall reign in life by one, Jesus Christ**" (emphasis added).

In the kingdom of God, there are no minnows but only masters because of the grace of God. Those who rise to become loyalty legends, however, must first identify their help is from God and not man (see Jeremiah 17:5-8).

In Hebrews 13:5-7, this power of God's grace to make you loyal to the end is illustrated. It says, "*Let your conversation be without covetousness; and be content with such things as ye have: for he hath said, I will never leave thee, nor forsake thee. So that we may boldly say,* **The Lord is my helper, and I will not fear what man shall do unto me. Remember them which have the rule over you, who have spoken unto you the word of God: whose faith follow,** *considering the end of their conversation*" (emphasis added).

The power to overcome and defeat every enemy starts with God's help otherwise called the grace of God. In Revelation 1:4-6, Elder John prays for the Church saying, "**Grace be unto you,** *and peace, from him which is, and which was, and which is to come; and from the seven Spirits which are before his throne; And from Jesus Christ, who is the faithful witness, and the first begotten of the dead, and the prince of the kings of the earth. Unto him that loved us, and washed us from our sins in his own blood, and hath* **made us kings and priests unto God** *and his Father;...*" (emphasis added).

God has given us grace to reign and operate in divine dominion here on earth. Failure to walk in it is tantamount to denying or frustrating the grace of God He has given us. Apostle Paul said in Galatians 2:20-21, "*I am crucified with Christ: nevertheless I live; yet not I, but Christ liveth in me: and the life which I now live in the flesh I live by the faith of the Son of*

*God, who loved me, and gave himself for me. **I do not frustrate the grace of God:**....*" (emphasis added).

A believer who wants to live a life of loyalty must let grace work in him or her instead of frustrating it through carnal living. According to Revelation 11:15-17, "*The kingdoms of this world are become the kingdoms of our Lord, and of his Christ; and he shall reign for ever and ever... because thou hast taken to thee thy great power, and hast reigned.*" God has given the church power to reign. All that is required is for the church, like Jesus, to take that power and to rule and reign with it!

THE THEORY OF THEOCRACY

In 1991, I prayed one of the most dangerous prayers ever to come out of my mouth. I asked God, as the sons of Zebedee and their mother did in Matthew 20:21-22, to grant me sit at His right hand even if it means drinking of the cup of suffering He once drank from.

I prayed that prayer of James and John - that made them martyrs and core-loyalists for the Kingdom (see Acts 12:2 and Revelation 1:9 respectively) -, and everything turned around overnight.

I saw astronomical growth spiritually, increased revelation from God's word, whole-hearted worship, excited evangelism and passionate prayers, but at the same time I felt opposition such as never before.

I experienced rejection and revulsion from erstwhile friends and family, failure at exams I, otherwise, normally would have passed and became beleaguered with health issues from a prolonged period of fasting while in school.

In the throes of these crises, however, I developed an intimacy with God that I had never had before. I learned to hear His voice, discern his Spirit and taste His power. I moved from mediocrity to mastery, from waywardness to wisdom, from foolishness to faith and from pallid to powerful. Every day was a fresh encounter with God and God's grace was multiplied upon my life.

Looking back now, I see God was preparing me through those trials and temptations for the future He had for me in ministry and medicine. These encounters were not designed to break me, but to make me strong as I leaned more and more on His ever-sufficient grace.

You don't need to make the devil smaller by making Jesus bigger!

- Dr. Jesse Duplantis (Jesse Duplantis Ministries Destreham, Louisiana USA)

GRIT OF A SOLDIER

"There be three things which go well, yea, four are comely in going: A lion which is strongest among beasts, and turneth not away for any; A greyhound; an he goat also; and a king, against whom there is no rising up" (Proverbs 30:29-31).

Grit is defined by the Webster's English Dictionary as unyielding courage. It represents undaunted courage in the face of challenging and near-impossible circumstances. True grit is found in the heart of a lion that *"...turns not away for any..."* (Proverbs 30:30) and produces a loyalty that makes *"...kings against whom there is no rising up"* (Proverbs 30:31).

The life that goes well and becomes a loyalty legend to his or her generation is first born in the heart of individuals who refused to cower. These ones conquer their enemies through faith and patience. In Hebrews 6:12, the writer of the book of Hebrews advises the church *"That ye be not slothful, but followers of them who through faith and patience inherit the promises."*

Nobody and nothing can stop a man or woman with the heart of a lion! This kind of believer fears only God and will not back down to or for anyone else. In 2 Timothy 1:6-7, Paul says, *"Wherefore I put thee in remembrance that thou stir up the gift of God, which is in thee by the putting on of my hands. For God hath not given us the spirit of fear; but of power, and of love, and of a sound mind."*

It takes a heart of courage to birth a life of vision and loyalty to the call of God. If there is no courage, the gift will lie fallow and die unexplored.

When the spirit of faith dissolves fear and when the spirit of dominion overcomes doubt, the gift of God empowering the individual is released to touch their world.

MUSTARD SEED FAITH THAT MOVES MOUNTAINS

Jesus told his disciples in Mark 11:22-23 "*...Have faith in God. For verily I say unto you, That whosoever shall say unto this mountain, Be thou removed, and be thou cast into the sea; and shall not doubt in his heart, but shall believe that those things which he saith shall come to pass; he shall have whatsoever he saith*" (Mark 11:22-23).

He had spoken to the fig tree because it had told him in no uncertain terms, according to Mark 11:14, that it was impossible for him to get any food from it. The Lord Jesus replied it saying "*...No man eat fruit of thee hereafter for ever...*" (Mark 11:14) and within 24 hours his words were reality.

The Bible says in Mark 11:20, "*...the fig tree dried up from the roots and Peter calling to remembrance saith unto him, Master, behold, the fig tree which thou cursedst is withered away.*" Those who do not become dissuaded or discouraged by their opposition speak to their mountains, not about them. They conquer their enemies with a faith that speaks (2 Corinthians 4:13), instead of one that is shuttered or cowers in its midst.

The secret to the faith that moves mountains is not its quantity but its quality. Jesus said in Matthew 17:20, "*If ye have faith as a grain of mustard seed, ye shall say unto this mountain, Remove hence to yonder place; and it shall remove; and nothing shall be impossible unto you.*"

The mustard seed is the smallest of all seeds, but faith of its size has the courage and quality of conviction that makes God available to it! The words of Jesus saying "*...Have faith in God...*" (Mark 11:22) in the original Greek is interpreted "Have the faith of God." Until the church stops settling for a cheap imitation of the God-kind of faith, the "mountains" bedeviling her existence will continue.

BATHSHEBA: SPINELESS SEDUCER OR SCHEMING SPIRIT?

Bathsheba succumbed to King David's invitation to an illicit affair in the palace, either out of fear or in order to obtain favor from the King. She was married to Uriah the Hittite, who was one of David's mighty men (see 2 Samuel 23:39), and exhibited a lack of grit when faced with betraying her erstwhile faithful husband.

Rather than stand up for her God-ordained relationship, she scampered into bed with David and cried "crocodile" tears when her husband died at the war front (see 2 Samuel 11:26). At the death of her first child, King David "...*comforted Bathsheba his wife, and went in unto her, and lay with her: and she bare a son, and he called his name Solomon...*" (2 Samuel 12:24).

Bathsheba lost her sense of loyalty as a result of her lack of grit. She lacked courage to stand up to anyone, and as a result she fell for anything that came against her. For example, after Solomon had become King in, she retorted again to fear when faced with opposition.

In 1 Kings 2:13 she asked Adonijah, an erstwhile competitor for the throne with her son, "...*Comest thou peaceably? And he said, Peaceably.*" Even though the king's mother, she was still afraid of Adonijah, and out of fear asked King Solomon that "...*Abishag the Shunammite be given to Adonijah thy brother to wife...*" (1 Kings 2:21).

Her lack of spiritual strength cost her first marriage and, on this occasion, nearly cost Solomon his throne (see 1 Kings 2:22). People who are disloyal don't have principles or philosophies. Rather, they pander to people's whims and caprices. In 1 John 4:18, the Bible says "...*perfect love casteth out fear: because fear hath torment. He that feareth is not made perfect in love.*"

Bathsheba's legacy was eclipsed by fear of man. Her disloyalty to husband and son were a result of her disenchantment and disaffection emotionally. She was moved by fear. As a result, she lost relevance in palace affairs. After her advice to King Solomon failed, in I Kings 2:21, she was relegated in the scheme of things and never mentioned again in Solomon's reign.

Bathsheba's inability to eliminate the fear of man, cost her the influence she could have exerted on King Solomon when he became beleaguered with foreign wives, had she attained the fear of God. Her lack of grit in the spiritual eventually manifested in her disloyalty in the secular. This lack of influence on Solomon, may have eventually dovetailed his reign and cost Bathsheba a progeny of Kings and Queens that could have outlived her.

DAVID WILKERSON: GOD'S AGENT OF CHANGE

David Wilkerson (1931-2011) was a youth pastor in rural Pennsylvania when God called him to the inner city life of New York City. He had seen an artist's profile of six kids, who belonged to a gang called the dragons, and were being sentenced to prison for the murder of a fifteen year old poliomyelitis patient.

Their faces expressed despondency, hopeless, and dismay and David felt the Lord telling him to leave the comfort of his pastorate in rural Pennsylvania to set up a new ministry base in Brooklyn, New York.

That was in 1958, and nearly fifty years later Teen Challenge, which David formed on arriving Brooklyn New York City, is a global household name. It has the highest rate of success for recovering addicts staying sober and drug-free (97%), and has touched lives around the globe. Ex-residents include Nicky Cruz, Steve Hill, etc). The teen challenge organization, now an affiliate of the Assemblies of God, has a presence in over 1,000 locations, offices in over 77 countries of the world, with more than 173 residential programs and 241 centers in the USA.

David Wilkerson, in 1971, re-located to Texas and started another organization called world challenge designed to bring the ministry of the word of God to the world. This arm of the ministry printed world-wide tracts and teachings that were shipped all around the world, and organized teen-themed crusades designed to reach the lost with the saving gospel of the Lord Jesus Christ.

In 1986, while walking down Time Square, after a street rally to reach the lost of New York City, God directed David to start a Church in downtown New York City. They bought out the famous Mark Hellinger cinema hall, after initially using rented facilities, and the Times Square Church was born. It encompassed thousands of New Yorkers' from over a hundred different nations and from this ministry church base missions, ministers' conferences and humanitarian aid were given.

After more than fifty years of marriage and ministry, the curtains were drawn on this General of the faith's life as he travelled on the roads of Texas. He was killed in a head-on collision and died instantly. His wife, though injured in the car crash, died nine months later from complications arising from cancer and not the car crash.. David Wilkerson's legacy, however, continues today in the thousands of men and women whose lives have been forever changed through the ministries he founded. As stated in a tribute by Nicky Cruz, at his death "David Wilkerson was like somebody who was not only my spiritual father, but much more than that is gone."

Environment determines one's Elements in life!

CHAPTER FORTY NINE

GATHER FOR STRENGTH

"They go from strength to strength, every one of them in Zion appeareth before God" (Psalm 84:7).

There is no loyalty legend who does not gather in faith with the saints. In the day when God makes up His jewels (Malachi 3:17) or legends, He gathers them *"...that feared the LORD (AND) spake often one to another: (so that) the LORD hearkened, and heard it, and a book of remembrance was written before him for them that feared the LORD, and that thought upon his name"* (Malachi 3:16).

Two categories of believers will characterize the last days' church: those who gather for strength and those who don't. In Hebrews 10:24-25, the Bible says, *"...let us consider one another to provoke unto love and to good works: Not forsaking the assembling of ourselves together, as the manner of some is; but exhorting one another: and so much the more, as ye see the day approaching."*

Those who start fast go alone, but those who last long go together. Those who gather for strength during life's journey become loyalty legends. They are those who *"...hold fast the profession of our faith without wavering..."* (Hebrews 10:23). They are those *"...planted in the house of the Lord (and) who) flourish in the courts of our God"* (Psalm 92:12).

True loyalty legends sharpen one another as *"iron sharpeneth iron; so a man sharpeneth the countenance of his friend"* (Proverbs 27:17). They are not isolationists, but integrationists who build bridges instead of walls! These ones don't forsake the gathering of the saints together but, rather build

266

each other up. In Romans 14:7-8, Paul declares that *"…none of us liveth to himself, and no man dieth to himself. For whether we live, we live unto the Lord; and whether we die, we die unto the Lord: whether we live therefore, or die, we are the Lord's."*

BUILDING BLOCKS FOR BREAKTHROUGH

The Bible calls the Church *"…lively stones…built up* (as) *a spiritual house…to offer up spiritual sacrifices, acceptable to God by Jesus Christ"* (1 Peter 2:5). Just as dissimilar blocks or stones in structure or content produce formidable infrastructure, so does diversity in the body of Christ guarantee a breakthrough.

The format of the New Testament church is unity in diversity. In 1 Corinthians 12:6-7 the Bible says, *"…there are diversities of operations, but it is the same God which worketh all in all. But the manifestation of the Spirit is given to every man to profit withal."*

The outcome of this unity in diversity is seamless splendor. 1 Corinthians 14:26 says, *"…when ye come together, every one of you hath a psalm, hath a doctrine, hath a tongue, hath a revelation, hath an interpretation. Let all things be done unto edifying."* It is the diversity of the gifts of the Spirit that guarantees Christians breakthrough.

The power of a spiritual gathering is in its spiritual edification. In Psalm 133:1-3, the Bible says "Behold, *how good and how pleasant it is for brethren to dwell together in unity! It is like the precious ointment upon the head, that ran down upon the beard, even Aaron's beard: that went down to the skirts of his garments; As the dew of Hermon, and as the dew that descended upon the mountains of Zion: for there the* LORD *commanded the blessing, even life for evermore."*

Jesus sent out the disciples two by two by Jesus, in Luke 10:1, for fellowship and fruitfulness. The wise man said in Ecclesiastes 4:9-12, *"Two are better than one; because they have a good reward for their labor. For if they fall, the one will lift up his fellow: but woe to him that is alone when he falleth; for he hath not another to help him up. Again, if two lie together, then they have heat: but how can one be warm alone? And if one prevail against him, two shall withstand him; and a threefold cord is not quickly broken."*

In the Old Testament, the warrior was considered more potent when with another than when alone. Deuteronomy 32:30 says, "…*one chase a thousand, and two put ten thousand to flight….*" True legends are not "lone-rangers" but team players who incorporate God's philosophy into their team. Abraham fought and took back all the conquered properties and people of Sodom and Gomorrah because "*Mamre the Amorite, brother of Eshcol, and brother of Aner…were confederate with Abram*" (Genesis 14:13).

In the New Testament, Paul asserts by the Spirit of God, "*I have planted, Apollos watered; but God gave the increase. So then neither is he that planteth any thing, neither he that watereth; but God that giveth the increase. Now he that planteth and he that watereth are one: and every man shall receive his own reward according to his own labor. For we are laborers together with God…*" (1 Corinthians 3:6-9).

God in the midst of His church sanctifies and supplies increase if the Church remains one. Nothing moves the hand of God as quickly as the unity of the brethren. In John 17:21-23, Jesus Christ prayed, "*That they all may be one; as thou, Father, art in me, and I in thee, that they also may be one in us: that the world may believe that thou hast sent me. And the glory which thou gavest me I have given them; that they may be one, even as we are one: I in them, and thou in me, that they may be made perfect in one….*"

CONNECTION FOR CONSECRATION

When God's people mix themselves with the multitude, strength is not available. He said, in Hosea 7:7-9, "*…all their kings are fallen: there is none among them that calleth unto me. Ephraim, he hath mixed himself among the people; Ephraim is a cake not turned. Strangers have devoured his strength, and he knoweth it not….*"

Strength is symbolic of loyalty legends, but it manifests through right relationships. Those who mix themselves with the wrong people lose their strength, but those who are rightly connected are consecrated.

In Jeremiah 12:8-9, God said the idolatrous nation of Israel who "*…crieth out against me: therefore have I hated it. Mine heritage is unto me as a speckled bird, the birds round about are against her; come ye, assemble all the beasts of the field, come to devour.*"

The word *speckled* as utilized in Jeremiah 12:8-9 means variegated or varied shapes, sizes and colors. It represents different sets of beliefs and standards. These people had no iota of commitment or loyalty whatsoever. It was only a matter of their vice, and not what God valued, that mattered. Such individuals "...have *dealt treacherously...;*(and so) *believe them not, though they speak fair words unto thee*" (Jeremiah 12:6).

The church that connects spiritually grows together in consecration and loyalty! In Colossians 2:19, Paul described "...*the Head, from which all the body by joints and bands having nourishment ministered, and knit together, increaseth with the increase of God*" as the secret to the supernatural.

The united church is the undefeatable church. It is the church that conquers territories and broods no opposition. As God said about the people of Babel, "*Behold, the people is one, and they have all one language; and this they begin to do: and now nothing will be restrained from them, which they have imagined to do*" (Genesis 11:6).

BETTY BAXTER: GOD'S HAND MAIDEN FOR MIRACLES!

Betty Baxter (1927 -) was brought up in a Christian home in Minneapolis, Minnesota. Ever since she was a child, she had known nothing but pain. She suffered from severe scoliosis, which had crippled her to the point of incapacitation.

After giving her life to Jesus, she understood that the will of God was to heal, not hurt; to deliver, not destroy. Without bitterness, grudging, or envy, she waited devotedly for God's healing stream.

One day, while in a coma, Jesus appeared to her and told her he would heal her on the first day of autumn at 3pm. She asked her mother to buy her a blue dress and white shoes for the occasion. Her mother told her God had given her the same date and time for her healing. Their expectation was pumped, and they waited earnestly.

The day Jesus healed her, Betty stood up straight and, for the first time, stood taller than her three-year-old brother. There was no scar or surgical incision. In less than a second, she was straightened by the power of God.

Betty's parents, siblings and neighbors witnessed the miracle. The local metropolitan newspaper reported the story. Betty went on to become a healing evangelist alongside Oral Roberts, sharing her testimony at his crusades. She functioned in the office of an evangelist, and retired in 2003 from active preaching after a visit to California.

Betty Baxter's story has brought thousands, if not millions, to the cross of Jesus Christ and reawakened the power of devotion in capturing Jesus' attention.

Those who stoop to worship mammon will stand to lose what matters most in life!

CHAPTER FIFTY

GIVING WITH SIMPLICITY

*"Having then gifts differing according to the grace that is given to us, whether prophecy, let us prophesy according to the proportion of faith;… Or he that exhorteth, on exhortation: **he that giveth, let him do it with simplicity**;…"* (Romans 12:6,8).

The word of God is sacrosanct on the doctrine of giving to release increase; Genesis 8:22 says *"While the earth remaineth, seedtime and harvest, and cold and heat, and summer and winter, and day and night shall not cease."* It is a universal law that will last as long as the earth remains. The presence of alternate seasons, that the Western Hemisphere is currently experiencing confirms the veracity of seed and harvest. The Lord of the harvest is our Master - the Lord Jesus Christ. Only He can bequeath to you increase from what you have sown.

2 Corinthians 9:6 says *"He which soweth sparingly shall reap also sparingly; and he which soweth bountifully shall reap also bountifully."* The secret to an abundant harvest with sufficiency in all things is sowing abundantly; for with the measure you give so will you receive. The Israelites in Haggai vividly demonstrate the result of not giving according to the increase a person receives. Haggai 1:9 says *"Ye looked for much, and, lo it came to little; and when ye brought it home, I did blow upon it. Why? saith the LORD of hosts. Because of mine house that is waste, and ye run every man unto his own house"*.

Nothing changes what is in your hand faster than placing it in God's hand. The Bible says in Proverbs 19:17, that *"He that hath pity upon the poor lendeth unto the LORD; and that which he hath given will he pay him again".* There is a credit rating in heaven and if your credit ratings are positive you can rest assured that God will not watch you in need without opening the resources of heaven to meet that need.

The proof of your faithfulness in giving is a reflection of your loyalty to God and His kingdom. The Lord Jesus told his disciples, *"if therefore ye have not been faithful in the unrighteous mammon, who will commit to your trust the true riches?"* (Luke 16:11). In a nutshell, Jesus was stating that those who fail to be faithful with money cannot be loyal to anything or anyone of greater value.

THE POWER OF THE TITHE

Money is a great servant but a poor master! It mirrors what your soul prioritizes and is a reflection of your value system. In Luke 12:33-34, Jesus says *"Sell that ye have, and give alms; provide yourselves bags which wax not old, a treasure in the heavens that faileth not, where no thief approacheth, neither moth corrupteth. For where your treasure is, there will your heart be also."*

If all that matters to an individual is money, that is where his or her heart will be. Mammon is the only other competitor with God for the human heart. The Bible says, in Matthew 6:24, "No man can serve two masters: for either he will hate the one, and love the other; or else he will hold to the one, and despise the other. **Ye cannot serve God and mammon**" (emphasis added).

The power of the tithe is that it testifies to God about your loyalty. It tells God that He is your sufficiency, source and strength. God has made believers *"...priests for ever after the order of Melchizedek"* (Psalm 110:4). Just as King of Salem received tithes of Abraham in Genesis 14:18 and as referred to in Hebrews 7:11-17, believers must be faithful to pay their tithes and offering.

Those who tithe and give offerings faithfully reap true riches like loyalty. In Deuteronomy 14:28-29, God says *"at the end of three years thou shalt bring forth all the tithe of thine increase the same year, and shalt lay it up within thy gates:...that the LORD thy God may bless thee in all the work of thine hand which thou doest."*

Also, in Ezekiel 44:30, God says *"And the first of all the firstfruits of all things, and every oblation of all, of every sort of your oblations, shall be the priest's: ye shall also give unto the priest the first of your dough, that **he may cause the blessing to rest in thine house**"* (emphasis added).

Lastly, God commands the church in Malachi 3:10 saying *"Bring ye all the tithes into the storehouse, that there may be meat in mine house and prove me herewith, saith the Lord of hosts, if I will not open the windows of heaven, and pour out a blessing, that there shall not be room enough to receive it."*

Those who are faithful to tithe receive the power to stay loyal to God. In Malachi 3:11-12, God says that for those who pay their tithe, He "… *will rebuke the devourer for your sakes and he shall not destroy the fruits of your ground: neither shall your vine cast her fruit before the time in the field. And all nations shall call you blessed: for you shall be a delightsome land…."* Increased loyalty is the *sine-qua-non* for those who lay the tithe or ten percent down at God's commands.

BARNABAS: THE WEALTHY WORSHIPPER!

Barnabas was not your conventional follower of Christ. He came from a pedigree of wealth and fortune. The Bible says, in Acts 4:36-37 that he was a Levite, who lived in Cyprus and was independently wealthy enough to finance the gospel with the sale of his property.

The scriptures say, *"And Joses, who by the apostles was surnamed Barnabas (which is being interpreted the son of consolation), a Levite, and of the country of Cyprus, having land, sold it, and brought the money and laid it at the apostles' feet."*

Barnabas was acknowledged by all who knew him as an encourager. He built up men, instead of tearing them down or tarnishing their reputation. He was nominated to the apostleship of Judas (Acts 1:23), and even though he lost the position to Matthias, Barnabas left a legacy of service in the kingdom that still reverberates today.

Folklore and history acknowledge him as the founder of the New Testament Church in Cyprus and as hazarding his life in loyalty for the gospel. In Acts 15:26, the Bible says Paul and Barnabas were *"Men that have hazarded their lives for the name of our Lord Jesus Christ."*

It was, however, not until he made a financial commitment to God that honor as a worshipper manifested! The Bible says he *"...lay it (the money) at the apostles' feet"* (Acts 4:37) and began a missionary ministry that brought thousands to the knowledge of the Christ.

Until believers lay the treasures of this world down, they cannot rise to be blessed or loyal to God's agenda. The Psalmist concurs and states, in Psalm 50:14-15 *"Offer unto God thanksgiving; and pay thy vows unto the most High and call upon me in the day of trouble: I will deliver thee, and thou shalt glorify me."*

MULLER: ROBBER OF THE CRUEL STREETS!

In 1836, the German-born missionary George Muller decided to start an orphanage for the wandering and abused children of Bristol. He raised over one million pounds (equivalent to nearly a hundred million pounds in today's estimation) and was able to care for over seventeen thousand orphans in his lifetime.

He took them off the street, housed them at the five Ashley Downs orphanages, gave them an elementary education, and at their age of graduation (which was fourteen for boys and seventeen for girls), gave them a coin in the left hand and a Bible in the right.

He told them they would never lack for the coin in their left hand if they held on to the Bible in their right hand. George Muller took dependence on God's supernatural supplies to an unprecedented level.

As a pastor, he refused to collect a salary from his church, Bethesda Chapel, and decided to never ask anybody for finances. He went ahead to stop the renting of church pews to wealthy families in his church and opened up all church seats to all comers.

He, while working with the orphanages and church, never lacked financially or materially. He pastored the same church until his death at Ninety three years of age and never collected a salary or stipend for his numerous travels abroad.

An orphan who lived in one of the homes tells how, on one occasion, they had no milk or bread in their house. As the three hundred residents were about to get ready for school, they sat down at the breakfast table and George Muller thanked God for the meal.

After his prayer, a baker brought enough bread for all three hundred orphans saying God woke him up in the night to bake bread for the orphans. As he was departing, a milkman brought ten jugs of milk saying his cart had broken down right in front of the orphanage and wanted to contribute the milk to the orphanage rather than leave it at the mercy of urchins.

On another occasion, he interrupted the tepid prayer of Captain Dutton and asked God to clear the fog threatening their prompt arrival in Quebec, Canada. To the downright disbelief of the captain, who came to be known as Holy Joe in his later transformed life, the fog immediately cleared and he was able to arrive as scheduled.

George Muller was a great man in life and in death. On his death tens of thousands came to view his hearse. He was called by the *Bristol Times* *"a robber of the cruel streets… who was raised up for the purpose of showing that the age of the miraculous was not past[1]."*

1. Warne, Frederick G (1898). *George Müller: the modern apostle of faith.* Fleming H. Revell. p. 230.

If you wake up in the Morning and you recognize yourself you are not dead to self yet!

– Smith Wigglesworth (1859-1947)
Apostle of Faith/Evangelist

CHAPTER FIFTY ONE

GLORY FOR THE SUPERNATURAL

"That He (God) would grant you, according to the riches of His glory, to be strengthened with might by His Spirit in the inner man" (Ephesians 3:16).

Glory is the birthright of a living church and the signature of the soon-to-be raptured church. In Ephesians 5:25-27, the Bible says "...*Christ also loved the church, and gave himself for it; That he might sanctify and cleanse it with the washing of water by the word, That he might present it to himself a glorious church, not having spot, or wrinkle, or any such thing; but that it should be holy and without blemish."*

God is coming for a glorious church, not for a garbage church. If the church denies the glory in her midst, she also forfeits the purpose of God to remain loyal. In Romans 8:29-30, the apostle Paul says "...*whom (God) did foreknow, he also did predestinate to be conformed to the image of his Son, that he might be the firstborn among many brethren. Moreover whom he did predestinate, them he also called: and whom he called, them he also justified: and whom he justified, them he also glorified."*

Every believer was created for glorious living. Until a believer, however, gives up everything for the glory, there will be no invasion of the supernatural on their natural. One of the signature attributes of glory is that it builds a hunger for more of God. In 2 Corinthians 3:17-18, the Bible says, *"Now the Lord is that Spirit: and where the Spirit of the Lord is, there is liberty. But we all, with open face beholding as in a glass the glory of the Lord, are changed into the same image from glory to glory, even as by the Spirit of the Lord."*

The apostle Paul prayed for the early church that they would taste of His glory and through the encounter with Shekinah, "...(be) *strengthened with might (spiritually), ...and be filled with all the fullness of God."* Glory starts the relay to loyalty; without it, the road to loyalty is full of dread, drudgery and disaster.

ISAIAH: FROM GLORY TO GLORY

When Isaiah saw the glory in Isaiah 6:1-3, he *"...saw also the LORD sitting upon a throne, high and lifted up, and his train filled the temple. Above it stood the seraphims: each one had six wings; with twain he covered his face, and with twain he covered his feet, and with twain he did fly. And one cried unto another, and said, Holy, holy, holy, is the LORD of hosts: the whole earth is full of his glory."*

Glory gives a greater thirst for God. It abolishes self, and births the supernatural. When the glory of God filled the temple at the dedication, *"...the priests could not enter into the house of the LORD, because the glory of the LORD had filled the LORD's house"* (2 Chronicles 7:1-2).

The glory is the habitation zone of the church, and like David, believers must yearn for it if they are to maximize their loyalty to God. David cried out, in Psalm 63:1-2, saying *"...my soul thirsteth for thee, my flesh longeth for thee in a dry and thirsty land, where no water is; To see thy power and thy glory, so as I have seen thee in the sanctuary."*

The aftermath of such hunger for his supernatural glory was his *"...soul followeth hard after (God and His)...right hand upholdeth (him)"* (Psalm 63:8). The mandate of the church is to restore the glory, not rubbish it! A life lived without His glory breeds disloyalty, but a life lived in glory births loyalty legends. David said in Psalm 63:11, *"the king shall rejoice in God; every one that sweareth by him shall glory: but the mouth of them that speak lies shall be stopped."*

THE GLORY ZONE

There is a place where glory is standard. That area is called the glory zone, and it is the right of every believer. Jesus Christ prayed, in John

17:21-22, "*That they all may be one; as thou, Father, art in me, and I in thee, that they also may be one in us: that the world may believe that thou hast sent me. **And the glory which thou gavest me I have given them;** that they may be one, even as we are one*" (emphasis added).

Where the glory of God is, signs and wonders follow. Psalm 85:9 says "*Surely his salvation is nigh them that fear him; that glory may dwell in our land.*" Salvation is always in sync with His glory, and loyalty is the byproduct of a life of supernatural glory. In Zechariah 2:5, God said to His church, "*I...will be unto her a wall of fire round about, and will be the glory in the midst of her.*"

The latter-days church is a glory-filled church! In Isaiah 60:1-3, God says "*arise, shine; for thy light is come, and the glory of the LORD is risen upon thee. For, behold, the darkness shall cover the earth, and gross darkness the people: but the LORD shall arise upon thee, and his glory shall be seen upon thee. And the Gentiles shall come to thy light, and kings to the brightness of thy rising.*"

It takes a supernatural glory to bring a spirit of loyalty in the body of Christ. Elder James says, in James 5:7, "*...the husbandman waiteth for the precious fruit of the earth, and hath long patience for it, until he receive the early and latter rain.*" There can be no abiding and precious fruits of loyalty, until the former and latter rains of glory are released upon a believer's life.

WILLIAM BOOTH: SOLDIER IN GOD'S ARMY

William Booth (1829-1912) started the Salvation Army in 1865 after leaving the Methodist Church, where he had been ordained a minister in 1858. He married Catherine Booth in 1855 and together they had nine children.

William gave his life to Christ in 1845, while working as an apprentice pawnbroker in his home city of Nottingham, England. Soon after, he joined the Methodist church and began holding itinerant evangelistic campaigns in streets and alleys.

Meanwhile, he was ordained as a minister of the Methodist church in 1852, but left in 1861. He was barred by the Methodist hierarchy from preaching to Methodist congregations, and instead William went into the back streets of London canvassing for lost souls.

On one occasion, while preaching in East London, a group of missioners heard him preach and invited him to hold meetings in a tent they had purchased in an old Quaker's graveyard. The meetings were immensely successful and it caused the birth of *The Christian Mission* in 1865 with William Booth as the General Superintendent.

The Christian Mission held daily evening and Sunday morning services in London, mostly because the poor and downtrodden who thronged their meetings were not welcome in any Churches nearby. In these Churches eyes, their past had eroded their future potential and they were held culpable for their past misdeeds.

William Booth and his team of evangelists, however, went for the worst and the "least of these" (Matthew 25:45). In a space of ten years (1867-1874), the ministry had grown from ten full-time workers to 1,000 volunteers and forty two evangelists.

In 1878, William Booth changed the name of the organization to *Salvation Army* and from the slums of East London, Salvation Army is currently in 124 countries with over 175 languages being spoken. Its global reach was preceded by William Booth's missionary reach that saw him travel over 5,000,000 miles and preach over 60,000 sermons.

The Salvation Army today has over 1.8 million adherents, and serves more than 200 million meals annually. It maintains philanthropy and purity as pillars of its vision till date, is the largest provider of shelter and food to the hopeless and a bastion of fervent preaching that has etched its philosophy on world leaders all around the world.

*I will rather die trusting
God than live in unbelief!*

– Smith Wigglesworth (1859-1947)

CHAPTER FIFTY TWO

GREATNESS OF THE SCRIPTURES

"I commend you to God, and to the word of his grace, which is able to build you up, and to give you an inheritance among all them which are sanctified" (Acts 20:32).

The word of God or the scriptures is the power of God. In Romans 1:16, Apostle Paul says *"...I am not ashamed of the gospel of Christ: for it is the power of God unto salvation to every one that believeth; to the Jew first, and also to the Greek."*

It takes power to live a loyal life, but a life bereft of the word of God cannot be strong or loyal. In Isaiah 37:27, God mocks the adversaries of Israel saying they conquered *"...inhabitants* (that) *were of small power,* (and so) *were dismayed and confounded...."*

The scriptures give direction and consequently strength, but where there is *"...confusion* (there will be)*...every evil work"* (James 3:16). The greatness of the scriptures lies in its ability to encourage, strengthen, inspire and give direction.

Paul said, in Romans 15:4, that *"whatsoever things were written aforetime were written for our learning, that we through patience and comfort of the scriptures might have hope."*

Loyalty is hinged on hope, but without the comfort of the scriptures life is hopeless. Believers who don't give place to the word, have inadvertently given place to the enemy in their hearts. Psalm 119:9 says *"wherewithal shall a young man cleanse his way? by taking heed thereto according to thy word."*

THE WORD OF GOD: STEALTH, STRONG AND SURE!

The word of God is *"...a more sure word of prophecy. Knowing this first, that no prophecy of the scripture is of any private interpretation for the prophecy came not in old time by the will of man: but holy men of God spake as they were moved by the Holy Ghost"* (2 Peter 1:19-21).

It does not come back void but *"...goeth forth out of His mouth (and) shall not return unto Him void, but it shall accomplish that which He please, and it shall prosper in the thing whereto I sent it"* (Psalm 55:11).

A life built on the word of God is, therefore, not shaken by circumstances or situations but stands strong in the climes of life. Jesus said, *"....the scripture cannot be broken...."* (John 10:35) and the Psalmist added, in Psalm 119:89, *"for ever, O LORD, thy word is settled in heaven."*

The scriptures are the most powerful force on earth, when mixed with faith. Hebrews 4:2 says, *"unto us was the gospel preached, as well as unto them: but the word preached did not profit them, not being mixed with faith in them that heard it."* The secret to a life of power that is unstoppable and immoveable is a life built on the word of God.

That is why Jesus told Peter, in Matthew 16:18, *"...upon this rock* (or heavenly revelation) *I will build my church; and the gates of hell shall not prevail against it."*

The word of God is also stealth in its activity. It is described as the *"...engrafted word, which is able to save your souls"* (James 1:21). The word "engrafted" is from the Greek word *emphutos* which means rooted, innate, implanted or to spring up and bring into living union with a successfully engrafted shoot.

The word of God works under ground and in unseen avenues to save souls, according to James 1:21. True power is not temporal, but eternal. It lasts the distance and finishes its course. The word-backed life sustains a power-filled Christian but a word-lacking believer is *"of small power... (and) as the grass of the field,...the green herb, the grass on the housetops, and as corn blasted before it be grown up"* (Isaiah 37:27).

The difference between character and charisma in the kingdom of God is the word of God! Not every believer remains ever-green through trials ad temptations, and the cause is lack of the stealth but strong and sure word.

284

THE FAIL-PROOF WORD

Of all the servants Jesus told *"occupy till I come"* in Luke 19:12-26, only the servant who hid his talent in the ground and failed to bring commensurate returns to the master, died pauperized and destroyed. Instead of being promoted, like the rest of his fellow servants, he had what little he had *"...taken away from him"* (Luke 19:17). The dysfunctional life begins when one goes aberrant to Gods word for its only when we hearken to his voice and obey Him that we can truly live. The word may make us strangers to our contemporary times, but keeps the believer current with the heavenly realms where true life is.

In Psalm 119:18-19, the Psalmist prayed saying *"Open thou mine eyes, that I may behold wondrous things out of thy law. I am a stranger in the earth: hide not thy commandments from me."* The consequence of obedience may be to be ostracized but it will guarantee a fail-proof life for eternity.

Jesus Christ called His church strangers, as a result of His sanctified word. In John 17:14, He says *"I have given them thy word; and the world has hated them, because they are not of the world...."*

The power of the word makes you live like a stranger in an insane world. It causes you to live in the clouds and, yet walk on the earth! It takes you from being a normal natural man to being supernaturally abnormal in the eyes of the world!

The Bible says, *"...Enoch walked with God, and he was not; for God took him"* (Genesis 5:24). You can't see glorious things from God's word and remain in the same place in life.

Something changes when you see what no else can see. You become what no one has ever been, and like they said of Jesus, they will say *"...we have seen strange things to day"* (Luke 5:26).

SMITH WIGGLESWORTH: GOD'S GENERAL OF FAITH

Smith Wiggleworth (1859-1947) pioneered a faith movement that still lives on today. He trail blazed a healing, miracle and deliverance ministry that saw more than fourteen people raised from the dead, hundreds of cripples, blind and deaf individuals healed and thousands saved. He gave his life to Christ as a teenager, but did not go into full time ministry till he was forty eight years old. He had moved from the Episcopal church to the Wesley Methodists and then, while in the Salvation Army, married his wife, Polly, on May 2nd 1882.

He later joined a group of the newly baptized Pentecostals and after receiving the power of the Holy Ghost began to preach with signs and wonder following. Though trained a plumber, Smith Wigglesworth left the trade as a demand for his ministry grew. He travelled all over the world, including New Zealand, Asia, South Africa, preaching the gospel.

He was a stickler for the word of God, and the power of God. On one occasion, when Lester Sumrall came to visit him he asked him *"what is that under your arm?"* Sumrall said he had a newspaper under his arm and Smith Wigglesworth said *"I do not allow lies into this house and that newspaper was full of lies."* At this point, Lester Sumrall threw the newspaper into the bush and hurriedly entered the house.

He once told someone, *"if the Spirit will not move, I will move the Spirit."* He believed the word of God over the feelings of men! Even though he suffered from troubling kidney stones, and had a daughter who was deaf he continued to preach and believe God for his healing.

He did not change the Word of God to satisfy the World, and did not alter his faith to satisfy his feelings. He stood on the word of God and said, *"I am not moved by what I see. I am moved only by what I believe. I know this-no man looks at appearances if he believes. No man considers how he feels if he believes. The man who believes God has it."*

Only a life lived
in celebration, not
condemnation, of the
saving acts of Jesus
can be truly loyal.

PART IX

CONCLUSION

"I can do all things through Christ that strengtheneth them..." (Philippians 4:13).

There is a spirit of falsehood jeopardizing the faith of the modern-day American church. In a mirror-image of Noah's day, the people are living in wanton vulgarity while the end draws nigh (see Matthew 26:37-39). The Bible describes the last-days generation as *"...lovers of their own selves, covetous, boasters, proud, blasphemers, disobedient to parents, unthankful, unholy, without natural affection, trucebreakers, false accusers, incontinent, fierce, despisers of those that are good, traitors, heady, high minded, lovers of pleasures more than lovers of God"* (2 Timothy 3:2-4).

The end-time church is a generation that must face and conquer traitors and trucebreakers with truth. Truth is the panacea to our world's dizzying moral conundrum and it is found only in the person of Jesus Christ (John 14:6) and in the word of God (John 17:17).

In Zechariah 8:16-17, God adjures Israel saying *"these are the things that ye shall do; Speak ye every man the truth to his neighbor; execute the judgment of truth and peace in your gates: And let none of you imagine evil in your hearts against his neighbor; and love no false oath: for all these are things that I hate, saith the LORD."*

God detests falsehood and wants believers to abhor falsehood and pursue loyalty to one another and to God. If a believer thinks no evil of his fellow man, he or she cannot conjure up evil against such a one. The spirit of falsehood makes a believer a caricature of their destiny and a sad reflection of their "supposed-to-be" life.

THE FOUR THINGS GOD HATES

There are four things God hates, but swearing falsely in particular irks Him. In Zechariah 8:16-17, the Bible says *"These are the things that ye shall do; Speak ye every man the truth to his neighbor; execute the judgment of truth and peace in your gates and let none of you imagine evil in your hearts against his neighbor;* **and love no false oath: for all these are things that I hate,** *saith the* LORD*"* (emphasis added).

Anytime the Bible lists an item as the last occurrence, it denotes something that requires the greatest attention. The last word is characteristically considered the most consequential of a person's words and God's last word here is for the believer to love no false oath!

There is a rise in brazen animosity, bare-faced cold-blooded lying and criminal falsehood in our society today. There is a dearth of truth and even those who should speak the truth lie without grimacing at falsehood. They lie and love their lies, instead of hating false oaths as God recommended in Zechariah 8:17. The burden of this generation is they not only hate good, but also love evil!

In the book of Jude, the Bible says *"…others save with fear, pulling them out of the fire; hating even the garment spotted by the flesh"* (Jude 23). The believer must hate sin and not love any form of falsehood if they truly fear God. In Proverbs 8:13, the Bible says *"the fear of the Lord is to hate evil: pride, and arrogancy, and the evil way, and the forward mouth do I hate."*

The spirit of falsehood causes believers to perish and lose the healing God earmarks for them. The Bible says in Proverbs 21:28, *"A false witness shall perish…"* and in Hosea 7:1, God adds that *"when I would have healed Israel, then the iniquity of Ephraim was discovered, and the wickedness of Samaria: for they commit falsehood; and the thief cometh in, and the troop of robbers spoileth without."* Too many sicknesses and premature deaths are rooted in disloyalty and falsehood!

LOOK, LIVE AND LOVE

Until you see what God is doing, you can't become everything He has earmarked you for. In 1 Corinthians 2:9-10, Apostle Paul says "...*Eye hath not seen, nor ear heard, neither have entered into the heart of man, the things which God hath prepared for them that love him. But God hath revealed them unto us by his Spirit:...*"

Those who see into the spiritual realm capture eternity. In 2 Corinthians 4:18, the Bible says "*while we look not at the things which are seen, but at the things which are not seen: for the things which are seen are temporal; but the things which are not seen are eternal.*" Real living is not found in seeing the temporal, but fixing our eyes on the unseen and following divine patterns, like Jesus did in John 5:19.

True life, however, must love to really live! If there is no love, God is not present for "...*God is love*" (1 John 4:8). In John 5:19-20, Jesus explained this mystery of look, live and love. He said, "...*the Son can do nothing of himself, but what he seeth the Father do: for what things soever he doeth, these also doeth the Son likewise. **For the Father loveth the Son, and sheweth him all things that himself doeth**: and he will shew him greater works than these, that ye may marvel*" (emphasis added).

When love is present, those who look find life and it takes a heart of love and an eye that looks to cement a life in concrete loyalty to God. The Holy Spirit, speaking in Hebrews 2:14-15, encourages believers to "*follow peace with all men, and holiness, without which no man shall see the Lord: looking diligently lest any man fail of the grace of God; lest any root of bitterness springing up trouble you, and thereby many be defiled.*"

It is only a believer that loves God and people that can look diligently into the spiritual realm and see the grace of God at work. Such believers' are core loyalists in God's army and live a *Zoe* type of life even on earth.

JOHN WESLEY: HEAD IN HEAVEN, FEET ON THE EARTH

John Wesley (1703-1791) famously told fellow believers' to have heads in heaven and feet on the earth. He emphasized living a Godly life that had earthly relevance. He said "Do all the good you can, By all the means you can, In all the ways you can, In all the places you can, At all the times you can, To all the people you can, As long as ever you can!"

When he faced opposition from the Church that had ordained him as a minister – the Church of England – he left and started preaching to thousands in cemeteries. When accosted by the authorities for preaching outside the Church, he told them "I look upon all the world as my parish; thus far I mean, that, in whatever part of it I am, I judge it meet, right, and my bounden duty to declare unto all that are willing to hear, the glad tidings of salvation."

The son of an Anglican clergyman, John left the Anglican Church and started an itinerant ministry that, after his death, birthed the Methodist Church. He travelled over 250,000 miles, gave out thousands of pounds to charitable causes and preached over forty thousand sermons in his lifetime or an average of three sermons a day! He criss-crossed America and Europe preaching the gospel, and at his death he had established a movement made up of schools, theological seminaries, orphanages, thousands of ministers and more than a hundred and thirty five thousand members.

He had no children, and he married a widow called Molly, who abandoned him after seven years of marriage. He said, "I did not forsake her, I did not dismiss her, I will not recall her." He dedicated himself to studying the word of God, and left over four hundred publications. He was instrumental the great awakening in America, alongside George Whitfield, and spoke out on social issues such as prison reform and the abolition/emancipation movement. He counted politicians and royalty as personal friends and when he died in 1791, he was acknowledged as "the most beloved man in Great Britain."

Do all the good you can,
By all the means you can,
In all the ways you can,
In all the places you can,
At all the times you can,
To all the people you can,
As long as ever you can!

– John Wesley (1703-1791) Evangelist/
Founder of the Methodist Church

Contacts

This ministry, Faith and Power Ministries, is dedicated to showing the power of God once again to this generation. It is dedicated to ushering in the last days' glory of God and, in the course of doing so, turning lives around for the kingdom of God.

Our email is tobemomah@yahoo.com. We can be contacted via email or via our websites www.tobemomah.com or on www.faithandpower ministries.org. I currently reside in West Monroe, Louisiana and can be reached at P.O Box 550 West Monroe, Louisiana 71294 U.S.A.

Other Books by the Author

1. **Tobe Momah.** *A General and a gentleman* (biography of General Sam Momah) –Spectrum books 2003
2. **Tobe Momah.** *Between the systems, soul and spirit of man* (a Christian doctors view on sickness and its source) – Xulon press 2007
3. **Tobe Momah.** *Building lasting relationships* (a Manual for the complete home) – Xulon press 2006
4. **Tobe Momah.** *Metrobiology – A Study of life in the city* 1ST ed (a Doctor's Daily Devotional) – Xulon Press 2008
5. **Tobe Momah.** *Pregnancy: Pitfalls, Pearls and principles* – Westbow Press 2011
6. **Tobe Momah.** *Ultimate Harvest: Five F.A.C.T.S on Fruitfulness and how to grow the American Church again* - Westbow Press 2012
7. **Tobe Momah.** *From Edginess to Eagerness…taking the Church back to willing service* - Westbow Press 2012
8. **Tobe Momah.** *Fear no Evil…by hating evil* – Westbow Press 2013
9. **Tobe Momah.** *Fear no Evil…by hating evil (A daily devotional)* - Westbow Press - 2013
10. **Tobe Momah.** *S.T.E.P,S to the altar …Why a glorious generation is living ashamed at the altar* - Westbow Press - 2014
11. **Tobe Momah.** *Healing Lives…True Stories of Encouragement and achievement in the midst of sickness!* Westbow Press – 2014.
12. **Tobe Momah.** *Stay In Tune (S.I.T)…Challenging an always going but Godless culture!* – Advanced Global Publishing 2015
13. **Tobe Momah.** *Stay In Tune (S.I.T)…Living Daily in His Presence (a Daily Devotional)* – Advanced Global Publishing 2015.

14. **Tobe Momah**. *The Death Knell called Depression! –* Advanced Global Publishing 2015.
15. **Tobe Momah**. *Heirs not Helpers: Raising a generation of plunderers who are not just pleaders.* Advanced Global Publishing 2015
16. **Tobe Momah**. *Healing Lives (II): Another One Hundred true stories of Encouragement and Achievement in the Midst of sickness.* Westbow 2016.